NEW TESTAMENT BASICS for CATHOLICS

"If you've ever opened up your Bible and felt lost, then read *New Testament Basics for Catholics*. John Bergsma has an amazing gift for making scripture clear and easy to understand. This book will transform your understanding of the Good News."

Brant Pitre
Author of *Jesus the Bridegroom*

"John Bergsma makes the New Testament come alive in this very readable introduction. *New Testament Basics for Catholics* lays out the plan of scripture and helps the reader to see and remember it by entering into the mind of Matthew, Luke, Paul, and John so that he can grasp the details and put them into the big picture. A masterful book!"

Lawrence Feingold
Associate Professor of Theology and Philosophy
Kenrick-Glennon Seminary, St. Louis

"Packed with nuggets of wisdom, Bergsma gives the reader a feast by offering timeless insights to get the most out of your Bible. Catechists, parents, and teachers can use it for their own personal edification and unpack the New Testament within their own families. *New Testament Basics for Catholics* will hold a prominent and permanent place upon my bookshelf. Rare is the book that can take something so deep and make it simple enough for a beginner to understand. This is the work of a master teacher."

Mark Hart
Author of *Behold the Mystery: A Deeper Understanding of the Catholic Mass*

"Nobody alive teaches the biblical basics as clearly and memorably as John Bergsma. In this book he helps us to see subtle touches that the ancient authors of the New Testament intended us to see, but often get lost in translation. Bergsma makes *New Testament Basics for Catholics* as vivid as our memories and enables us to apply the scriptures to our own lives."

Mike Aquilina
EWTN host, writer, author, and speaker

"There is no better introduction to the New Testament than *New Testament Basics for Catholics*. Dr. Bergsma's book is clear and simple, but it runs deep. He is gifted at making connections and communicating great mysteries in words that are a pleasure to read."

Scott Hahn
Author of *Angels and Saints*

"A brilliant book done in a brilliant way. *New Testament Basics for Catholics* is an easy way to understand the big picture of the New Testament. A must for anyone wanting to learn more about Jesus and the early Church."

Kevin Cotter
FOCUS Senior Director of Curriculum

NEW TESTAMENT BASICS for CATHOLICS

JOHN BERGSMA

Founded in 1865, Ave Maria Press is a ministry of the United States Province of Holy Cross.

www.avemariapress.com

Paperback: ISBN-13 978-1-59471-582-2

E-book: ISBN-13 978-1-59471-583-9

Cover design by Katherine J. Ross.

Text design by Andy Wagoner.

Illustrations rendered by Katherine J. Ross.

Printed and bound in the United States of America.

Library of Congress Cataloging-in-Publication Data
Bergsma, John Sietze.
New Testament basics for Catholics / John Bergsma.
pages cm
Includes bibliographical references.
ISBN 978-1-59471-582-2 -- ISBN 1-59471-582-3
1. Bible. New Testament--Introductions. 2. Catholic Church--Doctrines. I. Title.
BS2330.3.B47 2015
225.6'1--dc23

2015016905

Contents

Introduction: An Overview of the New Testament

You could make a good argument that the New Testament is the world's most influential book. More than two billion people on the globe claim to follow its main character, a certain Jewish carpenter-turned-religious teacher named Jesus who was from Nazareth in the north hills of Israel. People inspired by the ideas of this book invented the university and the hospital. They explored the planet, named countless locations, wrote down new languages, established the modern calendar, and built buildings—schools, churches, hospitals, monasteries, and convents. What is it about this book that motivated them to do all that and more?

Actually, the New Testament isn't one book: it's many books or half a book. It's many books because it's a collection of twenty-seven biographies and letters written by the close friends and followers of that Jewish teacher who changed the world. It's also half a book because it's the second of the two major parts of the holy book of Christians, usually called "the Bible." "Bible" comes from the Greek word *biblos*, which just means "book." For much of human history, books were rare, and the most important one, which spoke of God, purpose, meaning, love, and eternal life, was not just *a* book but *the* Book—the Bible.

The Bible itself is a huge book. In reality, it's a collection of seventy-two books consisting of around 750,000 words, depending on language and translation, written by many authors over a period of a thousand years. Who can get a handle on all that information?

It seems easier to deal with the New Testament alone. We call it the "second half" of the Bible, but we all know it's really much less than half the length of the Bible as a whole. It's a fifth the size of the Old Testament. Still, even the New Testament can seem daunting, and in some ways it's harder to organize than the Old Testament. Although the Old Testament is longer, it only tells one basic story line. By breaking it into periods and covenants, we were able to get a fairly good "bird's-eye" view of it in *Bible Basics for Catholics*.

The same approach won't quite work for the New Testament because the first four books (together almost half the New Testament) tell the same story of Jesus' life again and again. So we can't tell a single story line and cover the New Testament. We'll need a different approach.

The first step is to recognize that the New Testament is a whole world in itself. People can and do spend their whole lives studying just parts of it. So we have to be content with not covering every detail. Second, we should recognize that if we aim for *most* but not *all* we *can* simplify the New Testament into manageable, memorable pieces.

I have found that by focusing on just four authors, one can get a fairly good grasp of the New Testament. Between them, these four authors wrote around 85 percent of the New Testament. They are Matthew, Luke, Paul, and John. In what follows, we'll draw and introduce each one in turn. First, let's draw Matthew.

Matthew

To identify him, we've given him a bag of cash in his left hand. This reminds us that Matthew was a tax collector before his conversion to Christ. Tax collectors made a bundle of money. In his right hand, we've given him a quill, a sign of a "scribe," a professional writer and scholar of ancient times. It seems likely that Matthew was a Jewish scribe before or during his time as a tax collector. Jewish scribes studied the scriptures and religious law. Because they had to be careful writers and record keepers, they had the necessary skills to be tax collectors if they so desired.

According to the Church's ancient tradition, Matthew wrote the first gospel, which was eventually placed at the start of the collection of New Testament books. It is fitting that the Gospel of Matthew should begin the New Testament. Matthew stresses the similarity (or *continuity*) of the Old and New Testaments. He shows how Jesus' words and deeds in the New fulfill prophecies in the Old. His book makes a good transition between the two. With twenty-eight chapters and 1,068 verses, Matthew makes up about one eighth of the New Testament.

Our next main author is Luke. We'll draw him like this:

Luke

St. Luke has two distinguishing features. We've given him one of those classic head mirrors that doctors used to wear, plus a stethoscope. According to Colossians 4:14, St. Luke was a physician by training. That's not dogma. We can't be absolutely sure it's true, but it is plausible. Certainly, St. Luke's writing style shows that he was well educated in Greek culture, and medicine was an attractive profession for a well-educated man in ancient times.

Tradition also tells us that St. Luke associated with the Blessed Mother and even painted a portrait of her. That's why we've placed an icon of the Blessed Mother in his left hand. Again, we can't be absolutely sure he painted her portrait, but we may be confident that he knew her well. In fact, we are indebted to St. Luke for recording most of what we know about the life of Our Lord's mother. All five of the Joyful Mysteries, for example, come from St. Luke's gospel. Without Luke, we would have only a few comments about the Blessed Mother in Matthew 1 and two important scenes (the wedding at Cana and the Crucifixion) where she appears in the Gospel of John (Jn 2 and 19). St. John Paul II was convinced that St. Luke got his information about the life of the Blessed Virgin and the childhood of Jesus (Lk 1–2) directly from the Blessed Mother herself.[1] This is the common tradition of the Christian people down through the ages. In any event, we will leave him with the Marian icon in his hand to show his close relationship with her.

St. Luke stands out for several reasons. He is the only Gentile (non-Jew) to write any part of the New Testament. He is the only New Testament author to write a book of history: the Acts of the Apostles. Without it, we would have almost no record of the first thirty years of the Church's existence. Finally, St. Luke wrote more of the New Testament than any other person. The Gospel of Luke is the longest book of the New Testament, and together with its sequel Acts, it makes up well over one quarter of the whole.

Luke was a close companion and coworker of our third author, St. Paul. We draw St. Paul like this:

Paul

You'll note that in Paul's right hand is a sword. This is St. Paul's distinguishing mark in most religious art. The sword represents the Word of God, and St. Paul famously encouraged Christians to "take . . . the sword of the Spirit, which is the word of God" (Eph 6:17). He was also beheaded with a sword.

In Paul's left hand is a letter. This reminds us that the only writings we have from Paul are his letters (or *epistles* in older English). The thirteen letters of St. Paul—nine to churches (Romans to 2 Thessalonians) and four to individuals (1 Timothy to Philemon)—make up the middle of the New Testament. St. Paul was the greatest missionary of the early Church, and he was constantly on the move, preaching the Gospel. He didn't have time to sit and compose books, so all his theology is contained in letters he sometimes had to dash off quickly to churches or people in crisis.

The letters under Paul's name (Romans through Philemon) make up 20 percent or one fifth of the New Testament. If St. Paul also wrote the anonymous "Letter to the Hebrews," his writings would account for one quarter of the New Testament—just shy of his companion Luke.

In modern times, especially in the West, St. Paul has been considered the greatest theologian among the New Testament authors. But in ancient times, especially in the East, that honor would go to the fourth and last of our main authors, the apostle John. We draw St. John like this:

John

St. John is just slightly shorter than the rest of our authors to remind us of his youth. It's probable he was the youngest of the apostles and outlived the rest. In his left hand is the eucharistic cup, which reminds us that he records the most extensive teaching about the Eucharist in the entire New Testament (this teaching can be found in John 6). His right hand is upraised in a traditional sign of priestly blessing. Early Church tradition remembers St. John serving as a priest and pastor of the Church into his old age.

Five books are attributed to John: his gospel, three letters (epistles), and the Book of Revelation. Scholars dispute his authorship of some or all of these, but we'll accept the Church's tradition and discuss contrary opinions later. Together, these books make up about 20 percent or one fifth of the New Testament.

So here we are!

These four men give us the vast majority of the New Testament. Of course, modern scholars have cast doubt on whether they wrote the books that bear their names. But I think there are good reasons to trust the traditions of the Christian people about who wrote their most precious texts.[2] So, if we concentrate on getting to know these four, we'll get the "big picture" of this holy book. It's true there are other New Testament authors—such as Mark, Peter, James, and Jude—who wrote smaller works that are still important. But to include everyone at once would be biting off more than we can chew. At a later stage of study, after we're comfortable with the basics of the New Testament, we can turn our attention to them as well.

Now we need a common theme of the New Testament to tie it all together. It's not difficult to come up with one; we can take our theme from Jesus's preaching: "Repent! For the *kingdom of God* is at hand!" (Mt 4:17, emphasis added; see Mk 1:15). From beginning to end, the New Testament is about the *kingdom of God.*

First, we will take a look at St. Matthew, whose gospel explains to us that *the kingdom of God has come!* St. Matthew shows that Jesus fulfills the prophecies and expectations of the people of Israel about the return of the kingdom of David, even if he does it in an unexpected way. Jesus, who is both the Son of David and the Son of God, has established one kingdom on earth and in heaven that is both the kingdom of David and the kingdom of God. St. Matthew's gospel is rich in connections with the Old Testament, especially the prophets. He will "connect the dots" for us to show how the Davidic Covenant is restored in Jesus' Eucharistic Covenant.

Our next author will be St. Luke. St. Luke shows us that *the kingdom of God grows!* We say this because, in addition to his wonderful gospel, St. Luke gives us the Book of Acts, which shows us the early *growth* of the Church. The Church is the form of the kingdom of God on earth. St. Luke shows us the kind of things the Church must always do to continue growing.

St. Luke's mentor and guide, St. Paul, is our third author. St. Paul's letters instruct us on how to live together within the Church, which is the kingdom of God on earth. We'll title our study of St. Paul "Living in the Kingdom!" Studying all of St. Paul's letters would be too much, so we'll concentrate on the one that is often thought to be his most important: Romans.

It's fitting to end with St. John because his writings traditionally include the Book of Revelation, which shows the end of history and the final state of the kingdom of God in its heavenly perfection. His gospel, too, paints a powerful picture of what the Church is meant to be, its final goal. Therefore, we call our unit on St. John "The Kingdom Perfected!"

I should say a word about Bible translations. This book is best if you read it along with your own Bible. I use the Revised Standard Version, especially the Second Catholic Edition. My quotations will be from that version, but if they ever differ, it will be because I've changed a word to more closely reflect the original language (Hebrew or Greek). Any words in a verse that I have changed will be italicized to show that the word is my translation.

Now let's get started!

One

The Old Testament as "Prequel: Episodes 1–6"

Because the New Testament is the second half of a much longer book, if you begin reading it by itself, you can find yourself lost in the story line. Imagine watching a famous movie for the first time but starting halfway or more into the plot: for example, starting *The Sound of Music* with the Trapp family's final concert before fleeing from Austria. You might be a bit confused. Who are these people and why are they singing? Why don't the German soldiers want them to leave? Or compare it to watching the Star Wars series but beginning with *Return of the Jedi*. Why do Luke Skywalker, Princess Leia, and Darth Vader seem to have some deep connection?

Some people have read the Bible for much of their lives but *only* the New Testament. That's a little like watching *The Sound of Music* regularly but always starting from the final concert or watching *Return of the Jedi* over and over without episodes 1–5.

In my first book, *Bible Basics for Catholics*, I made a quick tour of the whole Bible, starting with Genesis and using stick figures to help us remember the main stages of Bible history. If you've never really studied the Bible before, I recommend starting with *Bible Basics for Catholics*. But for folks who can't read *Bible Basics* first or have already read it but need some reminders, we are going to do a quick review of the story line of the Bible.

The central idea in the Bible is "covenant." A covenant is a way of making a person part of your family by swearing an oath to them. To put it technically, covenant is the extension of kinship by oath. Marriage and adoption are the two most familiar forms of covenant.

One of the prayers at Mass sums up the story of the Bible this way: "Time and again you offered them covenants, and through the prophets taught them to look forward to salvation."[1] The story of the Bible is the story of God offering covenants to human beings. It's the story of God trying to make us part of his family. In the Old Testament, God made at least six major attempts to make humans his family by covenant. Think of them as "Episodes 1–6" if you will.

God offered the first covenant to the first man and woman, Adam and Eve, at the beginning of human history. Man and woman lived as son and daughter of God in a place of peace and perfection that the Bible calls the Garden of Eden. As son of God, Adam also enjoyed the privilege of being a king, priest, and prophet over all the world, and Eve shared in these roles with him. We can sketch a little picture of this situation like so:

Adamic Covenant

The meanings of the different parts of this sketch are explained in *Bible Basics*. For now, we just remember the basic fact that Adam and Eve lived as children of God, at peace with God and nature.

The situation of peace did not last, however. Adam and Eve wanted pleasure, appearances, and pride more than a loving relationship with God as their father. They thought they would get what they wanted if they disobeyed God. Deceived by Satan, they ate the fruit of the one tree in the garden that God had put off limits. They thought they would gain godlike power and knowledge, but the only knowledge they gained was that they were naked, that is, weak and helpless. Since they had broken their relationship with God as father, they had to leave the peace of the Garden of Eden and strike out on their own.

Humanity did not do well trying to live outside a relationship with God. Human history quickly went from bad to worse, until "the wickedness of man was great in the earth, and that every imagination of the thoughts of his heart was only evil continually" and "the earth was filled with violence" (Gn 6:5, 11). This wasn't just a description of prime-time television or the content of what's playing at the local cinema; it was reality, and God had to do something.

So he sent a great flood to wash the earth clean. But he singled out one good man, Noah, as a kind of New Adam to restart human history with his own family. Noah, of course, built the famous ark in which he, his family, and many animals were preserved. The ark, a kind of floating garden, came to rest after the flood on Mt. Ararat, a kind of New Eden. After the flood was over, God reestablished the *covenant* of Adam with Noah. Noah offered a sacrifice as a sign of his gratitude to God, and God sent a rainbow as a sign of his love for Noah.

Noah and his family were now in a family relationship with God. This is the sketch to help us remember:

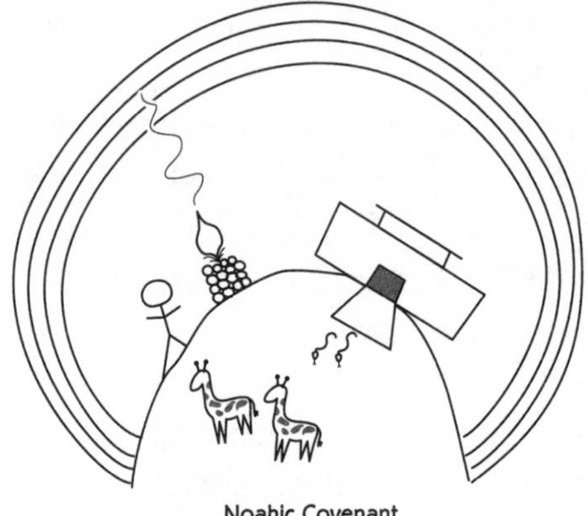

Noahic Covenant

But after the flood, Noah was not much more successful than Adam. Noah himself sinned against God, using his freedom and God's good gifts to get drunk (Gn 9:20–27). His son Ham took some kind of advantage of his drunkenness, and the result was curse and shame entering Noah's family and conflict between Noah's sons. Noah's descendants again refused to live as children of God and even gathered together to build a great tower (the "Tower of Babel") as a sign of their rejection of God (Gn 11:1–9).

At this point, God could have sent another worldwide judgment such as the flood, but instead, he decided to choose one man, Abraham. God would work with this man and his children to restore blessing to the whole human family. He invited Abraham into a *covenant*: a family relationship with himself. God did this in several stages (see Genesis 15 and 17).

The climax came when God tested how much trust Abraham had in God as his Father. God asked, *Abraham, would you be willing to risk sacrificing your own son to me?* Abraham, with the cooperation of his son Isaac, responded *Yes*. But God was not interested in Isaac actually being sacrificed.

It was a test of faith. Abraham and Isaac had showed a kind of trust or faith that defied all expectation. God called off the sacrifice. Then he swore an oath to Abraham on the mountain where Isaac had been laid on the altar. This oath confirmed God's covenant with Abraham. God promised him, "I will surely bless you . . . and by your *seed* [descendant] will all the nations of the earth be blessed" (Gn 22:16–18, my own translation).

We can sketch Mt. Moriah, the mountain Abraham climbed to sacrifice his "only begotten" son Isaac to God, in this way:

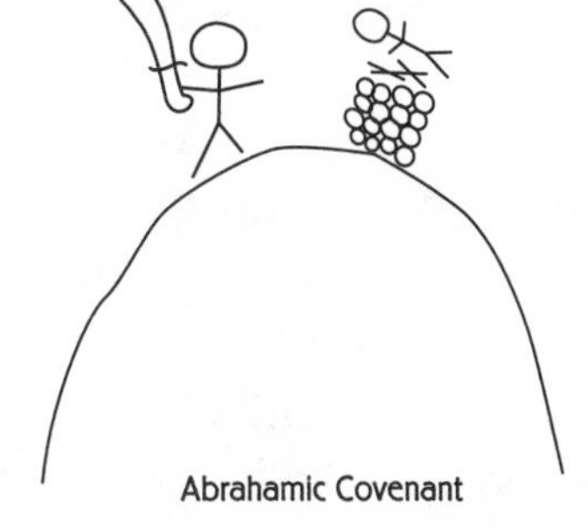

Abrahamic Covenant

Of course, this story raises many questions, and I discuss some of them in *Bible Basics for Catholics*. For now, let's recognize that Mt. Moriah bears an uncanny resemblance to another mountain, Mt. Calvary. On Moriah, Abraham the father laid his "only begotten" son Isaac on the wood of sacrifice to God. On Calvary, a different "only begotten son" (Jn 3:16) would be laid on the wood. He would give his life as a sacrifice of love for God and humanity. In other words, Mt. Moriah is a "type" or image of Mt. Calvary.

Mt. Moriah was a turning point or watershed moment in human history, where the path of salvation began to head unfailingly toward its destination. After God's covenant oath to Abraham on Moriah, there was not a catastrophic fall similar to Adam's or Noah's. There were difficulties, to be sure, but among all the difficulties, God began to fulfill his promises to Abraham step by step.

As privileges of the covenant, God had given Abraham three specific promises:

- He would become a "great nation,"
- He would get a "great name," and
- Through his "seed" (descendant) all the nations would be blessed.

After the death of Abraham, God began to fulfill the first promise. He arranged for Abraham's family to travel to Egypt, a land where food was plentiful and war was rare. There, Abraham's children were fruitful and multiplied until they became a "great nation." All they needed now was their own land to live in, so God sent them a leader and savior, Moses. Moses brought them out of Egypt and led them east to Mt. Sinai in the desert, where he gave them a "constitution" based on the Ten Commandments. Here, too, God made a covenant with Abraham's children. This covenant goes under different names:

- "The Mosaic Covenant" because Moses arranged it;
- "The Sinai Covenant" because it was established at Mt. Sinai; or
- "The Old Covenant" because it would later give way to the New Covenant in Jesus Christ.

At the top of Mt. Sinai, Moses sprinkled lamb's blood on the Israelites and on God's altar. This showed that God and Israel now shared one blood (Ex 24:8). They were family. Israel was the "firstborn son" of God (Ex 4:22) as Adam had been. Here's Moses getting the Ten Commandments from God, who appears on Mt. Sinai in a storm:

Mosaic Covenant

Moses' face is shining with God's presence.

But just like Adam, Israel also broke the covenant. In just forty days, Israel turned away from God and went back to worshiping the animal idols of Egypt (Ex 32). But Moses pleaded for the people, and God forgave them. God renewed the covenant, but he added many more laws as a kind of penance for Israel's sins (Ex 34–Lv 27). Here's the icon we use to remember the breaking of the Ten Commandments and the adding of more laws:

Israel still needed some space of their own to live in, so after a year at Sinai, Moses led them through the wilderness toward the Promised Land. The Israelites, however, rebelled against God at least ten times in the wilderness. A journey of a few weeks ended up taking forty years. God had to change the covenant after each rebellion until it took its final form in the Book of Deuteronomy. There, the covenant laws were sometimes harsh and somewhat like martial law or a "crack-down" against crime. Moses was not happy with Israel after their forty years of rebellions in the wilderness. Here he is, delivering the laws of Deuteronomy:

After Moses's death, his lieutenant Joshua led Israel into the Promised Land. Israel lived in the land under the rules of Deuteronomy for generations, with little change in their relationship with God. But hundreds of years after Moses, the people of Israel finally asked God for a king to rule over them, and the second king they got was a remarkable man, a "game changer" in the history of salvation: David.

Anointing is pouring or smearing oil on someone's head. In ancient times, this was done to single people out for a special role as king, priest, or prophet. David's anointing was special because he was open to God's Spirit. When the prophet Samuel anointed David as king over Israel, the Holy Spirit came down and remained on David "from that day forward" (1 Sm 16:13). God blessed David in all that he did. He rose to power, replacing his father-in-law Saul as king.

David made the worship of God his royal priority, and God was pleased. He granted to David a covenant, a special relationship in which David and his sons would enjoy the status of sons of God. God would watch over David and his heirs, expanding their kingdom till it covered the whole earth. In this way, God's blessings would flow from the king first to Israel and then to all the earth.

We draw this little icon to help us remember David and the covenant he received as king on Mt. Zion, also known as Jerusalem. Beside the king is the Temple built by Solomon, David's son:

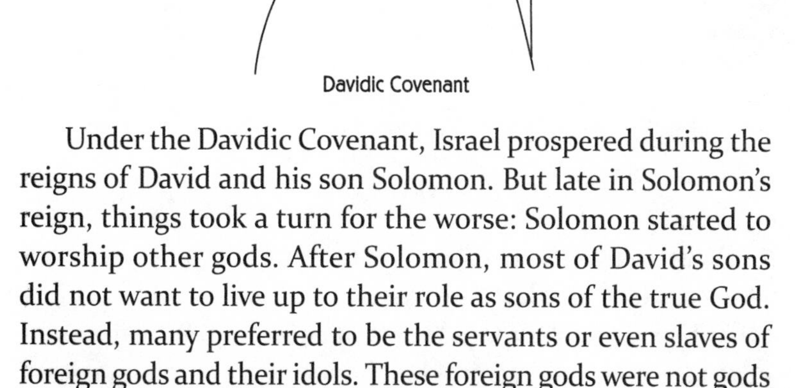

Davidic Covenant

Under the Davidic Covenant, Israel prospered during the reigns of David and his son Solomon. But late in Solomon's reign, things took a turn for the worse: Solomon started to worship other gods. After Solomon, most of David's sons did not want to live up to their role as sons of the true God. Instead, many preferred to be the servants or even slaves of foreign gods and their idols. These foreign gods were not gods at all; sometimes they were even demons.

As a result, the kingdom of Israel split into northern and southern kingdoms. Both began to decline. Over about three hundred years, enemies destroyed first the northern and then the southern kingdom and took the people into exile. What was God doing during this time? He sent the great prophets to warn his people to turn back to him. These were the famous prophets, men such as Isaiah, Jeremiah, and Ezekiel.

The prophets preached a basic, two-part "first the bad news and then the good news" message to Israel. The bad news was God was sending judgment because the people had broken the Mosaic Covenant, especially the Ten Commandments. The good news was God would make a new covenant restoring all the blessings promised to David.

Here's a sketch of a prophet preaching in Jerusalem. The images of the Davidic Covenant are in dotted lines because they are a future reality. Sometime in the future, God will send a new Son of David who will build a better temple and restore the kingdom of Israel:

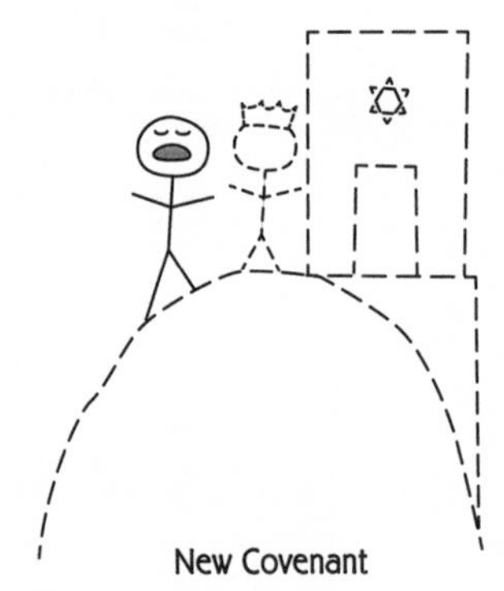

When we open the New Testament and begin to read, Israel is still in this last, "prophetic" stage of salvation history. It has been several hundred years since any of the great prophets had walked the earth, but their writings remained, and many Israelites were convinced that the time of fulfillment was very near. The promised son of David might arise at any moment, take control of Jerusalem, and restore the kingdom.

In fact, there were two significant "false alarms" just before and during the lifetime of Jesus. Rulers arose who seemed, briefly, to be fulfilling the prophecies. But then their dynasties disintegrated and hopes were dashed.

The first cause of false hope was the Maccabees (or "Hasmoneans"), an Israelite priestly family from the central hill country. Men from this family rose up to overthrow the Greek-speaking forces that were oppressing Israel in the mid-100s BC. The Maccabees eventually won Israelite independence around 164 BC, formed a government around 140 BC, and ruled until 37 BC. Some of their later rulers took the title "king."

At the height of their power, the Maccabees extended the kingdom of Israel almost to the borders of David and Solomon. Jerusalem, their capital, became very wealthy. It looked as if the promised restoration of the kingdom was at hand, but there was one problem: the Maccabees had the wrong genealogy. The prophets had promised a king from the line of David. But the Maccabees were descendants of Levi, the tribe of priests, not kings. So the Maccabees eventually faded, and the Roman Empire became the true ruler of Israel.

After the Maccabees, another dynasty arose; this one started by Herod the Great, one of the most remarkable men in ancient history. Herod was a nobleman from the region south of Israel. He married into the Maccabean family and went to Rome, where he convinced the Roman Senate to appoint him king of Israel. Returning to Jerusalem with a Roman army, he easily ousted any opposition and established himself as ruler of the land. He reigned from 37 BC to 4 BC, and his descendants reigned after him until AD 66.

At least twice during the Herodian dynasty, the borders of Israel expanded almost to the limits of David and Solomon's kingdom, and Jerusalem became extremely wealthy. The vast number of Jews who came on pilgrimage from around the Mediterranean to celebrate the great Jewish feasts at Herod's rebuilt Temple brought great wealth to the city. Once more, it appeared the prophetic visions might be fulfilled.

But there was one problem: Herod had the wrong genealogy. He was not a son of David. He wasn't even fully Jewish: his father was an Edomite, a descendant of Esau, a traditional enemy of Israel. Neither he nor his sons could be the fulfillment of the prophecies. Of course, many Jews may have dreamed of assassinating the unpopular Herod and replacing him with a descendant of David. For that reason, Herod was paranoid about assassination attempts and also persecuted people who had Davidic blood. But for all his efforts and those of his sons, the Herodian dynasty eventually declined. The Romans deposed the last descendant of Herod in AD 66.

When Jesus was born near the end of Herod's reign, the Jews were in the middle of having their hopes raised and dashed for the second time by a dynasty of rulers who did not have the right bloodline to fulfill the prophecies. This helps explain why the New Testament begins the way it does, as we will see in the next chapter.

Here's our summary sketch of the six covenant "episodes" that precede the New Testament:

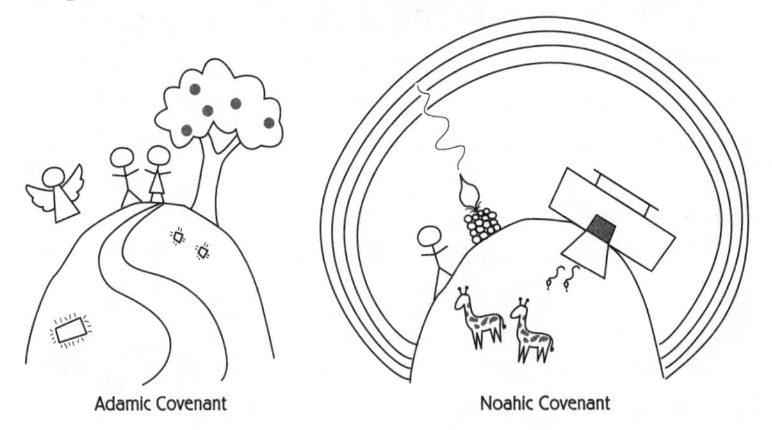

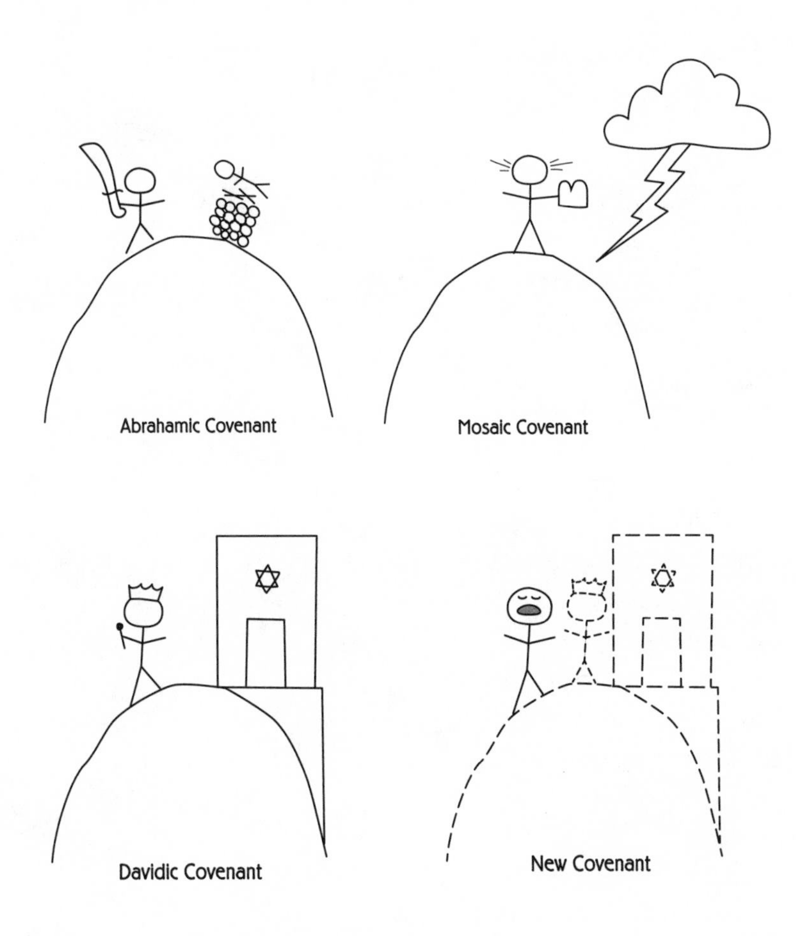
Abrahamic Covenant
Mosaic Covenant
Davidic Covenant
New Covenant

Part I

The Kingdom of God Has Come!

Matthew

Two

The Gospel of Matthew

Most Americans don't care much about genealogies. We move around too much and don't place enough emphasis on family ties. In fact, many of us would have a hard time clearly remembering the names of any ancestors before our own grandparents.

In many parts of the world, the attitude is different. I went on a pilgrimage to Israel some years ago. Our guide turned out to be an Arab Catholic. Not knowing anything about Arab Christians, I thought he must be a recent convert from Islam. "How long have you been Catholic?" I asked. "Oh," he said, "about *eight hundred years*." His family clan had become Catholic in the time of the Crusades (1200s) and had been living in the land of Israel near Nazareth since that time. Genealogies are often very important to families in the Middle East, where history and culture are deep.

Matthew begins his gospel with a genealogy. This may not be the way to grab the attention of Americans, but it *certainly* caught the attention of ancient Jews who were waiting for a king with the right genealogy. After two failed dynasties (the Maccabees and the Herodians) of kings with wrong family lines, Jews would have been very interested in someone who could prove his descent from the right man: King David.

We'll pick up with Matthew 1, the genealogy of Jesus, in just a minute. First, let's get an overview of this gospel.

Bird's-Eye View of Matthew

Anytime you are going to tell a long story, you have to organize it somehow. St. Matthew likes to organize Jesus' teachings by topic. Five long sermons by Jesus, each on a separate topic, make up the backbone of his gospel:

1. The Sermon on the Mount (Mt 5–7)
2. The Mission Sermon (Mt 10)
3. The Parables of the Kingdom Sermon (Mt 13)
4. The Mercy Sermon (Mt 18)
5. The End Times Sermon (Mt 24–25)

Matthew "glues" these five long sermons together with narration about Jesus' travels, miracles, and other deeds. Finally, he puts the Christmas story at the beginning of his gospel and the Easter story (really the Triduum) at the end. That gives us a biography of Jesus that begins with Christmas, ends with Easter, and has five main blocks:

The Christmas story ("infancy narratives"): Mt 1–2

Book 1: Jesus announces the kingdom: Mt 3–7

Book 2: Jesus sends out the royal officers: Mt 8–10

Book 3: Jesus teaches on the hidden kingdom: Mt 11–13

Book 4: Jesus teaches on the forgiving kingdom: Mt 14–18

Book 5: Jesus teaches on the end of the kingdom: Mt 19–25

The Easter story (Triduum): Mt 26–28

Of course, a long time ago there was another famous teacher of Israel, a man who had a miraculous childhood, had a difficult career, and faced much opposition but finally led Israel in a sacred meal of salvation, made a covenant between them and God, and taught them God's laws. That was Moses:

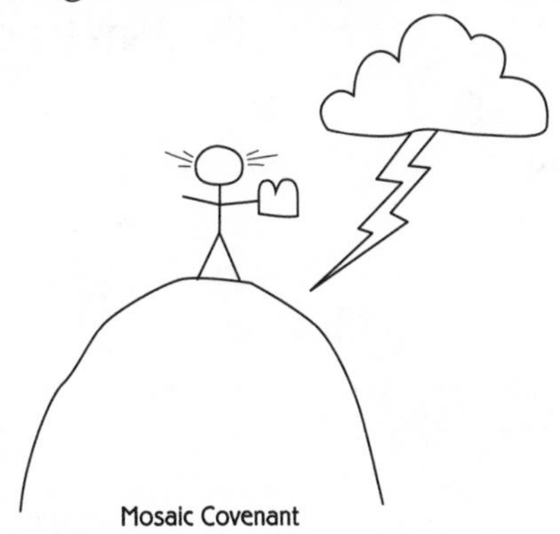

Mosaic Covenant

According to tradition, Moses wrote five books, the first five books of the Bible: Genesis, Exodus, Leviticus, Numbers, and Deuteronomy.

Was Matthew trying to paint Jesus as a new Moses with five new books? It's possible. He certainly does portray Jesus as a new Moses in many important places in the gospel. So, for the sake of memory and learning, it can be helpful to compare Moses with Matthew's portrait of Jesus:

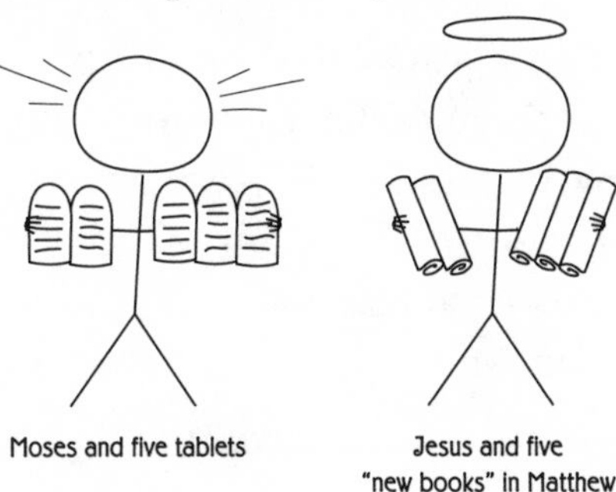

Moses and five tablets

Jesus and five "new books" in Matthew

That's our overview of Matthew. Now let's start reading!

Matthew's Christmas Story: The Genesis of Jesus

Matthew begins, "The book of the genealogy of Jesus Christ, the son of David, the son of Abraham" (1:1). Stifle that yawn! There is a lot going on here! In one sentence, Matthew has connected Jesus to three of the most important men in the Bible: Adam, David, and Abraham.

First, by beginning with "the book of the genealogy of Jesus Christ," Matthew makes a connection to the only other place in the Bible where this phrase occurs: Genesis 5:1: "This is the book of the generations of Adam." Matthew is saying Jesus is a New Adam. We've opened a new chapter, a whole new book, in human history. Imagine that!

Second, by calling Jesus "*the* Son of David" Matthew identifies Jesus as the one who would restore the covenant and kingdom of David. There were many descendants of David running around in Israel in those days. Some scholars think certain towns (such as Nazareth) were almost entirely made up of folks with Davidic blood.[1] But Jesus is not just "*a* son of David," he is "*the* Son of David," about whom the prophet Nathan had prophesied, "When your days are fulfilled . . . I will raise up your *seed* after you, who shall come forth from your body, and I will establish his kingdom. He shall build a house for my name, and I will establish the throne of his kingdom for ever. I will be his father, and he shall be my son" (2 Sm 7:12–14).

Third, by calling Jesus "*the* Son of Abraham," Matthew identifies Jesus as the one who would fulfill all the promises of the covenant to Abraham. Every Jew was "*a* son of Abraham." But Jesus was "*the* Son of Abraham," about whom God spoke to Abraham: "I will establish my covenant with you and with your *seed* after you" and "by your *seed* shall all the nations of the earth be blessed" (Gn 17:7, 22:18). As we recall from the

Old Testament, God's covenant with Abraham included three major promises: great nationhood, great name (royalty), and universal blessing to the nations. Jesus would establish the great nation of Abraham (the Church), receive the great name (King of kings and Lord of lords), and spread blessing to all the nations (the outpouring of the Holy Spirit).

So in one sentence, Matthew connects Jesus with three of the greatest key figures in Bible history and suggests what Jesus' life and ministry will mean for the world. Not bad!

Proceeding through Jesus' genealogy, we run into a lot of names that are hard to pronounce. Pity the young deacon who has to proclaim this at the Christmas Vigil! At the end, we note that Matthew has arranged the genealogy into three sets of fourteen (Mt 1:17). Why? Fourteen is the number of David. Hebrew has no vowels, and the consonants double as numerals. David's name spelled in Hebrew is DVD. *D* is the fourth letter of the Hebrew alphabet, and *V* is the sixth. Add the values up, and it comes to fourteen. Jesus' genealogy is fourteen three times: a "triple David" or "David cubed." Matthew arranges it this way to make it easy to memorize and drive home the Davidic connection.

Now let's look at the genealogy again. Matthew starts with Abraham because Abraham was "father of the Jews," and Matthew writes his gospel for Jews in particular. He traces Jesus' line through David and Solomon, of course, because it is important to show Jesus is the crown prince, the heir to the throne of Israel. But then,

> Four of these names are not like the others,
> Four of these names just don't belong,
> Can you tell which ones are not like the others
> By the time I finish my song?

Can you spot them? Of course! Four *women* are mentioned in this genealogy: Tamar, Rahab, Ruth, and Bathsheba—and *such* women! If women were included at all in ancient genealogies, it was for some special reason: perhaps they were queens or national heroines. But Matthew's women are not the "usual suspects," not the great holy matriarchs Sarah, Rebekah, and Leah.

Instead, they are . . . well, let's just retell their stories.

Do you remember Tamar? She was Judah's daughter-in-law, probably a Canaanite. She was married to two of Judah's sons, both of whom were rascals that God struck down. But when she was widowed, through no fault of her own, Judah refused to provide for her. What did Tamar do? She put on a cocktail dress and some spike heels (or the ancient equivalent) and hung out along the side of the road to catch Judah's eye (see Gn 38). She ended up having two boys by her father-in-law: Perez and Zerah. The vast majority of the tribe of Judah, that is, the Jews, descended from these two boys, both the product of this very, um . . . *unusual* relationship!

How about Rahab? She was the Canaanite "proprietor" of her own "establishment" in the red-light district of Jericho. The Israelite spies ran into her place of business to hide when they were scouting out the city (Jo 2). She survived the capture of the city and ended up doing well for herself, marrying Salmon, a nobleman from the tribe of Judah.

And Ruth? She was not Jewish either; she was a woman of the country of Moab, widowed after marrying a man of Judah. She was a woman of faith and loyalty, who accompanied her old mother-in-law back to Judah to care for her. However, there was that one sketchy scene in Ruth 3 where she hatched a plot to "reel in" her boyfriend, Boaz, after a party at night, using a lot of perfume and "attractive" clothing. That scene is the sole reason the Book of Ruth has a PG-13 rating. But nothing happens, and it all turns out good. Boaz marries Ruth, and they live happily ever after.

If only Bathsheba's story were so happy! Hers is one of the most painful in the Bible. Matthew doesn't even mention Bathsheba's name; he just says, "David was the father of Solomon by *the wife of Uri'ah*" (Mt 1:6, emphasis added). Ouch! Matthew, did you have to bring that up? David and Solomon were the two greatest kings of Israel, but the link between them involves a sordid tale of adultery and murder. Uriah was a Gentile, a Hittite (from modern-day Turkey) and a devout convert to the faith of Israel. His wife Bathsheba (we don't know her nationality) was one of the prettiest women in David's kingdom, and Uriah himself was one of David's "top brass," a high-ranking war hero. David took a fancy to Bathsheba one day when Uriah was out of town, and when Bathsheba found out she was pregnant by David, the king decided to cover his tracks by having Uriah killed in battle. Then, he married Uriah's widow himself. The whole episode was the moral low point of David's entire career (2 Sm 11), a personal disaster that spun his family out of control and led to further abuse, murder, betrayal, and war.

So Matthew, why bring that up? In fact, why mention *any* of these four women, all of whom were *Gentiles* (or at least married to one) and had, shall we say, *checkered* personal histories? For many good reasons!

1. Jesus would later be despised as one who hung out with "tax collectors and prostitutes," that is, men associated with Gentiles and women of ill repute. Matthew points out that the great Jewish kings David and Solomon descended from such people.
2. Jesus and his apostles would be criticized for inviting sinners, marginal women, and Gentiles into the New Covenant. Matthew shows that God had already brought such people into the Old Covenant.

3. Slander was spread about the Blessed Mother. Some Judeans claimed she was not a virgin before the birth of Jesus. Matthew contrasts the purity of Jesus' birth with some of the impure unions in the ancestry of David and Solomon. Matthew is saying, *If you Judeans want to accuse people of impurity, let's talk about the ancestors of Solomon, your greatest king!*

God is merciful. He works his salvation despite our sins and failings. Even in the Old Covenant, God brought fallen, imperfect people into the center of his covenant family. He still does this, even more so in the New Covenant, where people of any ethnic background, regardless of their sins, mistakes, or baggage, are welcome to come to God.

The Birth and Childhood of Jesus *(Matthew 1:18–2:23)*

In contrast to the questionable relationships that formed the bloodline of Israel's great kings, Jesus is born to a father and mother in a completely pure relationship. He is conceived in the womb of his mother Mary, a virgin engaged to a righteous man, Joseph, heir to the throne of David. God explains to Joseph in a dream that the child is conceived by the Holy Spirit, a fulfillment of a famous prophecy: "Behold, a virgin shall conceive and bear a son, and his name shall be called Emmanuel" (Is 7:14). It is often said that Matthew misquotes Isaiah 7:14 here, since the original Hebrew of Isaiah does not use the word for "virgin" (Hebrew, *betheulah*) but for "maiden" (Hebrew, *almah*). The truth is that there is such overlap between the meaning of these Hebrew words that Jewish translators themselves, hundreds of years before Matthew wrote, chose the Greek word "virgin" (*parthenos*) to render Isaiah 7:14. Matthew, writing in Greek, cites this verse in the well-known Jewish-Greek translation (the Septuagint) familiar to most of his readers.

The prophecy of Isaiah 7:14 was uttered seven hundred years before Matthew wrote, and it probably predicted the birth of good King Hezekiah of Judah in exaggerated, poetic language. But prophecies often have more than one fulfillment. Matthew knows that Jesus is more truly "born of a virgin" than Hezekiah was and that Hezekiah was merely a sign of God "being with" Israel but that Jesus *truly* is "God with us," *Emmanu-el* in Hebrew. Jesus fulfills the prophecy better than Hezekiah himself did. That's why Matthew quotes it.

As we move on into the infancy and childhood of Jesus, Matthew continually shows us two things: Jesus is Israel's King and Jesus is the "True Israel," or Israel-in-one-person.

While he is still a child in Bethlehem, "wise men" come from the East searching for him, and when they find him they worship him with "gold, frankincense, and myrrh." The last time wise men from the East came to Israel looking for a king was in the reign of Solomon. If you doubt me, go back and read 1 Kings 4:29–34, where Solomon's wisdom "surpassed . . . all the people of the East," and men came from every land to hear his wisdom. Solomon attracted all these international wise men when he was at the height of his career, but Jesus is already attracting them as a toddler! The gifts also remind us of Solomon. No one had more gold than Solomon (1 Kgs 10:14–22), and "frankincense and myrrh" together are only mentioned elsewhere in the Bible in the Song of Solomon, where they are romantic perfumes worn by Solomon and his bride. The visit of the magi marks Jesus as a bridegroom-king, like Solomon, from his very childhood.

King Herod hears from the wise men about the birth of this new king. He sends soldiers to kill any male children in the region born near when the wise men first saw the prophetic star that announced his birth. King Herod, as we mentioned earlier, was not of the line of David and wasn't even fully Jewish. He was an impostor. He and everyone else knew it. Herod also knew that most Jews would have been very happy if he, Herod, suddenly died under mysterious circumstances and got replaced by a Jew with David's blood.

So, Herod was terribly paranoid and was in the habit of killing people who might pose a threat to his throne, including his wives and sons. The "slaughter of the holy innocents," which probably amounted to the killing of a dozen to twenty baby boys in the vicinity of Bethlehem, was such a small event in comparison to Herod's other massacres and murders that other contemporary historians didn't even bother to record it.

St. Joseph, much like his namesake Joseph, "Prince of Egypt," is gifted with supernatural dreams. The dreams drive him to flee with the Holy Family to Egypt, whose capital city Alexandria was the "New York" of its day, a center of Jewish culture, with the largest Jewish population outside the land of Israel. For Jews fleeing political trouble in Israel, Alexandria was the logical place to flee. Not only was it close but also one could easily melt in and "get lost" in one of the city's two huge Jewish quarters. But years later, when Joseph hears that Herod is dead, he takes the family back to Nazareth.

Nazareth was a little village in the north (Galilee), probably settled by Davidic kinsmen, who may have named their town "Little Branch" (*Nezereth*) after the famous prophecy that a "branch" (Hebrew, *nezer*) would come forth from David's line (Is 11:1). Matthew refers to this prophecy, "He shall be called a *Nazarene*" (Mt 2:23), that is, he shall be the branch the prophets announced.

Matthew gives us no more information about Jesus' childhood. The next we know, Jesus is an adult, beginning his public ministry in response to the preaching of John the Baptist. What was Jesus doing for about thirty years in Nazareth?

Christians call these the "silent years" of Jesus life, during which he probably worked at home, learning his father's craftsmanship and taking care of his mother after the death of Joseph, who passed away when Jesus was a young man.

Although we know so little of these years, they are very important to us. Don't most of us work for years on end, out of the public eye, with our days made up of simple things such as getting up to go to work, buying groceries, cleaning the house, and taking care of other family members? The silent years of Jesus remind us that he too—God himself!—worked for many years unnoticed by the world, taking part in "the daily grind." As we go about the toil of our quiet lives, we know Jesus understands and is close to us.

Book 1 of Matthew: Jesus Announces the Kingdom

John the Baptist bursts onto the stage of history with his shout, "Repent, for the kingdom of heaven is at hand!" John was the original "hellfire and brimstone" preacher. He made quite the scary figure in his hair garment, with a leather belt, honey dripping from his beard, and bee stings on his arms! John looked like a survivor of God's coming judgment day. People may have been baptized just to avoid ending up looking like him!

John the Baptist

The heart of John's message was, "I baptize with water for repentance, but he who is coming after me is mightier than I." This one to come sounded very intimidating—who would this be, who would "baptize with the Holy Spirit and fire"?

Jesus, too, came to John to be baptized. Why should Jesus be baptized? He has no sin. Even John protests: "I should be baptized by you!" But Jesus says, "It is fitting to fulfill all righteousness." What does that mean? In part, it means that Jesus' baptism fulfills many themes and prophecies in scripture.

As Jesus comes up from the water, the Holy Spirit hovers as a dove and the voice of God the Father speaks. We recognize images of the creation story: God spoke the word, and the Spirit came down to hover over the waves (Gen 1:1–2). The creation comes up from the water. So the baptism is like a new creation event, and, in fact, Jesus is the new creation. This reminds us of how Matthew began: "The book of the genealogy of Jesus," comparing Jesus to Adam.

The voice of God the Father speaks at the baptism: "This is my beloved Son, with whom I am well pleased!" Here, the voice of God echoes a line from the ancient coronation hymn of the Davidic kingdom, the song sang when each new king mounted the throne. We know this hymn as Psalm 2, and the key line goes:

> I will tell the decree of the Lord:
> he said to me:
> "You are my Son!
> Today I have begotten you!" (v. 7)

It's as if Jesus, the Son of David, is beginning his reign and his heavenly father sings a bit of the hymn for the occasion!

But there's more. The Father says, "my *beloved* son," which harks back to a famous incident, the near sacrifice of Isaac in Genesis 22, that famous chapter where Isaac is called (in the ancient translations) the *beloved* son of Abraham three times. So not only is Jesus the royal Son of David beginning his reign but also he is a New Isaac, a "beloved son," who will go to the same mountaintop to offer his life in sacrifice.

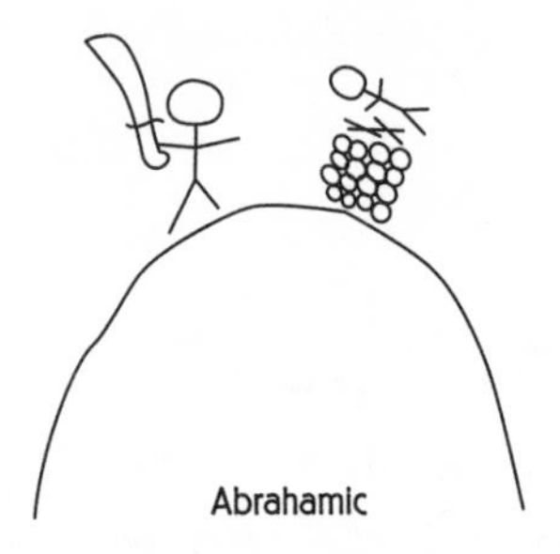

We said earlier that Matthew stresses two themes: Jesus as King of Israel, and Jesus as the True Israel. So let us take note: the Israelites went down to Egypt at the end of Genesis; they stayed there and then left, passing through the waters of the Red Sea before wandering in the wilderness for forty years, facing many trials and tests. Jesus went down to Egypt and stayed there but now passes through the waters of the Jordon before entering the desert to wander for forty days, where he faces many trials and tests. Jesus is the mystical Israel, and he has to experience in his own person what the nation as a whole endured.

But he is also their great king. And we note that the greatest of Israel's kings, Solomon, began his reign by being *washed* and *anointed* at a source of sacred water, the spring called Gihon, in the city of Jerusalem (1 Kgs 1:38–40). The reigning priest, Zadok, and the ranking prophet, Nathan, presided at this washing and anointing. Then Solomon was charged to keep the Law of Moses (1 Kgs 2:1–4) before beginning his reign (1 Kgs 2:12).

Likewise, Jesus is *washed* and *anointed* at another source of sacred water, the Jordon, by John the Baptist, who had legitimate priestly status from his father Zechariah (Lk 1:5) and was the ranking prophet of his day. Then Jesus enters the desert, where he keeps the Law of Moses against the tests of the devil, and returns to begin his reign with the cry, "Repent, for the kingdom of heaven is at hand!" So the sequence baptism-temptation-preaching follows patterns from both Israel's history and the history of the royal family.

The Temptation *(Matthew 4:1–11)*

Jesus is driven out into the desert, where he fasts and prays for forty days. "Afterwards" he is hungry (Mt 4:2). Why is he not hungry until after forty days? People who fast for long periods usually get over hunger pains within about five days, when the body shifts to burning body fat. After that, hunger is calm until all body fat is consumed. Then the body starts to break down muscle, and the pangs resume. At this point, one is literally dying of hunger.

Satan comes to tempt him three times: "Turn these stones to bread"; "Throw yourself down from the Temple"; and "Worship me for the riches of nations." We know this scene well. People don't notice, though, that Jesus responds three times, quoting the Book of Deuteronomy, which was the Law of Moses. As a royal son of David, he was responsible to keep the Law of Moses (Dt 17:18–20; 1 Kgs 2:1–4), and he does.

The temptations follow an ancient pattern: Satan appeals to Jesus' physical desires: "Turn these stones to bread!" He also appeals to Jesus' visual desire or greed, as he "showed him all the kingdoms of the world and the *riches* of them." Then there is the appeal to Jesus pride: "Throw yourself down from the Temple and let the angels catch you!" In other words, perform a big stunt and become a celebrity! These three basic temptations are called the *threefold concupiscence*, and St.

John summarizes them as "the lust of the flesh and the lust of the eyes and the pride of life" (1 Jn 2:16). They are the triple-headed monster of temptation that had already begun in the Garden of Eden, when Eve saw that the fruit was good for food, pleasing to the eye, and desirable to make one wise as God, that is, to become equal to God: an ego trip. Jesus is undoing our first parents' threefold surrender to sin.

According to the Law of Moses, the king of Israel had to resist the lust of the flesh by not having multiple wives, the lust of the eyes by not having much gold, and pride of life by not amassing huge numbers of war horses (i.e., military power; Dt 17:16–17). Jesus is the good King who resists these lusts and pride, even when starving in the desert. Solomon, however, amassed wives, gold, and war-horses, and fell into sin (1 Kgs 10:14–11:13). Jesus is greater than Solomon!

After the temptations are over, Jesus returns and begins to preach in the region of Galilee. This beautiful, well-watered northern part of Israel is marked by rolling hills and the delightful freshwater lake known as Gennesaret or the "Sea of Galilee." This part of Israel was the first region destroyed by Israel's enemies over seven hundred years before. The prophet Isaiah promised it would be the first region to see the Messiah, the anointed Son of David (Is 9:1–2). Matthew quotes the prophecy as he notes the beginning of Jesus' ministry (Mt 4:16), and Jesus continues John the Baptist's message: "Repent, for the kingdom of heaven is at hand" (v. 17).

A kingdom needs not just a king but also other officers to assist in governing, so Jesus begins to call his first disciples, the inner circle of Peter, Andrew, James, and John (Mt 3:18–22). After many miracles and much preaching in the area of Galilee (4:23–25), St. Matthew records the first and greatest of Jesus' major sermons: the Sermon on the Mount (Mt 5–7).

The Sermon on the Mount *(Matthew 5–7)*

The Sermon on the Mount has rightly been called the "greatest sermon ever preached," and one can hardly exaggerate its influence on human history. Only in heaven will we find out how many millions of people have been comforted, consoled, convicted, and converted by pondering this sermon. In the Catholic Church, it has always had a privileged place, and many of the Church Fathers considered it the perfect summary of Jesus' message, the Good News of the kingdom.

Many people confuse the Sermon on the Mount with the opening blessings or Beatitudes (Mt 5:1–12). But the Beatitudes are only the introduction. The whole sermon does not end until the last verse of chapter 7: "And when Jesus finished these sayings, the crowds were astonished at his teaching."

The sermon has roughly five parts. Jesus opens with blessings and encouragement (5:1–16) and then concludes with a series of warnings (7:13–27). In between, he teaches on law (5:17–48), piety or good deeds (6:1–18), and principles of living (6:19–7:27). The theme throughout is "the kingdom."

1. Blessings of kingdom citizens (5:1–16)
2. New laws for the kingdom (5:17–48)
3. Piety in the kingdom (6:1–18)
4. Principles of kingdom living (6:19–7:27)
5. Warnings for kingdom citizens (7:13–27)

We should not miss the comparison of Moses and Jesus. A long time ago, Moses went up on Mt. Sinai and delivered divine laws to guide God's people. Now Jesus goes up on the mountain of the Beatitudes and delivers a new set of instructions for God's people.

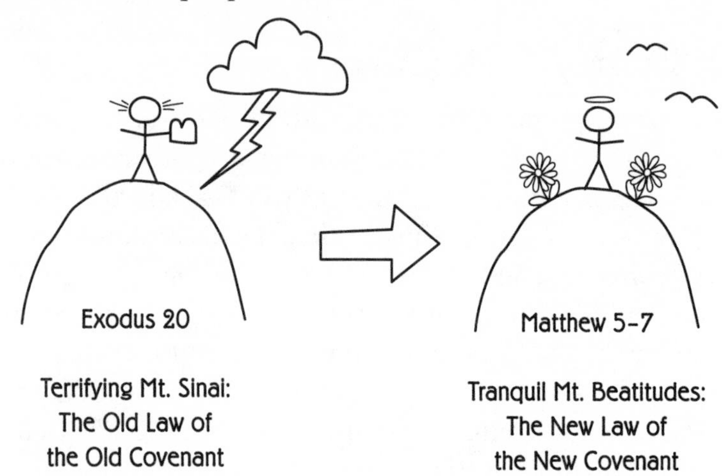

However, Jesus is greater than Moses. In fact, the second section of Jesus' sermon is made up of six contrasts where Jesus corrects the Law of Moses or the way folks interpreted it:

MOSES SAID:	JESUS SAYS:
No killing . . .	No anger or hatred! (vv. 21–26)
No adultery . . .	No sexual lust! (vv. 27–30)
No undocumented divorce . . .	No divorce at all! (vv. 31–32)
No false oaths . . .	No false speech ever! (vv. 33–37)
Practice justice . . .	Practice mercy! (vv. 38–42)
Love your neighbor . . .	Love your enemy! (vv. 43–48)

In Jewish thought, Moses was the Great Prophet. No one was higher than Moses except God himself. When Jesus adjusts, adds to, and even corrects Moses' law, one thing is clear: Jesus is claiming to be higher than Moses. Jesus is acting like God.

We said that the theme of the Sermon on the Mount is *the kingdom of heaven* (or *"of God"*). I want to show you that this theme is clear at the beginning, middle, and end of the sermon.

The Sermon on the Mount begins with the famous "Beatitudes," a word from Latin meaning "blessings." There are eight main ones, numbered here:

1. Blessed are the poor in spirit, for theirs is the kingdom of heaven.
2. Blessed are those who mourn, for they shall be comforted.
3. Blessed are the meek, for they shall inherit the earth.
4. Blessed are those who hunger and thirst for righteousness, for they shall be satisfied.
5. Blessed are the merciful, for they shall obtain mercy.
6. Blessed are the pure in heart, for they shall see God.
7. Blessed are the peacemakers, for they shall be called sons of God.
8. Blessed are those who are persecuted for righteousness' sake, for theirs is the kingdom of heaven.

   Conclusion: Blessed are you when men revile you and persecute you and utter all kinds of evil against you falsely on my account. Rejoice and be glad, for your reward is great in heaven, for so men persecuted the prophets who were before you.

Each of these eight main beatitudes has the form "Blessed are the *x*, for they shall *y*." The conclusion follows and expands on the blessing for persecution. Let's notice that the *first* and *last* beatitude both promise the same reward:

1. Blessed are the poor in spirit, *for theirs is the kingdom of heaven* (Mt 5:3, emphasis added).
8. Blessed are those who are persecuted for righteousness' sake, *for theirs is the kingdom of heaven* (Mt 5:10, emphasis added).

Jesus begins and ends his blessings on the same theme: the kingdom of heaven. Ancient teachers often began and ended their speech or writing with the same idea. Scholars call this pattern an *inclusio*. Ancient teachers used it to indicate their main point. So the main point of the Beatitudes is *the kingdom of heaven*, and we may say the Beatitudes are *blessings for kingdom citizens*.

The citizens of the kingdom of heaven, however, have qualities we would not expect. They are poor, mournful, meek, hungry, thirsty, merciful, pure, peace loving, and persecuted. They are, in short, the kind of people the rest of the world walks all over and mocks. How different this is to what we (and the ancient Jews) would expect! Shouldn't citizens of a heavenly kingdom be rich, happy, satisfied, powerful, and invincible? Take note: Jesus preaches the kingdom of heaven, but *his view of the kingdom is different from what everyone expects!*

Now let's look at the kingdom theme in the middle of the sermon. The middle section of the sermon is on piety (religious good works), and the middle act of piety is prayer (Mt 6:5–15). Here, Jesus teaches us the Our Father:

> Pray then like this:
> Our Father who art in heaven
> Hallowed be thy name.
> Thy kingdom come,
> Thy will be done,

> On earth as it is in heaven.
> Give us this day our daily bread;
> And forgive us our debts,
> As we also have forgiven our debtors;
> And lead us not into temptation,
> But deliver us from evil. (Mt 6:9–13)

The second request of the prayer, after blessing the name of God, is "thy kingdom come." The Lord's Prayer is a kingdom prayer. What does it mean for God's kingdom to come? It means that his will is done on earth just as it is in heaven.

The rest of the prayer has a close relationship to the Beatitudes. We pray for our daily bread because we are the poor, hungry, and thirsty. We pray for forgiveness of debts because we are the merciful who have already forgiven our debtors. We pray to avoid temptation because we want to be pure, and we pray for deliverance from evil because we are persecuted. The Lord's Prayer is not a prayer for the wealthy, powerful, prideful, satisfied, and judgmental. It's a prayer for the downtrodden who seek peace, mercy, and righteousness more than wealth, power, fame, and glory. It's a prayer for the kingdom citizens described by the Beatitudes.

Now let's go to the end of Sermon on the Mount. Jesus concludes with a famous parable about two men who built their houses on very different foundations:

> Every one then who hears these words of mine and does them will be like a wise man who built his house upon the rock; and the rain fell, and the floods came, and the winds blew and beat upon that house, but it did not fall, because it had been founded on the rock. And every one who hears these words of mine and does not do them will be like a foolish man who built his house upon the sand; and the rain fell, and the floods came, and

> the winds blew and beat against that house, and it fell; and great was the fall of it. (Mt 7:24–27)

Like many other Americans, I learned this parable growing up through a favorite Vacation Bible School song:

> The wise man built his house upon the rock [three times]
> And the rain came tumbling down!
> The foolish man built his house upon the sand [three times]
> And the rain came tumbling down!
> The rain came down and the floods came up [three times]
> And the foolish man's house went SPLAT! [handclap]

> So build your house on the Lord Jesus Christ [three times]
> And the blessings will come down!

The kids' Bible song does get the major point of the parable: Jesus' teachings are a "firm rock" on which to build the "house" of one's life. So far, so good. However, there is a lot more to this parable.

"The wise man who built his house upon a rock" is a loaded phrase for an ancient Jewish audience. Who was the famous "wise man" who built an enormous "house" on top of a famous "rock"? It was none other than Solomon, the wisest man who ever lived, who built the House of God, the Holy

Temple, on a huge rock formation at the top of Mt. Moriah (2 Chr 3:1), now called the "Temple Mount." The Muslim shrine called the "Dome of the Rock" now stands near the site, where Jewish tradition holds that Abraham attempted to sacrifice Isaac so long ago.

So the "wise man who built his house on the rock" is a quiet reference to Solomon, the greatest of Israel's kings. The message of the parable is, if you follow my (Jesus') teachings, you will be like Solomon the great king. This promise of a kind of royalty for the faithful disciple of Jesus concludes this sermon that began with the blessing of the "kingdom of heaven." So from beginning to end, the Sermon on the Mount is a "kingdom sermon," a description of how to live and behave as part of the kingdom of heaven.

But as we have seen, there's not a hint in the Sermon on the Mount that the kingdom of heaven is going to have a standing army and navy, a geographical capital, a system of taxation, a program of world conquest, or any of the other things the kingdoms of this world typically have. The kingdom of heaven defies our expectations. It requires us to undergo a conversion in the way we see the world.

Book 2 of Matthew: Jesus Sends Out the Royal Officers

(Matthew 8–10)

In the Sermon on the Mount (Mt 5–7), Jesus announced that the kingdom was here and taught his followers how to live as part of it. In the following chapters of Matthew (Mt 8–10), Jesus continues to do things that show he is the King. He also chooses twelve royal officers to help him lead his growing kingdom.

All of Jesus' miracles in these chapters point to his authority as king. A centurion comes to Jesus to beg him to heal his sick servant. Jesus offers to come to the house to deal with the servant directly. But that's not necessary! "Only say the word, and my servant will be healed." The centurion regards Jesus as a kind of spiritual Caesar who just has to speak and immediately all the hidden powers of the universe jump to do his will.

Some of Jesus' mighty works link him directly to David and Solomon, the great kings of Israel's history. For example, in Matthew 8, Jesus first calms a storm at sea with a word (vv. 23–27) and then casts out demons from two crazed demoniacs (vv. 28–34). The Jews remembered Solomon having these kind of powers: in the Book of Wisdom, Solomon claims that divine wisdom granted him "to know the structure of the world and the activity of the elements" and "the powers of spirits" (Ws 7:17–20). In rapid succession, Jesus demonstrates power over the "structure of the world" and "the elements" at the Sea of Galilee and then overcomes "the powers of the spirits" with the demoniacs. Jesus has Solomon-like power and wisdom.

Solomon, of course, was remembered as the greatest bridegroom of Israel. He had more brides than anyone else: seven hundred, according to 1 Kings 11:3! The great love poem of the Bible, the Song of Songs, features him as the male lead. Psalm 45, the royal wedding psalm, describes one of his weddings. Solomon inherited a bridegroom role from his father David. When David first became king of Israel, the elders of Israel said to David, "We are your bone and flesh" (2 Sm 5:1), echoing Adam's famous words to Eve at the first wedding in human history (Gn 2:23–24). Then, David and Israel made a covenant together that he should be their king (2 Sm 5:3). Marriage is a kind of covenant. David's relationship to his people was like a marriage. As king, he and his sons after him were a kind of bridegroom to the people as bride (2 Sm 17:3). Solomon, the greatest of David's sons, was a great bridegroom figure.

Bridegroom King

Getting back to Matthew, we find that, shortly after his calming of the sea and healing of the demoniacs, Jesus calls himself "the bridegroom": "Then the disciples of John came to him, saying, 'Why do we and the Pharisees fast, but your disciples do not fast?' And Jesus said to them, 'Can the wedding guests mourn as long as *the bridegroom* is with them? The days will come, when the bridegroom is taken away from them, and then they will fast'" (Mt 9:14–15, emphasis added). The prophets also described God as bridegroom of Israel (see Hosea 2:14–23). As Son of God and Son of David, Jesus is both the divine bridegroom of the prophets and the royal bridegroom like David and Solomon.

Even the blind can see who Jesus really is, as shown a few verses later when two blind men greet Jesus by crying out, "Have mercy on us, Son of David." Son of David is a royal title; they are recognizing him as the promised king. He heals them and also a mute man, fulfilling what Isaiah had said about the day when God would come to save Israel: "The eyes of the blind shall be opened . . . and the tongue of the mute sing for joy" (Is 35:5–6).

When Solomon ruled over all Israel, at the height of his power, he appointed "twelve officers over all Israel, who provided food for the king and his household" (1 Kgs 4:7).

Twelve officers over the Kingdom

So it's no surprise when, after "preaching the gospel of the kingdom" in "all the cities and villages," Jesus takes time to call his twelve disciples and give them authority to do the same things he is doing. They are not to go to the Gentiles or Samaritans but to "the lost sheep of the house of Israel."

Their message is simple: "The kingdom of heaven is at hand" (Mt 10:5–7). While on their preaching journey, they will live according to the Beatitudes: They will be poor, carrying nothing with them (vv. 8–10). They will be peacemakers, bringing peace to the homes they visit (v. 13). They will be pure of heart, as "innocent as doves" (v. 16). And they will be thoroughly persecuted for the sake of Jesus (vv. 17–23). Jesus grants to them his very own authority, such that anyone who accepts the apostles will be as good as accepting Jesus himself: "He who receives you receives me" (v. 40). To embrace the King's officer is to embrace the King himself.

The apostles continued their ministry as officers of the King in their lifetimes, but before they died, they appointed other men to continue their ministry, whom they called "overseers." These men served as officers of the King in the next generation and appointed others to serve after their death, down to the present day. It is still the case that embracing these royal officers, these "overseers," is to embrace the King himself. In Greek, "overseer" is *episkopos*, which eventually morphed into the English word "bishop."

Book 3 of Matthew: Jesus Teaches on the Hidden Kingdom *(Matthew 11–13)*

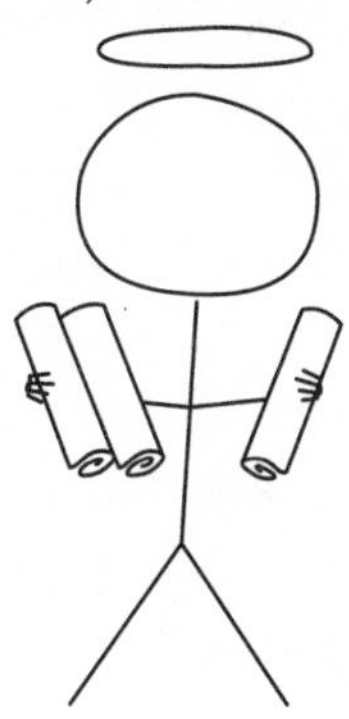

In the movie classic *Charade* (1963), the widow (Audrey Hepburn) of an American soldier searches for weeks with a CIA agent (Cary Grant) to find a fortune left behind by the widow's late husband. The only clues are some random personal belongings and a letter found on her dead husband's body. After much fruitless searching, the pair finally realize that the late husband's fortune is all tied up in the three extremely rare and valuable stamps used on the otherwise plain-looking envelope containing his last letter. In other words, the fortune had been right in front of them the whole time, "hidden in plain view."

There is a similar theme in Matthew 11–13. The kingdom of heaven has arrived with Jesus, who is the King. But people cannot recognize the "kingdom in plain view."

Many of Jesus' miracles and teachings in chapters 11–12 show a lack of recognition of the kingdom. For example, Matthew 11 opens with John the Baptist sending messengers to Jesus to confirm that he really is the Messiah, the King of Israel (Mt 11:2). Locked up by King Herod and suffering in a dark dungeon, even John was beginning to wonder if Jesus had really brought the kingdom. Jesus tells John's disciples to go back and tell him that they had seen the prophesied signs of the age: the healing of the blind, lame, lepers, and the deaf (see Is 35).

Jesus then teaches about John the Baptist, again emphasizing people's lack of recognition. John is the greatest of the prophets. Both he and Jesus have been preaching the kingdom of heaven. John emphasized fasting and self-denial. Jesus gave his blessing to joy and feasting. Despite this, the leaders of the Jews believed neither John nor Jesus. Regardless of how the message was presented, they would not recognize the coming of the kingdom. Even though Jesus performed incredible miracles in some of their greatest cities, they would not accept his preaching.

Later, in Matthew 12, we discover that even exorcisms do not impress the Pharisees. Although Jesus casts out demons publically, they do not accept that he has come from God nor do they believe his message of the kingdom. They say he is in the service of Satan, casting out demons by Satan's power! How backward they have become, such that good has become evil to them and evil, good! They cannot recognize the signs of the kingdom or the power of God's Spirit. They perceive the Spirit as evil; therefore, they cannot be forgiven since the Holy Spirit is the agent of God's forgiveness.

Hypocritically, the scribes and Pharisees come to request a sign from Jesus to prove that his preaching is from God (Mt 12:38). Apparently, all the healings and exorcisms have not been enough. What more do they want Jesus to do? Sensing their lack of sincerity, Jesus refuses to give them a sign; the only sign they will have will be the "sign of Jonah"—that is, Jesus will be dead for three days, as with Jonah's three-day death in the belly of the whale (12:40–42). Jesus' contemporaries are much more blind than the Gentiles in the Old Testament; although many Gentiles recognized God at work in the Israelite kings and prophets, the Pharisees and other leaders cannot recognize God's King walking among them.

This leads right into Matthew 13, a homily of Jesus about the kingdom of heaven in which he tells seven kingdom parables. The common theme in all the parables is that the kingdom is unexpected and not easy for everyone to recognize.

The Parable of the Sower (Mt 13:1–9) describes the "word of the kingdom" as seed that falls on hard, rocky, thorny, or good soil, which represents four different kinds of people. Only those who are "good soil" recognize the "word of the kingdom" for what it is, embrace it fully, and "bear fruit."

The Parable of the Weeds and the Wheat (Mt 13:24–43) describe the kingdom of heaven as a field planted with wheat, with weeds sown in between by a criminal. The owner of the field, unwilling to damage the wheat, leaves the weeds in place until harvest.

The Church Fathers correctly saw this weed-strewn field as an image of the Catholic Church. There are many hypocrites and insincere persons mixed into the visible Church in every age. In fact, it often seems that the hypocrites are more noticeable than true believers just as weeds often stand straight and tall whereas ripe wheat often bends over due to its heavy ear of grain. So the weeds in a wheat field are more prominent than the wheat itself. It would be a mistake, however, to think that the Church was not the kingdom of heaven simply because hypocrites are mixed into the crop. Many Christians through the ages have broken with the Church, offended that there were sinful people within it. Various self-appointed "reformers" have broken off and attempted to establish "pure" or "sifted" churches, but this will not be accomplished until the final judgment. That is not to say there isn't a time and place to excommunicate someone who publically flaunts the teachings of scripture and the Church (see 1 Cor 5:9–13). Sadly, that's sometimes necessary. But only God can remove the hypocritical and insincere who don't call public attention to themselves.

The Parable of the Mustard Seed (Mt 13:31–32) teaches that the kingdom begins with a single small seed that dies in the ground, but that seed grows into an enormous bush for the birds to build a nest in its branches. This is like the Church, starting with the death of a single man, Jesus of Nazareth, and growing into the world's largest institution (1.2 billion people), as the mother of hospitals, schools, and universities, and as the world's teacher and conscience.

The Parable of the Leaven (or Yeast; Mt 13:33) describes the kingdom as yeast that works its way, unseen, through the whole batch of dough. This is the effect of the Church on society. Even when the Church is publically rejected or persecuted, ideas such as human dignity, care for the poor, forgiveness of offenders, and human rights come from the Gospel. They spread in a culture, but many don't even realize these are the effect of the Church.

Jesus concludes his homily with three more short parables on the hidden nature of the kingdom:

The kingdom is like a treasure hidden in a field (v. 44). It isn't obviously there. There aren't neon signs pointing to it. Someone has to be searching (digging) to come across it and realize its value. Again, the Church is like this field. Most people would never suspect its true value; only someone taking the time to investigate patiently would notice.

The kingdom is like a very valuable pearl (vv. 45–46). It can take a trained jeweler to tell the difference between a real or fake, a valuable or worthless pearl. Likewise, those who aren't careful or concerned can fail to recognize the value of a pearl and can fail to see the value of the Church.

Finally, the kingdom is like a fishing net that gathers fish of many kinds (vv. 47–50), which are not sorted out until the fishermen bring the net to shore. The Church Fathers understood the sea as the world and the net as the Church. The fishermen were the apostles and their successors, the bishops. The good and bad fish were saints and sinners in the Church. This parable is particularly important because it proves that the kingdom of heaven is present in this age. The kingdom is a net gathering fish, and the fish are not sorted out till the angels come for the final judgment. That means the kingdom exists *now*, gathering fish *now*. It is not a purely future reality, not simply a perfect age that Jesus will bring at the end of time.

I can hardly stress how important it is for Catholics to reflect on these seven parables of the kingdom in Matthew 13. Jesus came proclaiming that the kingdom of heaven had arrived. Liberal scholars say he was mistaken and died a failed prophet.

Some conservative Protestants say the Jews rejected the kingdom and so Jesus moved to "plan B," the Church, until a good time arrives to bring the kingdom back to the Jews. What these two camps have in common is that they believe the kingdom is some supernaturally perfect age, with Jesus ruling visibly from a throne in Jerusalem, and so forth. It is almost as if they had not read the description of the kingdom in Matthew 13!

The Catholic Church asserts that the kingdom has come, and it is present already in the Church. Everyone else scoffs at this: How can the Church be the kingdom? It's full of bad fish. It has weeds all through it. In some places, it's as small as a mustard seed or as hidden as yeast in dough. It's just an empty ordinary field like any other. It doesn't look any different than these faux pearls to us! But Jesus told us it would be this way. The visible Church will always appear contemptible to people without faith. Nonetheless, inside it, the kingdom of God is already present because Jesus the King lives in his Church.

Book 4 of Matthew: The Merciful Kingdom *(Matthew 14–18)*

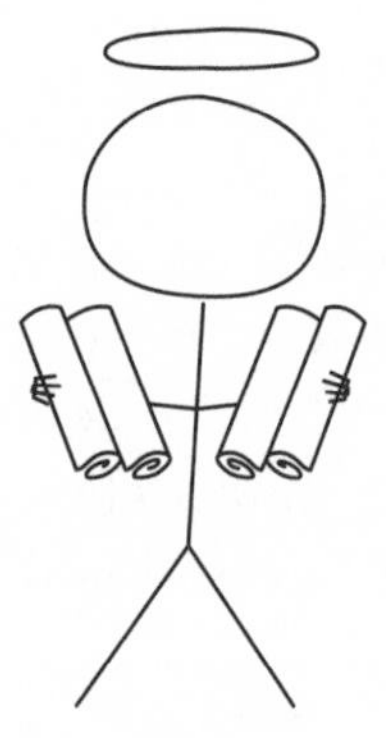

Mercy in God's kingdom is the dominant theme in the next "book" or unit of Matthew (chapters 14–18). Mercy and the forgiveness of offenses can be rare qualities in societies not influenced by the Gospel. Some cultures do not even regard mercy and forgiveness as a virtue, seeing it instead as a sign of weakness or a failure to enforce justice.

The theme of mercy is seen in several of the more important miracle stories and teachings in this book. Twice in this section, Jesus has mercy or "compassion" on the crowds that come to him, and he provides them food by multiplying loaves and fish (Mt 14:13–21; 15:32–39). After Peter's great confession of Jesus as the Son of God, Jesus gives him the power to "loose [things] on earth," and the Greek word "loose" can refer to release from sins (Rv 1:5). So Peter will have a role as "chief forgiver of sins." Finally, in Jesus' concluding homily in Matthew 18, he talks quite a bit about mercy and forgiveness. He gives instructions on forgiving one's brother (vv. 21–22) and tells the Parable of the Unmerciful Servant (vv. 23–35).

We can't discuss every story that is in these five chapters, so we'll concentrate on a couple of important ones that show how Jesus' kingdom is one of mercy. The two feeding miracles, one of five thousand and the other of four thousand, are important in this section of Matthew. Many think they are confused accounts of the same event, but they are not. The feeding of the five thousand takes place in Jewish territory, and the twelve basketfuls left over symbolize the restoration of the Twelve Tribes of Israel, the people of God. The feeding of the four thousand takes place in Gentile territory (15:21), and the seven basketfuls left over may symbolize the covenant with the Gentiles that the Messiah was expected to make (Is 42:6; Am 9:11–12; Zec 14:16–19). Seven is the number of the covenant (Gn 21:27–32). Jesus probably performed other feeding miracles during his three-year ministry, but only these two are recorded by the gospel authors.

When Jesus almost single-handedly feeds the entire company of five thousand Israelites in Matthew 14, we are reminded of not only the feeding miracle of Elisha (2 Kgs 4:42–44) but also the glorious times when David and his royal sons fed all Israel at the king's own expense. David provided a feast of bread and wine to all Israel when the ark was brought to Jerusalem (2 Sm 6). Solomon did the same thing at the dedication of the Temple (1 Kgs 8). The good kings Hezekiah and Josiah provided a Passover meal for the entire nation largely at their own expense (2 Chr 30:24; 35:7–8). So Jesus, the Son of David, feeding Israel at his own expense is part of a great royal tradition.

Of course, these feeding miracles point forward to the Eucharist, where the Son of David, Jesus, feeds us all at his own expense in the most profound way possible: he gives us his very body and blood for food. Matthew tells the feeding of the five thousand and four thousand in such a way that ancient readers would make the connection to the Eucharist. He recalls Jesus telling the people to *recline* and then *taking* the bread, *giving thanks* or *blessing* it (the Greek words "give thanks" and "bless" can be synonymous), *breaking* it, and *distributing* it to the people. The gospel authors use this sequence of words—*recline, take, give thanks, break,* and *distribute*—when retelling the account of the Last Supper when the Eucharist was established. Early Christians heard these words every week at the celebration of the Eucharist, so the first readers of Matthew's gospel were sure to recognize the connection with Jesus' miraculous feedings.

Jesus showed *compassion* and *mercy* on the crowds by feeding them, lest they faint from hunger while returning to their homes. The Eucharist continues to be a feast of *compassion* where Jesus the King feeds us, his subjects, at his own expense so that we don't faint from spiritual starvation during our earthly journey. It is the royal feast of mercy.

Themes of royalty and compassion are also present in one of the most important historical accounts in this part of Matthew. In Matthew 16:13–20, Jesus asks his disciples who people think he is and what they think he came to do. After getting a survey of responses, Jesus puts the question to the disciples themselves: What about you guys? Who do *you guys* say that I am? There was probably an awkward silence for a moment while the disciples fumbled mentally for what to say, until Peter stepped forward with boldness: "You are the Christ, the Son of the living God."

What Jesus said next is of great importance, and we need to work through it slowly. "And Jesus answered him, 'Blessed are you, Simon, Bar-Jona! For flesh and blood has not revealed this to you, but my Father who is in heaven. And I tell you, you are Peter [*petros*], and on this rock [*petra*] I will build my church, and the powers of hades shall not prevail against it. I will give you the keys of the kingdom of heaven, and whatever you bind on earth shall be bound in heaven, and whatever you loose on earth shall be loosed in heaven'" (Mt 16:17–19).

Now, we have to understand that the name "Peter" is from the Greek word for "rock" (*petra*, as in "petrified") only with a masculine ending on it: *petros*. This word was never before used as a man's name. So, in this passage, Jesus identifies St. Peter as the "rock" on which he will build his "church" that will overcome "hades." This is temple-building imagery. Jews knew the Temple in Jerusalem was built on a great natural stone slab called "the foundation stone" (Hebrew, *eben shettiyyah*), which they believed blocked up the shaft that led down to the realm of the dead: *Hades* in Greek or *Sheol* in Hebrew. So Jesus is comparing his Church to a new temple built on Peter.

Some interpreters argue that Peter is not the rock on which Jesus built the Church. They say that two *different* Greek words are used in the verse: *petros* and *petra*. So Peter (*petros*) is not the rock (*petra*) but something else is, such as his confession of faith in Jesus.

This problem of two different words for rock only arises because the gospels translate Jesus' words into Greek, the international language of the day (as English is today). In Greek, the word for rock, *petra*, has a feminine ending *a*, as with many English women's names: Sarah, Laura, Rebekah, Angelina, and so forth. So it can't be used as a man's name with changing the ending to the masculine, which is *os* in Greek: *petros*. In other words, you can't call a man "Rock-aleena"; you have to call him "Rocky."

But Jesus spoke the language of Jews of his day (Aramaic), and in that language, there is just one word for "rock": *kepha*. What Jesus said to Peter was, "You are *kepha*, and on this *kepha* I will build my church." This Aramaic word *kepha* gives us the name "Cephas" used for Peter in several places (Jn 1:42; 1 Cor 1:12, 3:22, 9:5, 15:5; Gal 1:18; 2:9, 11, 14).

The gist of all this is, in Jesus' spoken language, it was absolutely clear that Peter (*kepha*) was the rock (*kepha*) on which he would build his church, but a little confusion enters when Matthew translates Jesus' words into Greek.

Now let's look at the "keys of the kingdom" and the "binding and loosing." In the ancient kingdom of David, the officer in charge of the palace was the king's top advisor and right-hand man, the second most powerful person in the kingdom. Scholars call him "the royal steward," and he wore the keys of the palace tied to his shoulder as a sign of his office (Is 22:22). Only he had the authority to unlock or lock the palace, so he controlled access to the king. If you wanted to see the king, you had to go through the royal steward. No one but the king himself could contradict him; therefore, they used to say about the royal steward, "He shall open, and none shall shut; and he shall shut, and none shall open" (Is 22:22). Jesus echoes this line when he says, "Whatever you bind on earth will be bound in heaven, whatever you loose on earth will be loosed in heaven." So Jesus is making Peter his royal steward, his "big number two."

King

Royal Steward

Other Officers

Structure of the Kingdom

But "binding" and "loosing" had another meaning in Jesus' day. Jews used the phrase to speak about the authority to make official interpretations of religious law.

Religious law always needs to be interpreted. God said that on the Sabbath "you shall not do any work" (Ex 20:10), but what is "work"? Is starting a fire "work"? The Jewish teachers (rabbis) said yes, so they "bound," forbade, starting fires on the Sabbath day. Is taking a half-mile walk "work"? The rabbis said no, so they "loosed," permitted, short walks on the Sabbath.

So, in Matthew 16, Jesus is making Peter his "chief rabbi." Peter will interpret divine law. Heaven will guide him and back him up. As Catholics, we know this authority of Peter was passed on to his successors, the bishops of Rome, to our present day. That's why, when faced with new issues that require the interpretation of divine law, such as new biotechnologies, we look to the pope for guidance to determine what is right and wrong.

Finally, "binding" and "loosing" can refer to retaining or forgiving sins, as in Revelation 1:5: "[Jesus Christ] has *loosed* us from our sins." So Peter's power to "bind and loose" includes the authority to forgive sin. We see this also at the end of John, when Jesus breathes on the apostles after his resurrection and says, "If you forgive the sins of any, they are forgiven; if you retain the sins of any, they are retained" (Jn 20:23). Peter will be the "chief forgiver of sins." He seems to realize this, and a little while later, during Jesus' famous "Church Discourse" (Mt 18), he asks Jesus some practical specifics about forgiving sins (Mt 18:21–22).

Let's move now to that great homily that ends this section of Matthew. Sin and forgiveness are the main themes. Jesus begins by warning that those who cause children who believe in Jesus to sin will have a serious price to pay in the next life: "it would be better for him to have a great millstone fastened round his neck and to be drowned in the depth of the sea" (Mt 18:6). Millstones could weigh hundreds of pounds.

Sinning and causing others to sin is a very serious business! Jesus warns that if your hand, foot, or eye causes you to sin, you should cut it off in order to save your soul. Now the Lord did not mean this literally. Neither the apostles nor the other early saints made a practice of cutting off their body parts. This is an example of *hyperbole* (hi-PER-bow-lee): exaggeration for emphasis. Furthermore, it's not *really* our limbs or our organs that cause us to sin. Sin doesn't come from the hand or the eye; it comes out of the heart (Mt 15:19). Cutting off limbs would not stop us from sinning.

Since sin is so serious, should we live in fear of hell? No, we shouldn't because we have a loving father as a God. Jesus tells the Parable of the Lost Sheep: God is like a shepherd who would leave a flock of ninety-nine sheep to find and bring back just one that went astray. Therefore, when we go astray, we rest assured that God our Shepherd will come after us.

The apostles are under-shepherds who will have to decide whether or not to forgive the sins of other Christians, so Jesus gives advice about how to deal with sinners in the Church: First, go to the sinner and show him his sin personally. If he doesn't listen, bring one or two witnesses along. Finally, tell the whole Church about the matter, and if he will not listen to the whole Church, stop treating him as a fellow Christian.

Jesus then bestows on the apostles as a group the power to "bind and loose." As we saw above, this is the authority to interpret divine law and to forgive or retain sin. This power, given to the apostles as a group, was transmitted to their successors, the bishops. That's why we hold a gathering of all the Church's bishops (an "ecumenical council") to be *infallible*, that is, not able to go wrong.

Peter has a question about exercising his role of "chief forgiver" and asks if he should forgive the same sinner "as many as seven times"? Peter probably thought he was being generous, but Jesus responds, "I do not say to you seven times, but seventy times seven." "Seventy times seven" is 490, a special number in the Bible. In ancient Israel, every forty-nine years there was a jubilee year when all debts were forgiven. Four hundred ninety years is ten jubilee cycles, a period of perfect forgiveness. The number 490 represents the perfection of forgiveness.

Jesus ends his homily with the Parable of the Unmerciful Servant. We know this parable well. The kingdom of heaven is like a king whose servant owed him an impossibly large sum (one thousand talents, more than three hundred million dollars today). The servant pled for forgiveness, so the king forgave him. The servant then goes out and attempts to strangle another servant who owed him about three month's wages (one hundred denarii, about five thousand dollars). The second servant pled for forgiveness, but the first would have none of it and threw him in jail. Finally, the king hears the sorry story and calls the first servant in: "I forgave you all that debt . . . and should you not have had mercy on your fellow servant?" Jesus concludes, "So also my heavenly Father will do to everyone of you, if you do not forgive your brother from your heart" (Mt 18:23–35).

Unlike the kingdoms of the world, which were based on fear of punishment and vicious penalties for minor infractions, Jesus' "kingdom of heaven" would be based on *mercy* expressed in the forgiveness of sins, debts, and offenses. The foundational mercy for the whole kingdom is the mercy of the king, who forgives every one of us the enormous debt of our sin. Having experienced God's forgiveness, we practice forgiveness toward others.

It's hard to feel how radical Jesus' teaching about the kingdom was back in his day. Nowadays, due to the influence of Christianity, principles of forgiveness and mercy are written into the law codes of many countries. We've become used to thinking that forgiveness and mercy are virtues. So now we try to rehabilitate, and not merely punish, criminals. This is the quiet effect of the Gospel, like the leaven in the dough. It wasn't always like this. Moreover, there is still plenty of unforgiveness between persons, groups, and nations everywhere in our world today. There are still many of us who need conversion. Although Jesus has forgiven our one-thousand-talent debt, we can't manage to forgive the one-hundred-denarii debt of some family member, coworker, or friend. We have to relearn what it means to be a citizen of the kingdom.

Book 5 of Matthew: Jesus Teaches on the End of the Kingdom *(Matthew 19–25)*

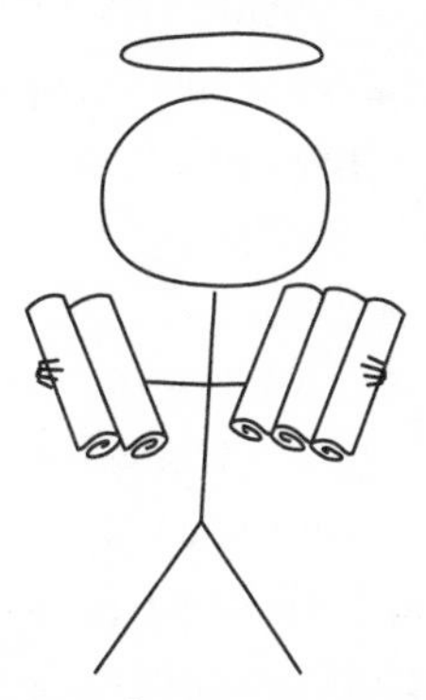

Jesus is now wrapping up his ministry, and in this last book of Matthew, we find him discussing the ends of things: the end of his life, the end of Jerusalem, and the end of the world.

Jesus begins with a set of teachings that are based on how things will be at the end of time in heaven. The Pharisees come to Jesus and ask him if divorce is lawful (Mt 19:3–12). Jesus says no. God made marriage to last forever; Moses only allowed it reluctantly because of men's stubbornness. The disciples are shocked: if marriage is permanent, it's better not to get married! Jesus agrees that those who are able should lead a single life and become "eunuchs for the sake of the kingdom of heaven." There were such voluntary "eunuchs" in Jesus' day. On the shores of the Dead Sea, at a site called Qumran, there lived a group of celibate Jewish men who prayed and worshipped together while waiting for the coming of the Messiah. We Catholics would call them monks. Jesus praises such men. They living a "heavenly" life because in heaven there will be no marriage (22:30). They are living *now* as everyone will live *in the end*.

A rich young man comes to Jesus in Matthew 19 and asks how to be saved. Jesus tells him to sell all his goods, give the money to the poor, and follow him. The rich young man is not up for this. He doesn't realize that there will be no possessions in heaven and that all one's property is going to decay in time. Not grasping this, he refuses to live *now* in the way that everyone will live *in the end*.

The apostles *have* left all their goods to follow Jesus, so naturally Peter wants to know what they will get in the end for their faithfulness. Jesus tells them: in the new world, when the Son of Man sits on his glorious throne, you will sit on twelve thrones, judging the twelve tribes of Israel. This is a clear reference to Solomon, who sat on his glorious throne (1 Kgs 10:18–20) and appointed twelve officers over the Twelve Tribes of Israel (1 Kgs 4:7; cf. Ps 122:5). Jesus' words may refer to a special honor the apostles will enjoy in the end at the final judgment. However, they will be fulfilled before then, too. In just a few months after saying these words, Jesus would ascend to heaven and take his seat on the glorious throne of his father. The apostles would begin their rule over the Church, the New Israel. They would enjoy spiritual thrones, that is, spiritual authority to govern the

Church, including supernatural power, as we see in the Book of Acts (see 4:32–5:16). The authority of the apostles would be passed on to their successors, the bishops, who now sit on thrones called *cathedras* (from Greek *kathedra*, "seat, throne") in big buildings called *cathedrals* all around the world.

The apostles will have a special place in the kingdom, but Jesus does not want them to serve him out of self-interest, out of some greedy desire to be a "big shot" in heaven. So he tells the Parable of the Vineyard, about several groups of vineyard workers who labor for different hours in the day, but each receive the same wage, a denarius (about fifty dollars). Now, the "vineyard" is a biblical symbol of the nation of Israel (see Is 5:1–5), so this parable connects with Jesus' promise that the apostles would rule the twelve tribes. What is the "denarius" that everyone receives? Probably Jesus himself. He is the wage that every faithful laborer will receive at the end of time. So, in a sense, all will receive the same reward.

James and John don't get the point. They send their mother to ask for the top two positions in the kingdom: to sit on Jesus' "right and left." Jesus says that decision is really not up to him. Actually, the ones who will sit on Jesus' "right and left" when he is acclaimed as king will be two thieves, each on their own cross! James and John didn't realize what they were asking! But Jesus warns them that "whoever would be first among you must be your slave" because the kingdom is about service, not about lording it over other people. Jesus turns the usual organizational hierarchy upside down. The worldly, or demonic, view of leadership looks like this:

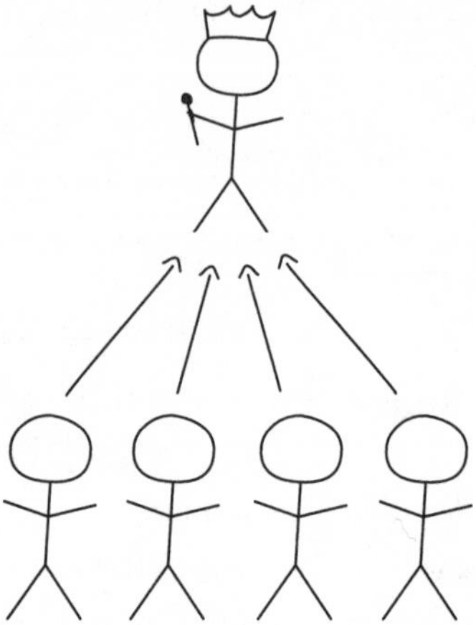

Service flows up from the people to the ruler. I use the term "demonic" intentionally because this is Satan's view of how things should work. The lesser exist for the greater and should serve the greater. This is the philosophy of the Nazis, of Friedrich Nietzsche, and of Ayn Rand. According to tradition, Satan fell from heaven when he realized he would be sent by God to serve puny humans, and that offended his sensibilities.

But Jesus teaches, "Whoever would be great among you must be your servant," which makes an organizational structure that looks like this:

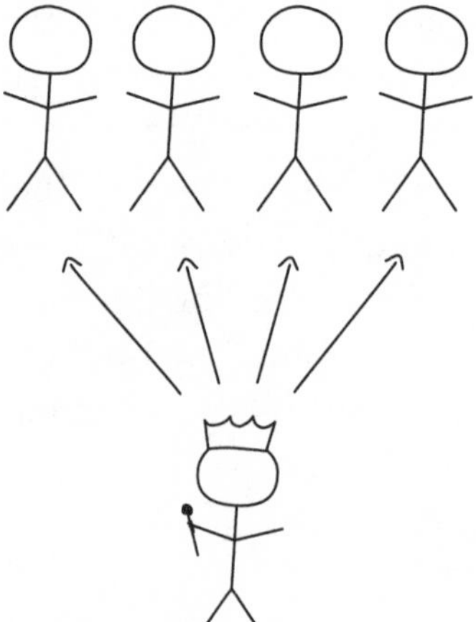

In the Church, those who are leaders should serve. Priests serve their parish; bishops, their diocese; and the pope, the universal Church. So we call the pope *servus servorum Dei*, "servant of the servants of God." This is an upside-down kingdom. That doesn't mean they don't have any authority should be doormats, but the authority is given for the purpose of serving everyone else.

Now it is time for Passion Week. Jesus begins the last week of his life by riding into Jerusalem on a donkey. This is a reenactment of Solomon's entrance into Jerusalem on a donkey the day that he became king. Five hundred years earlier, the prophet Zechariah had predicted that another king would come one day and enter Jerusalem on a donkey just like Solomon. Zechariah had described it poetically: "Your king comes to you . . . humble and riding on an ass, on a colt the foal of an ass" (Zec 9:9). Just to make sure that the crowds realize the prophecy is being fulfilled, Jesus gets both a donkey and a donkey's foal and uses them both to ride into town. The crowds get the point and go wild with excitement: a miracle-working prophet is riding into the royal city in the style of Solomon of old! The time has come for all the prophecies to be fulfilled! They throw branches and clothes on the road to give him the "red carpet" treatment.

Solomon, the son of David, built the first Temple, and ever afterward, the royal sons of David had the responsibility for maintaining it. Jesus' first act upon entering Jerusalem in royal procession is to go inspect the Temple. He finds it defiled by unscrupulous merchants, so he kicks them all out.

The leadership of Jerusalem is none too happy about all this, so Jesus delivers several teachings about their fate. He curses a fig tree on the way into Jerusalem, which immediately withers. The fig tree is a symbol of Jerusalem itself; since Jerusalem does not repent at the arrival of the Messiah, God's own Son, the city will fall under a curse of destruction. The leadership of Jerusalem is like a son who tells his father he will obey but never follows through (Mt 21:28–32). They will find themselves outside of God's kingdom while repentant tax collectors and harlots will enter it.

The leaders of Jerusalem are like workers in the vineyard that represents Israel. They have control of the vineyard but won't obey the owner. They kill all the owner's messengers (the prophets) and finally his Son (Jesus). Therefore, they won't escape punishment from the owner. God's kingdom, which is also the kingdom of Israel, will be taken from them and given to others, namely, the apostles and their successors.

The following day, Jesus returns to Jerusalem and begins a "wisdom contest" against all comers in the royal city. A wisdom contest is when a sage takes up a teaching position in a public place and all come to challenge him. If he defeats all comers, he gains the right to keep teaching. We see Solomon engaged in a wisdom contest in Jerusalem in the Book of First Kings, where people come from all nations (1 Kgs 4:34), especially the Queen of Sheba, to "test him with hard questions." The Pharisees, Sadducees, and others will now come to test Jesus, the one "greater than Solomon."

Before the wisdom contest begins, Jesus makes a kind of opening statement with his Parable of the Marriage Feast. In this parable, God the Father is the king, Jesus is the son getting married, and the marriage feast is the new Passover (the Eucharist) that Jesus is about to celebrate. The invitees are the leaders of Israel, the people who ought to welcome the coming of Israel's Messiah, but they reject the invitation and even abuse the messengers. So the king sends his troops to burn their city—a reference to the destruction of Jerusalem, which would take place in less than forty years (ca. AD 70). Riffraff from the streets (that is, the Gentiles) are recruited to fill the kings' banquet hall (the Church), which is now filled with "both good and bad," reminding us of the weeds, the wheat, and the net. A guest, however, shows up with no wedding garment (good deeds; see Rv 19:8), so the host tosses him out. Sometimes this is necessary in the Church (see 1 Cor 5:9–13).

The leaders of Jerusalem, both Pharisees and Sadducees, don't fully understand the parable, but they can figure out that they are the butt of it, the ones whose city will be burned. So they become determined to ruin Jesus' reputation and career by any means possible.

The Pharisees come first, asking him whether it is lawful to pay taxes to Caesar. They think they have him trapped. If he says yes, they will tell the crowds, *This man cannot possibly be a prophet of God. He supports the pagan, tyrannical, immoral Roman regime that is oppressing us, God's true people!*

If he says no, they will immediately go to the Roman authorities and say, *Arrest this man! He is trying to start a revolution by telling everyone to stop paying their taxes to Caesar!*

Jesus responds, *Whose image and inscription are on the coins?*

Caesar's, they say.

Then give to Caesar what is Caesar's and to God what is God's (Mt 22:21).

The point is, according to Genesis 1:26 and 28, the image and likeness of God are stamped on every human being. Therefore, as far as Jesus is concerned, you can give all your money back to the government that printed it and then give your whole self to God. It's similar to what he said to the rich young ruler: "Sell what you possess . . . and come, follow me" (Mt 19:21). After all, there's no material wealth in heaven, so you might as well start now.

The Pharisees are unwilling to follow this advice. Jesus uncovers their hypocrisy because, on the one hand, the Pharisees very much enjoyed the wealth made possible by the stability of the Roman government and its internationally recognized currency. On the other hand, they resented paying the taxes that made the Pax Romana (the "Roman peace") possible. Jesus is pointing out that if you want to enjoy the benefits of Rome, you have to pay Rome's dues.

The Pharisees have whiffed. Next up to bat are the Sadducees. The Sadducees consisted of the high priestly families who controlled the Temple and everyone whose livelihood depended on them. They were the original religious "professionals," people who make their living working for religious organizations but don't personally have faith and even look down on the people who do.

The Sadducees would only accept the first five books of the Bible (Genesis through Deuteronomy, a.k.a. the Torah, Pentateuch, or Books of Moses) as scripture. Since the resurrection and the life to come are never directly described in these books, the Sadducees did not believe in them. In fact, they thought the whole idea of a future life was ridiculous. It would create insolvable conundrums, such as the one they present to Jesus: One woman was married to seven brothers in turn, each of whom married her and then died and left her to his next brother in line. Now, in the resurrection—*if* there is a resurrection [snicker]—to whom will she be married? That is to say, *Look, Rabbi Jesus, isn't all this resurrection stuff a bunch of ridiculous nonsense?*

Jesus responds, *You are wrong because you do not know the scriptures and the power of God. First, there is no marriage in heaven. Second, there is a life to come, and it is taught in the Books of Moses*, the only scriptures that the Sadducees accepted. Jesus quotes Exodus 3:6, where God says, "I AM the

God of Abraham, the God of Isaac, and the God of Jacob" and concludes, "He is not the God of the dead, but of the living." The argument here depends on the tense of the verb. If Abraham, Isaac, and Jacob were dead, God would have had to say, "I *WAS* the God of Abraham . . ." But that's not what God says. He *IS* the God of Abraham, which means Abraham is still alive! Jesus' answer is brilliant, and he does what no Jewish rabbi had succeeded in doing before him: he offered a proof of the life to come from the Books of Moses.

Let's notice how a view of *the end* has guided both of Jesus' answers. In the end, we won't have money—the answer to the Pharisees. In the end, there won't be marriage—the answer to the Sadducees.

Now, the Sadducees have whiffed. So all Jesus' opponents huddled up, trying to think of another stumper. One, a lawyer, came up with an honest question: "Teacher, which is the greatest commandment in the law?" (Mt 22:36). This question is not obviously hostile, but if Jesus gave an ill-considered response, he could discredit himself, alienate some of his audience, or get embroiled in a debate with other rabbis.

Jesus' answer is not entirely new; some rabbis had said similar things before him. But it is a great summary: "You shall love the LORD your God. . . . This is the great and first commandment. And a second is like it, You shall love your neighbor as yourself" (Mt 22:37–39). Thus, the whole moral teaching of scripture boils down to love of God and love of neighbor. This is now almost a cliché. We've heard it so often we no longer recognize the brilliant simplicity. The Pharisees and other experts in the law realized they could not argue against it.

Having defended himself from all challengers in this "wisdom contest," Jesus now goes on offense, posing a question to the Pharisees: *If the Messiah is the Son of David, how can*

David call him "my lord" in Psalm 110:1? A couple of assumptions are at work here. One is your descendant can never be your master because he owes you the honor due a father. The second is Psalm 110 is a prophecy of the Messiah. Now, the Pharisees accepted both these assumptions, so they are stumped. They cannot figure out why David would call the Messiah "my lord." In hindsight, we know what the answer is: because the Messiah is also God himself, true God and true man. But the Pharisees aren't ready to go there. They aren't ready to accept Jesus as the Messiah, much less that he is God himself walking among them.

Jesus has defeated the Pharisees, so now he really asserts his authority. In Matthew 23, Jesus spends the whole chapter warning the Pharisees about where they are going to *end up* unless they repent. With seven "woes" (vv. 13, 15, 16, 23, 25, 27, 29), he bluntly warns them that "upon you" will come the judgment for "all the righteous blood shed on earth." It is not that Jesus hates the Pharisees; rather, he uses a kind of "tough love." Some people are so far gone you have to risk being blunt with them. In fact, you *must* be honest with them because they *deserve* to be warned of the disaster that's ahead of them.

For the Pharisees, that disaster will be the destruction of their culture and capital city, Jerusalem. So Jesus laments over Jerusalem (23:37–39) and proceeds to the last great discourse of the Book of Matthew, the "eschatological discourse."

Eschatological (say "ess-SKAT-oh" + "logical") means "related to the end times." In Matthew 24–25, Jesus describes the "end times" of two things: Jerusalem and the world. When you read these chapters, you will find many things that clearly sound like the end of the world and the final judgment. However, scholars see many events in these chapters that were fulfilled in the siege and destruction of Jerusalem in AD 70.

Actually, Jesus is describing both things at once. Jerusalem was the Temple city, the "navel of the universe" whose Temple represented the whole cosmos. The Temple was decorated with images of the sun, moon, and stars. Jews viewed the cosmos as a macrotemple and the temple as a microcosmos.[2] Therefore, the destruction of Jerusalem and its Temple was a premonition of the end of the world. That's the key concept for understanding Matthew 24–25. When Jesus says, "this generation will not pass away till all these things take place" (24:34), it has a double meaning. A generation was sometimes calculated as forty years, and within less than forty years, all the tribulations Jesus described would fall on Jerusalem (see 23:37–38). On the other hand, the Greek *genea*, "generation," can also mean "kindred" or "race" (cf. Lv 25:41; Nm 10:30), and the human race will not pass away before God brings the final judgment.

Jesus finishes with three parables about being ready for *the end*: the Wise and Foolish Maidens (25:1–13); the Talents (25:14–30); and the Sheep and the Goats (25:31–46).

In the Parable of Maidens, it is clear that Jesus himself is the bridegroom whom the young women are expecting. Let's note how often Jesus uses bridegroom and marriage imagery to talk about the kingdom of heaven. We've seen it before throughout the gospel, most recently in the Parable of the Wedding Feast (22:1–14). Let's remember that the prophets spoke of the LORD as the husband of Israel, and the Davidic king was also a major bridegroom figure of the Old Testament. Jesus is both the LORD and the Davidic King. The Eucharist is the Wedding Feast where we receive his Body. But we are getting ahead of ourselves. In the Church's tradition, the "oil in the lamps" of the wise virgins was understood as a life of holiness. It is wise to live a life of love for God *now* and not wait to "get ready for Jesus" right before he comes for you either at the end of time or at the end of *your* time (that is, your death). In a special way, these "maidens" or "virgins" point forward to religious brothers and sisters who lead a life of celibacy so that they can devote themselves totally to "waiting for Jesus." They lead an end-times lifestyle today.

The Parable of the Talents reminds us that we are to be busy with the tasks God gives us while we wait for Jesus to return. Our Lord wants us to "grow" his kingdom during the time that we have, and he is not pleased with those who sit on their hands, hoping to get into heaven with the least possible effort in this life.

The Parable of the Sheep and the Goats warns that individual persons and entire nations will be judged based on what they did for "the least of these my brethren" (25:40). Whatever anyone does for a weak, sick, naked, thirsty, or imprisoned "brother" of Jesus, Jesus regards as being done to himself personally.

The original message of this parable was whatever kindness you show to a Christian (a "brother of Jesus"), Jesus regards as kindness to himself. Jesus and his followers are one. Even better is to say Jesus and his Church are one. In time, we've come to expand the meaning of this parable and take it as an exhortation to help all the poor, since any poor person might be a "brother" or "sister" of Jesus, unbeknownst to us.

Wow! We've come to the end of book five of Matthew, the book about the *end of the kingdom*. Notice how much of it was guided by the idea of "the end." Jesus has given much guidance for living based on the fact that, "in the end," we won't marry or hold property (Mt 19:3–12; 16–30; 22:15–33). Furthermore, most of his teaching has been taken up with warnings and parables about "the end" of time and the punishment or reward that people will receive.

Matthew's Easter *(Matthew 26–28)*

To keep it simple, we call this section "Matthew's Easter," but it might be better to call it "Matthew's Triduum" because these chapters give us the historical record of the events we celebrate on Holy Thursday, Good Friday, and Easter.

Matthew's account of the Last Supper and the institution of the Eucharist can be found in chapter 26. When a woman anoints Jesus with expensive perfume at a banquet in Bethany (only two miles from Jerusalem), Jesus compares it to anointing his body for burial (vv. 6–13). Perhaps tired of following a rabbi with an apparent death wish, Judas sneaks off to swing a deal with the chief priests to betray Jesus at the right moment (vv. 14–16). Meanwhile, Jesus has some other disciples prepare a room for them to celebrate the Passover in Jerusalem (vv. 17–19).

Let's look closely at how Jesus leads the disciples in the Last Supper. As they were eating, Jesus *took* bread, *blessed* it, *broke* it, and *gave* it to the disciples saying, "Take, eat; this is my body" (v. 26). Notice this sequence *take-bless-break-give*. It's the same sequence as the feeding of the five thousand (14:19). The disciples are reclining at the supper (26:20 in Greek) just as the five thousand lay down on the grass (14:19). Matthew is comparing these two meals. They are both miraculous suppers with the Messiah in which the Messiah supernaturally transforms natural food. Over the cup, Jesus says, "Drink of it, all of you; for this is my blood of the covenant" (26:27–28). There is only one place in the Old Testament where the precise phrase "the blood of the covenant" occurs and that is in Exodus 24:8, where Moses sprinkles blood on the altar (representing God) and on the people, declaring, "Behold, the blood of the covenant." What's the point? *What Jesus is doing on top of Mt. Zion with the twelve apostles is as earthshaking as what Moses did on Mt. Sinai with the twelve tribes.*

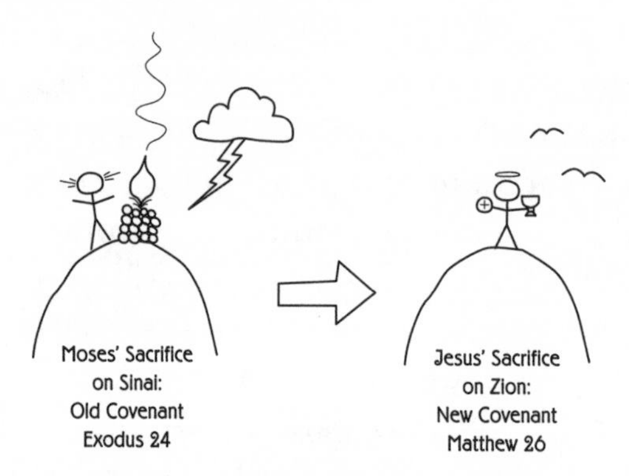

Only there is a change: Moses sprinkled the people with "the blood of the covenant." Jesus tells the apostles to drink of "*my* blood of the covenant" (emphasis added). Moses made the covenant with the blood of bulls (Ex 24:5). But bulls cannot bear the price for human sin. Jesus makes the New Covenant with his own blood.

Why is it "my *blood* of the covenant" (emphasis added)? Blood means family. We say he's "blood to me," meaning "he's a relative of mine," and we say "blood is thicker than water," meaning biological family relationships are stronger than other attachments. Again, we say, "He's a *blood* relative," meaning a family member by birth, not only by law. This is why the New Covenant is so brilliant. Covenant is family-making by oath. The oath ritual for the New Covenant is a meal where Jesus *gives us his blood to drink so we can share the blood of God*. We become God's "blood relatives"—his family.

The Bible says, "The life of the flesh is in the blood" (Lv 17:11). God didn't want his people sharing animal life, so in the Old Testament, drinking blood was forbidden (Lv 7:26–27). But God does want us to share divine life, so now drinking

Jesus' blood is commanded (Mt 26:27–28): "Drink of it . . . this is my blood of the covenant."

This blood of the covenant, Jesus says, "is poured out for many for the forgiveness of sins" (26:28). Sins were keeping us out of a covenant relationship with God in the first place. The eucharistic blood removes sins and makes us family at the same time.

Finally, Jesus says, "I shall not drink again of this fruit of the vine until that day when I drink it new with you in my Father's kingdom" (v. 29). That sounds as if Jesus is promising never to drink wine again ("the fruit of the vine") until the kingdom arrives. This is odd because there was still at least one cup of wine left to complete the Passover ceremony. Wasn't Jesus going to complete the Passover? Or was the Father's kingdom going to arrive before the end of the meal? Many people take it to mean that Jesus was speaking of a great feast he will share with all his followers when he returns at the end of time. But what does Jesus really mean by these words?

After drinking the eucharistic cup, the disciples sang "a hymn, [and] went out to the Mount of Olives" (v. 30). That also seems odd. The "hymn" would have been a set of psalms (Pss 115–118) known as the *Hallel*, sung near the end of the Passover service. After the *Hallel*, however, a final cup of wine was drunk and a last blessing was pronounced to end the meal.[3] Matthew, however, makes no mention of this. Instead, after the hymn, they "went out to the Mount of Olives." For someone who knows the Passover ritual, this sounds as if they left before the end. It would be like reading about a Mass celebration where priest and people leave the church after Communion, without saying, "The mass is ended. Go in peace. Thanks be to God!"

Why does the Last Supper seem to end without the drinking of the final cup of wine? Then, when Jesus goes to the Mount of

Olives, he prays there repeatedly: "My Father, if it be possible, *let this cup [or "chalice"] pass from me.*" And finally, he says, "If this cannot pass away *unless I drink it*, thy will be done" (Mt 26:39, 42; emphasis added).

Almost immediately after this, Judas arrives with soldiers and thugs from the authorities. They seize Jesus to drag him before the high priest and the Jewish council for a "kangaroo court." Jewish law forbade court cases to be tried at night.[4] False witnesses come forward to accuse Jesus, but the court can't find any convincing charge that would merit the death penalty, even though they were looking for one. Finally, the high priest tries a desperate move to get Jesus to incriminate himself: "I adjure you by the living God, tell us if you are the Christ." Jesus responds, "You have said so," which was an ancient slang such as our modern "you said it!" meaning, "that's right!" Then Jesus says, "Hereafter you will see the Son of man seated at the right hand of Power, and coming on the clouds of heaven" (Mt 26:63–64).

Long ago, the prophet Daniel had a vision of the future in which he saw "one like a son of man" coming "with the clouds of heaven" to appear before the heavenly courtroom where the "Ancient of Days" presides (Dn 7:13). This "Ancient of Days" is God himself, or as Christians we would say God the Father. Jesus is claiming to be the "Son of man" who will come before the "Ancient of Days" riding on the clouds.

But this idea of riding on the clouds doesn't just mean up in the sky. Riding on the clouds was a divine privilege; in paganism, the chief god rode on the clouds: Jupiter for the Romans, Zeus for the Greeks, Ba'al for the Canaanites, and Thor for the Norse. So the Son of Man is more than just a human being: he has divine power and authority. That's what Jesus is claiming for himself. The high priest senses this and tears his robe in pretended shock: You heard the blasphemy!

We don't need any more witnesses. *Well, that's convenient because it just so happens that we don't have any more witnesses and none of the ones we did have were any good.* As for tearing his robes—that was illegal for the high priest to do, according to biblical law (Lv 10:6; 21:10). As for the charge of "blasphemy," an intentional insult to the majesty of God, that was a real stretch. Although it's clear Jesus was claiming to be the Messiah, the words he spoke did not personally offend God in any way according to Jewish law. Nonetheless, the rest of the court jumped on the bandwagon of the "blasphemy" charge because it was the only excuse they could come up with to put Jesus to death. "He deserves death!" they all shout.

Meanwhile, Jesus' best friend Peter is out in the courtyard, telling all the bystanders that he's never even met this strange "Jesus of Nazareth" person they keep talking about around the fire (26:69–75).

In the morning, the chief priests take Jesus to Pilate to have him executed. Now, there are two reasons they did this. First of all, technically they did not have the authority to execute anyone because the Roman government kept that authority for itself. However, the Jewish council leadership could (and did) just lynch people when they got good and angry (Acts 7:54–59), so that was not the real reason they handed him over to Pilate.

There were at least two others. First, they were scared of Jesus and his popularity and what the reaction might be if it was found out that they had killed him. If there was a popular backlash about his death, they wanted it to be directed at the Romans, not themselves. Second, if the Romans killed him, it would be done by crucifixion, which was a particularly cruel and torturous means of death and carried with it a divine curse. According to Deuteronomy 21:22–23, anyone hanged on a tree becomes "accursed by God." This would discredit

Jesus' claim to be the Messiah. How could the true Messiah die a death that was accursed by God?

Now Pilate knew that the charges against Jesus were trumped up. When he interrogates Jesus himself, he can find no offense against Roman law, just as the chief priests could find no offense against Jewish law, certainly nothing carrying the death sentence. Jesus confesses only one thing. When asked by Pilate, "Are you the king of the Jews?" he responds, "you say so," which means "you said it!" But even that was no crime to claim to be the heir to the throne of a small, oppressed ethnic group.

Pilate tries a tactic to get Jesus off his hands. It was the custom to release a prisoner at Passover as a sign of goodwill on such a festive occasion. Pilate tries to manipulate this custom. He gives the crowd a choice of only two prisoners, both of whose first names were "Jesus": Jesus Barabbas and Jesus of Nazareth.

Barabbas was an unpopular man, a terrorist who had killed some fellow Jews during a riot. The people would surely choose to release this inoffensive Galilean rabbi rather than a terrorist, Pilate thought. But no! The chief priests and leaders plant their minions in the crowd and use their influence to get the mob to vote for Jesus Barabbas. Pilate is disgusted with the whole procedure and "washes his hands of the matter," a ritual making a public statement that he did not agree with what was happening. But was that enough to clear Pilate of responsibility for Jesus' death? Certainly not! Pilate had the authority and power to punish the guilty and protect the innocent. Jesus teaches us that all authority comes from God (Jn 19:11; Rom 13:1–7). It is immoral for a government official, then or now, to allow the innocent to be abused while they do nothing to stop it.

In fact, Pilate gave the Roman soldiers orders to follow the wishes of the chief priests and crucify Jesus. After mocking him as "King of the Jews!" they take him to the local place of execution, a hill known as the skull (Gol'gotha). There they nail him to his cross. As a small act of compassion, they offer Jesus soured wine spiked with a narcotic to dull the victim's pain. But keeping in mind his oath "not [to] drink again of this fruit of the vine until that day when I drink it new with you in my Father's kingdom," our Lord does not accept the drink (26:29, 27:34).

It was the custom to write the crime the victim committed on a sign at the top of his cross.

Pilate writes Jesus' crime: "This is Jesus the King of the Jews." In Latin, this would be "**I**esus **N**azarenus **R**ex **I**udaeorum," giving us the famous "INRI" acronym. Pilate was the local representative of the Roman government. By writing this sign, he was formally recognizing Jesus' claim to the throne of Israel. That's why the Gospel of John tells us the chief priests protested the way Pilate wrote Jesus' sign, but Pilate refused to change it.

There is great irony in the Gospel of Matthew. He began the gospel with a genealogy of Jesus, demonstrating that Jesus had the bloodline to claim David's throne. But his claim to the throne is only recognized by the authorities when he is being killed. The Roman soldiers, the chief priests, and the Roman governor himself all call him "King of the Jews" or "King of

Israel" (27:29, 37, 42). The only "throne" Jesus receives in this world is the Cross. This is ironic and paradoxical. But somehow it fits with the kind of kingdom Jesus has been preaching about since his first sermon (Mt 5–7). He is the King of the poor, the mournful, the hungry, the thirsty, the humble, and especially the persecuted. That's how he is when the authorities acclaim him as king. That's how he is in his death.

It's a lesson for us, too, to follow this King as his disciples. We are not going to get a throne on this earth for our efforts. This world does not react well to those who live Jesus' lifestyle, especially not if they speak the truth publically. If we reign with Christ in this life, it's going to be on a cross, like Jesus himself.

Jesus is near death as it draws near to three in the afternoon. About this time, Jesus cries out, "Eli, Eli, la'ma sabachtha'ni?" which is, "My God, my God, why have you forsaken me?" Many are troubled by this verse. Does this mean God the Father has completely abandoned Jesus the Son? Would God the Father likewise abandon me in my hour of need? What kind of God do we worship and believe in?

Surprisingly few people seem to notice that Jesus' words are the first line of Psalm 22: "My God, my God, why have you forsaken me? Why are you so far from helping me?" (v. 1). In ancient times, the Psalms were not numbered. The Jewish practice was to refer to biblical books or sections of books by their first line or at least a significant line. Any educated Jew would know exactly what Jesus was referring to by saying "My God, my God . . ." Think about this: nowadays in the United States, if someone says to you "Oh, say can you see?" it will probably start "The Star-Spangled Banner" running in your head. In the same way, for the Jews of Jesus' day, "My God, my God, why have you forsaken me?" would start Psalm 22 running in their heads.

When was the last time you read through Psalm 22? It's an interesting experience. You might try it right now. Chances are, you don't recall exactly how the Psalm goes. But look it over. And then ask yourself a question: How does the Psalm end? Does it end in despair or triumph? See for yourself. Below I've copied a few lines taken from the second half of the Psalm, beginning in verse 23:

> You who fear the LORD, praise him!
> all you sons of Jacob, glorify him!
> and stand in awe of him, all you sons of Israel!
> For he has not despised or abhorred
> the affliction of the afflicted;
> and he has not hid his face from him,
> but has heard, when he cried to him. . . .
> The afflicted shall eat and be satisfied;
> those who seek him shall praise the LORD!
> May your hearts live for ever!
> All the ends of the earth shall remember
> and turn to the LORD;
> and all the families of the nations
> shall worship before him. (Ps 22:23–27)

The whole Psalm is worth reading through carefully. However, these verses are enough to make our point: the Psalm ends with the triumph of God and the vindication of the suffering servant. In fact, "all the ends of the earth" (a reference to the Gentiles) shall remember this and turn to the God of Israel.

Now let me ask a final question: Do you think Jesus knew how Psalm 22 ended? You think he did? Good! So do I. So when we interpret Jesus' words from the Cross, we may say, *Yes, Jesus is suffering*. Momentarily there is the sensation that God is absent, that evil is having its day. But Jesus also knows the outcome. He knows that God's victory and the resurrection are to come.

Some of the bystanders think Jesus is calling for Elijah. Why is that? It's because they only speak Greek and cannot understand Jesus' Hebrew. All they can pick out are the syllables "eli–lah" from Jesus' second and third words ("Eli lama"), which sounds a lot like "eli-yah," the pronunciation of Elijah in Greek. But one of the bystanders does something very significant. He ran to get soured or cheap wine (Greek, *oxos*), put it on a reed, "and gave him to drink." Most English translations make it sound as if Jesus was offered the drink but make it unclear whether he took it. But the Greek indicates he drank; it would be better to translate as "gave him a drink" rather than "gave him to drink." If there was any confusion, John 19:30 removes all doubt: "*When Jesus had received the soured wine*, he said 'It is finished'" (emphasis added).

But wait, Jesus, didn't you say you were not going to drink again of the fruit of the vine until you drank it new in the kingdom of heaven? What do you mean by drinking now, and what do you mean by saying "It is finished"? *What* is finished?

There are several possible answers to that question, and perhaps many things come to a finish with Jesus' drink on the Cross, depending on how we look at it. However, one thing that was finished would be the Passover that he started days before with his disciples. We saw how they seemed to leave the Upper Room before drinking the last cup of the meal, with Jesus himself saying he would not drink again until he was in the kingdom. Then we saw the theme of the cup continue as Jesus went out to the Mount of Olives and prayed that the "cup" would pass from him. And he refused to drink the "fruit of the vine" when it was first offered, before his death was near. But now he does drink and immediately dies. The great Passover of God is completed, and the Passover "lamb who takes away the sins of the world" has died to bear the guilt of our sin.

But where is the kingdom Jesus promised? How can it have arrived at the moment Jesus dies? It does seem paradoxical, but St. Matthew records mysterious events that took place at the time of our Lord's death, mysterious events that pointed to the arrival of God's kingdom. The curtain in the Temple that kept people from seeing or worshipping in the Holy of Holies was miraculously torn in two. God's presence was now available to everyone. An earthquake split rocks and opened tombs, and many holy people from previous generations rose from the dead and milled around in the city of Jerusalem, appearing to many eyewitnesses. It was a mini-resurrection, as a sign that God's kingdom had broken into our reality and a sign of the end of times when the kingdom will become visible to all.

By these events Matthew, and hopefully we, too, are convinced that the kingdom arrived in power with the sacrificial death of Jesus. It's the arrival of the kingdom that helps explain Jesus' words at the end of the gospel, after he rose from the dead and had appeared to his disciples:

> All authority in heaven and on earth has been given to me. Go therefore and make disciples of all nations, baptizing them in the name of the Father and of the Son and of the Holy Spirit, teaching them to observe all that I have commanded you; and lo, I am with you always, to the close of the age. (Mt 28:18–20)

"All authority in heaven *and on earth* has been given to me," Jesus says, indicating that his reign *on earth* has begun already. The kingdom of Jesus is not only a heavenly reality. Psalm 2, an ancient prophecy about the Davidic King, says, "Ask of me, and I will make the nations your heritage, and the ends of the earth your possession" (v. 8). Jesus is saying that he has already received that universal authority. It only remains to send his servants, his officers and viceroys, out into the world to claim possession of his kingdom.

So he says, "Go, therefore, and make disciples of all nations." Note that he does not say, *Make churchgoers of all nations; Make converts of all nations;* or *Make people in all nations claim to be my followers*. No, he says, "make disciples." A disciple is a person who studies the teachings of a great man and imitates his lifestyle as accurately as possible. In a sense, a disciple is to be a "copycat." We are to be copycats of Jesus.

Becoming a disciple starts with Baptism: "Baptizing them in the name of the Father, Son, and Holy Spirit," Jesus says.

But it doesn't end with Baptism: "Teaching them *to observe all that I have commanded you*." Notice it does *not* say *teaching them all that I have commanded you* the way Plato or Confucius might be taught in a college philosophy course. Oh, isn't it interesting that Plato said such and such and Confucius this other thing? How quaint those old thinkers were! No. It says, "teaching them *to observe* all that I have commanded." Teaching information and teaching behavior are very different things. You can teach someone all about the physics of swimming and the buoyancy of the human body and that person will still not be able to swim. Teaching *about swimming* and teaching someone *to swim* are different. The apostles went out to teach people *to swim*, not to have PhDs in swimming science. Or better, the apostle's went out to teach people how to fish, not how to be students of fish genetics and behavior.

Christianity is not an academic subject; it is a lifestyle, and ultimately it's about how we live, not just what we think. Furthermore, no aspect of the Christian lifestyle is optional. Jesus did not say, "Teach them to pick and choose among my teachings which they will follow." No. Rather, he said, "Teach them to observe *all* that I have commanded." All the aspects of Christian faith and life are interconnected. If you give up on one, the whole robe begins to unravel. Jesus did not want to produce "cafeteria Catholics," those who pick and choose what they will obey among his teachings and those of his Church.

These last instructions of Jesus in Matthew 28:18–20 are a tall order, a tough command to follow. People usually call this passage "the Great Commission" because in it Jesus commissions his high officers with their "marching orders" until the end of time. Others joke that these verses are the "Great Omission" because Christians down through the centuries haven't carried it out. Let's make sure that's not true of us. I'm sure you're reading this book—and I'm certainly writing it—as part of an effort to learn Jesus' teachings more thoroughly so that we can live them more effectively.

* * *

Congratulations! You've come to the end of Matthew, the first of the four major authors of the New Testament. You've seen how, from the opening royal genealogy to the final "Great Commission," Jesus' life, death, and resurrection really have brought God's kingdom to earth. Now that we've worked through one gospel, the other gospels will go a little more quickly since we've covered the common ground already.

Part II
The Kingdom of God Grows!

Luke

Three

The Gospel of Luke

Now it's time to begin studying the writings of St. Luke, and it's hard not to be excited. I always feel joyful when I start teaching Luke and its sequel, the Acts of the Apostles, to my New Testament courses because the theme of joy runs through both books. The Gospel of Luke, in fact, begins with the account of the five Joyful Mysteries.

Why was St. Luke so joyful? He was probably joyful because he grew up a pagan and later in life heard the good news about Jesus Christ from the apostle Paul. Paganism didn't have a lot of joy in it. The pagan gods could be cruel and unpredictable. Plus, pagan religion wasn't always clear about what, if anything, a person could hope for in the next life. This was the culture St. Luke grew up in before he met the apostle Paul and heard him teach about Jesus Christ. St. Paul said God loved human beings so much that he had become one of them, had even suffered and died to prove his love for them. Jesus of Nazareth was God in the flesh: he showed the way to eternal life. Whoever trusted in him and followed his teachings could have confidence of a life to come in the loving embrace of God. This was such good news! How could one not be joyful to hear it? St. Paul's preaching radically change Luke's life forever.

As we mentioned before, St. Luke was a well-educated, Greek-speaking Gentile, the only Gentile to write any part of the New Testament. Although he was a Gentile, we will see that he knew the Jewish scriptures very, very well. He may have been a convert to Judaism before becoming a Christian.

If St. Matthew wrote his gospel primarily to Jews, St. Luke writes primarily to non-Jews (Gentiles). This explains many of the differences between these two gospels. For example, Matthew only traces Jesus' genealogy back to Abraham, the forefather of the Jews. But Luke traces the genealogy all the way back to Adam, father of the whole human race. Gentile characters play a bigger role in St. Luke's gospel, and St. Luke omits certain details about Jesus' life that non-Jews wouldn't understand.

St. Luke's gospel has some special emphases. Besides greater emphasis on Gentiles, he stresses the importance of prayer and the Holy Spirit. We see Jesus praying more often in Luke, and the activity of the Holy Spirit is mentioned more frequently. Women play a greater role. Luke tells us more about Jesus' relationships with women, how they helped his ministry and the growth of the Church.

St. Luke's gospel breaks down into four basic sections:

1. Jesus' childhood (the "infancy narratives," Lk 1–2);
2. Jesus' early ministry (Lk 3–9);
3. Jesus' final journey to Jerusalem (the "travel narrative," Lk 10–19); and
4. Holy Week (the "Passion narrative," Lk 20–24).

We can use some simple icons to help remember the four major parts of Luke's gospel. For the infancy narratives

(Lk 1–2), we'll draw a baby Jesus with a rattle and halo. (The Lord will forgive our simple art. He knows we mean well!)

During the early ministry (Lk 3–9), Jesus taught and performed miracles. To recall his teaching, we will draw him with his hand raised, making a point. To recall his miracles, we'll draw baskets of fish and bread, recalling the feeding of the five thousand (see Lk 9:10–17).

The travel narrative (Lk 10–19) all takes place while Jesus is headed toward Jerusalem for the last time. So we'll draw him walking determinedly toward Jerusalem.

To represent the Holy Week chapters of Luke (20–24), we will draw Jesus celebrating the Eucharist, which will remind us of two famous episodes in these chapters: the institution of the Eucharist (Lk 22:1–38) and the Emmaus Road event (Lk 24:13–35), when Jesus was "made known in the breaking of the bread" (24:35).

There is a good bit of overlap between the Gospel of Luke and the Gospel of Matthew, especially in Luke 3–9, the account of Jesus' early ministry. Most of the unique material in Luke can be found in the sections on Jesus' childhood (Lk 1–2) and his final journey to Jerusalem (Lk 10–19). Luke also adds some special touches to his record of the events of Holy Week. In what follows, we'll skip most of the material that we covered in Matthew and pay more attention to the stories and teachings that are unique to Luke.

Luke's Introduction

Ready to begin? Good! Let's jump into Luke. Here's the opening sentence: "Inasmuch as many have undertaken to compile a narrative of the things which have been accomplished among us, just as they were delivered to us by those who from the beginning were eyewitnesses and ministers of the word, it seemed good to me also, having followed all things closely for some time past, to write an orderly account for you, most excellent The-oph'ilus, that you may know the truth concerning the things of which you have been informed" (Lk 1:1–4).

That's quite a sentence! You can scarcely read it aloud in one breath. Let's notice several things:

First, this is a very elegant sentence. It's more complex than anything your average high school graduate could compose. St. Luke is showing off his good Greco-Roman education. He is saying, *Look at what I can do, world! I can rip off a sentence such as this without even breaking a sweat.* St. Luke had been educated at the best schools of his day, the ancient equivalents of Harvard and Yale. When he wanted to, he could compose Greek as elegant as the great philosophers and historians. High-class Greeks and Romans who read the opening of his gospel would immediately realize that they were dealing with an educated man of the world, not some back-hills faith healer or foot-stomping preacher.

Second, St. Luke tells us he is writing history, not mythology. He says he has "followed all things closely for some time past," which means he's made a personal investigation into the events he records. He draws on the testimony of "eyewitnesses" and writes an "orderly account" so that his readers can know the "truth." This is the language of history writing. By the time of St. Luke, Greeks had been writing histories for over four hundred years, since the days of the great historians Herodotus and Thucydides. The Greeks had very sophisticated ideas about how to write history and longstanding debates about the best way to go about it. Herodotus believed that one should record all the information one could and let the readers make their own judgment about what was true or not. Thucydides, on other hand, argued that one should only record information that one could personally verify. Luke clearly sides with

Thucydides. He presents only the information he has verified. That's what it means that he has "followed all things closely" and gotten the information from "eyewitnesses."

Luke mentions that "many" had already written about the life of Jesus. The Gospels of Mark and Matthew were already in existence when St. Luke wrote, and he certainly used Mark as a source, possibly also Matthew. But two gospels are not "many." There were a number of biographies of Jesus in ancient times that are now lost to us. The Church was very careful about which biographies of Jesus ("gospels") it approved. Of the many that were written, the Church chose only the best, the most accurate, and the most reliable.

St. Luke writes to "Theophilus." The name "Theophilus" means "one who loves God." Writing to Theophilus might have been a literary device. Perhaps St. Luke meant to write to "anyone who loves God." On the other hand, there may have been a real person by the name of Theophilus to whom Luke was writing. Interestingly, the only person by this name who lived at the same time as Luke happens to be a Jewish high priest.[1] If this was the Theophilus to whom Luke wrote, it was a very high-profile correspondence. Was St. Luke hoping to convert a very influential leader in the Jewish community? Even if he was, St. Luke was well aware that many others would read the account he wrote for Theophilus. In fact, there's reason to believe that St. Luke had the sense that he was writing new scriptures for God's people and his book would take a place with the books of the Old Testament.

For example, when we continue reading from Luke 1:1–4 to the stories of Jesus' childhood in Luke 1:5–2:52, St. Luke changes his Greek style. If the introduction was very elegant, educated Greek, the childhood stories are written in "biblical Greek," that is, in the style of the famous Greek translation of the Old Testament that almost all Jews knew (called "the

Septuagint", say sep-TOO-ah-jint). In other words, most of Luke 1–2 sounds "Bible-ish" for a Greek reader. It's like when I was growing up and my father and other older men would switch into "biblical English" when they prayed in public: "O Lord, we come to thee again in this evening hour." By using "thees" and "thous," the older men of my childhood imitated the classic King James Version of the Bible and made their prayers sound "biblical." St. Luke is doing something similar in his opening chapters. By telling the story of Jesus' childhood with "Bible language," he shows that the story of the Bible is continuing with the life of Jesus. Jesus is a great prophet like the prophets of the Old Testament—more than that, he is the King that the Old Testament predicted would return!

Part 1 of Luke: The Infancy Narratives *(Luke 1–2)*

St. Luke doesn't just use biblical style; he also writes based on biblical models. The Books of Samuel in the Old Testament told the story of the rise of David as king over Israel. However, the books back up and begin with the birth of Samuel, the prophet who found David and anointed him as king.

In the same way, St. Luke backs up his gospel to begin with the birth of John the Baptist, the new prophet who will identify and anoint Jesus, the new Davidic King. John is "Samuel" to Jesus' "David."

Zechariah, John's father, is a high-ranking priest who actually finds out about John's birth from an angel in the Temple when he is celebrating a very important liturgy: the burning of incense before God in the inner sanctuary. There, he sees the angel Gabriel. No one had seen Gabriel since he appeared to Daniel five hundred years before (Dn 9). At that time, he had told Daniel it would be about five hundred years until the Messiah, the "anointed prince," would come. Time's up! Now he's back to announce the Messiah's coming.

But the prophets had said Elijah would return before the Messiah, and that's why Gabriel comes to speak to Zechariah. He tells the elderly priest that he will have a son, to be named "Jo-hanan," that is, "the grace of the Lord." He will be a Nazirite like Samuel, drinking no alcohol, and he will "go before him in the spirit and the power of Eli'jah" (Lk 1:17).

John the Baptist was not literally Elijah raised from the dead, and so when people later asked him, "Are you Eli'jah?" he said no (Jn 1:21). However, John was the one the prophets spoke of when they prophesied that Eli'jah would return before the Messiah. For example, Malachi, considered the last of the Old Testament prophets, concluded his book by writing, "Behold, I will send you Eli'jah the prophet before the great and awesome day of the LORD comes. And he will turn the hearts of fathers to their children and the hearts of children to their fathers" (Mal 4:5–6). So Gabriel says of John, "He will go before him in the spirit and power of Eli'jah, to turn the hearts of the fathers to the children" (Lk 1:17). John would be the "Eli'jah" the prophets predicted.

What if you were an old man and an angel appeared to you one day at your worksite to tell you your elderly wife was going to have a baby? You wouldn't believe it, and neither did

Zechariah. So Gabriel made him unable to speak until the baby would be born.

The Annunciation *(Luke 1:26–38)*

Six months later, Gabriel is back in action, this time announcing the birth of the One for whom John was supposed to prepare the way. He goes to Nazareth in Galilee, to a virgin named Mary, engaged to a certain Joseph, a descendant of David. "Hail, full of grace, the Lord is with you!" he exclaims. This is quite an unusual greeting for an angel to give a human being. Literally, Gabriel calls Mary "one who has been graced," which St. Jerome translated *gratia plena* in Latin, "full of grace." Mary is taken aback by this appearance of an angel, but Gabriel reassures her:

> Do not be afraid, Mary, for you have found favor with God. And behold, you will conceive in your womb and bear a son, and you shall call his name Jesus [*y'shua*, "Salvation"].
> And he will be great, and will be called the Son of the Most High.
> And the Lord God will give him the throne of his father David.
> And he will reign over the house of Jacob for ever;
> And of his kingdom there will be no end. (Lk 1:30–33)

If you've been with me through *Bible Basics for Catholics*, you recognize that Gabriel is promising Mary that Jesus will fulfill the Davidic Covenant. In fact, Gabriel's words basically just summarize the key points of 2 Samuel 7, that famous chapter where God granted David a covenant of kingship.

But if Jesus is the Son of David who will rule from David's throne forever, why don't we see him enthroned in Jerusalem ruling over the Jews now?

Luke's gospel is going to answer that question.

After hearing Gabriel's announcement, Mary has an obvious question: *How is this going to happen, since I'm not married?*

Gabriel replies, "The Holy Spirit will come upon you, and the power of the most high will *overshadow* you" (emphasis added), using the same word for God's glory *overshadowing* the Tabernacle in the wilderness (Ex 40:35), such that Moses was not able to enter it. Mary is God's new tabernacle, a holy dwelling for his presence.

"Behold, I am the handmaid of the Lord; let it be done to me according to your word" (Lk 1:38). "Let it be done" in Latin is *fiat*. So we speak of Mary's *fiat* here, that is, her willingness to let God have his way with her. There is no doubt that St. Luke is holding her up as an example for us all. I realized that years ago, even as a Protestant preacher, when I had to preach this text each Advent season.

The Visitation *(Luke 1:39–56)*

Even in her pregnant condition, Our Lady still goes to the house of her elderly cousin Elizabeth to offer help during Elizabeth's own pregnancy and delivery. St. Luke tells the story in such a way that we can hear echoes of a great story from the Old Testament. Mary "arose and went with haste" to the hill country; when she greets Elizabeth, the baby John leaps "in her womb," and Elizabeth cries out with joy. This echoes the great event when David "arose" and "went" with the Ark of the Covenant up into the hill country of Judah, to Jerusalem itself, and there he leapt with joy before the Ark as the procession entered the city. Mary is like a new Ark of the Covenant. The Ark contained the Ten Commandments (the Word of God), the manna (bread from heaven), and the staff of Aaron the high priest. Jesus, in Mary's womb, was the Word of God, the bread from heaven, and our true high priest.

When Mary arrives at Elizabeth's house, the reaction is very unusual. Keep in mind the difference in status between these two women. Elizabeth is an elderly woman; she lives near Jerusalem, the capital city, and her husband serves actively in the temple as a priest, a high-class profession. All those things gave Elizabeth status in society. Mary, on the other hand, was a pregnant teenager, engaged to a blue-collar worker from the back hills. In the world's eyes, she was low status. Elizabeth was a wine, cheese, and "Grey Poupon" lady who finds her pregnant teenage "Big Mac" cousin from the north on her doorstep. How is she going to react?

She reacts by falling all over herself, as if Queen Elizabeth or the First Lady had decided to come for tea! "She exclaimed with a loud cry, 'Blessed are you among women, and blessed is the fruit of your womb!'" (1:42). "Blessed are you among women" is a Hebrew phrase that means "you are the most blessed of all women." Elizabeth acts as if it's a great *privilege* that her teenage cousin should *deign* to pay her a visit: "And why is this granted me, that the mother of my Lord should come to me? For behold, when the voice of your greeting came to my ears, the babe in my womb leaped for joy. And blessed is she who believed that there would be a fulfilment of what was spoken to her from the Lord" (vv. 43–45).

Why is there this overreaction? The key is the title Elizabeth gives Mary: "the Mother of My Lord." This is the title of the queen mother, the First Lady of the kingdom of David.[2] In ancient Israel, it was *not* the king's *wife* who ruled as queen but his *mother*. We see this especially in 1 Kings 2, where Solomon, the greatest of all Israel's kings, treated his mother Bathsheba with so much respect. When she came to visit him, he got up off his throne and bowed down to her. Then he had a throne brought for her to sit at his right hand and promised to give her whatever she asked (1 Kgs 2:19–20). You can bet there was no other person on the planet to whom Solomon, the great emperor, would bow down. But that was ancient court protocol. The queen mother was honored by everyone, even the king, and every request she made was supposed to be granted.

Despite Mary's poverty and her apparent low-class status in the eyes of the world, Elizabeth sees her for what she truly is: the Queen Mother of all Israel, and she treats her as such.

Some Christians have little use for Mary and criticize the Catholic Church for showing her honor. But showing honor to Mary, what we call "Marian veneration," is biblical and starts in the Bible itself. The first person to show Mary honor was the angel Gabriel, who called her "O woman who has been graced." Elizabeth is the second person and the first example of *human* veneration of Mary in history. As with St. Elizabeth, Catholics throughout history have recognized Mary as the Queen Mother of the House of David and treated her with royal dignity.

In response to Elizabeth, Mary is filled with the Holy Spirit and sings her great song, which we call the Magnificat (= "[My soul] magnifies") from its first word in Latin:

> My soul magnifies the Lord,
> and my spirit rejoices in God my Savior,

> for he has regarded the low estate of his handmaiden.
> For behold, henceforth all generations will call me blessed;
> for he who is mighty has done great things for me, and holy is his name.
> And his mercy [*eleos*] is on those who fear him from generation to generation.
> He has shown strength with his arm,
> he has scattered the proud in the imagination of their hearts,
> he has put down the mighty from their thrones,
> and exalted those of low degree;
> he has filled the hungry with good things,
> and the rich he has sent empty away.
> He has helped his servant Israel,
> in remembrance of his mercy [*eleos*],
> as he spoke to our fathers,
> to Abraham and to his *seed* forever. (1:46–55)

In Mary's song, Jewish readers would hear many echoes of the song Hannah sang over the birth of the prophet Samuel (1 Sm 2:1–10). Hannah's name is "Grace" in Hebrew, just as "Grace" is used as a woman's name today. Compare Mary and Hannah: one woman is "Grace;" the other is "full of grace." They both praise God for bringing down the proud and lifting up the humble. Mary probably had Hannah's song memorized, so it is not surprising that her Magnificat sounds similar.

Mary rejoices that "all generations will call me blessed," and her prophecy is fulfilled every time we pray the Hail Mary: "Blessed art thou among women, and blessed is the fruit of thy womb, Jesus." The Hail Mary is based on biblical texts and prophecy.

The word "mercy" is very important in Mary's song. Mary speaks of God "remembering his mercy," which is a strange way to speak in Greek or English. What does it mean to "remember mercy"? We don't talk like that. It only makes sense in Hebrew. St. Luke is translating the Hebrew phrase *zakar hesed*, which means "to call to mind" (*zakar*) "the bond of covenant faithfulness" (*hesed*). This word *hesed*, "covenant faithfulness," is very rich; it gets rendered *eleos* in Greek and *mercy* in English but means so much more than mercy. It's God's faithfulness to his sworn promises. Look at the last two lines of the Magnificat: "He has helped his servant Israel, in remembrance of his mercy [*eleos* = *hesed*], as he spoke to our fathers, to Abraham and to his posterity (literally *seed*) forever" (v. 54–55). Our Blessed Mother is describing the covenant with Abraham. When and where did God speak to "our father Abraham and to his seed forever"? This happened on Mt. Moriah, after Abraham almost sacrificed his "only begotten son" Isaac to God, and God said, "By myself I have sworn . . . because you have done this . . . I will indeed bless you . . . and by your *seed* shall all the nations of the earth bless themselves" (Gn 22:16–18).

Mary knows the baby in her womb will fulfill all the good promises God gave to Abraham by a covenant oath. Every time priests, religious, and other Catholics recite the Magnificat during Evening Prayer of the Divine Office (Liturgy of the Hours), we are thanking God for his faithfulness (*hesed*) to his covenant with Abraham.

If we fast-forward a little in Luke, after the birth of John the Baptist, we find that Zechariah, John's father, has very similar ideas to the Blessed Mother. When his tongue is finally loosed after the birth of his son, he praises God with his own song, the Benedictus, which we recite at Morning Prayer of the office. This is the beginning of it:

> Blessed be the Lord God of Israel,
> for he has visited and redeemed his people,
> and has raised up a horn of salvation for us
> in the house of his servant David,
> as he spoke by the mouth of his holy prophets from of old. (Lk 1:68–70)

Zechariah thanks God for acting to fulfill both the Davidic and the Abrahamic Covenant. "Visit" and "redeem" are covenant terms: when your covenant partner gets himself in trouble (as in, sold into slavery), you go "visit" him and "redeem" him (buy him back). A "horn of salvation" in the "house of his servant David" means a new Davidic king, a son of David who will restore David's kingdom and covenant. The "holy prophets from of old" spoke of this:

> Isaiah: "For to us a child is born, to us a son is given . . . of the increase of his government and of peace there will be no end, upon the throne of David" (9:6–7).

> Jeremiah: "Behold, the days are coming, says the LORD, when I will raise up for David a righteous Branch, and he shall reign as king and deal wisely" (23:5).
>
> Ezekiel: "And I will set up over them one shepherd, my servant David, and he shall feed them" (34:23).

So God is "remembering" not only the covenant with David but also the covenant with Abraham. A little later in the Benedictus, Zechariah utters three lines that mean the same thing: "To perform the mercy [*hesed*] promised to our fathers, and to remember his holy covenant, the oath which he swore to our father Abraham" (Lk 1:72–73). *Hesed* is covenant faithfulness. So to "perform *hesed*" means the same thing as "remember his holy covenant." And the "holy covenant" is the same thing as the "oath" God swore to Abraham because covenant is the *extension of kinship by oath*. And when did God swear an oath to "our father Abraham"? This happened only once, at the end of this event: "*By myself have I sworn* . . . because you have done this, and have not withheld your son, your only son, I will indeed bless you . . . and by your *seed* shall all the nations of the earth bless themselves" (Gn 22:15–18, emphasis added).

Together, Mary's Magnificat and Zechariah's Benedictus make up part of the heartbeat of prayer in the Catholic Church, recited daily in the evening and the morning respectively. Both prayers are full of the concept of *mercy*, which we have seen is a covenant concept, *hesed*. How often have we prayed these two canticles without realizing we were praising God for his covenant faithfulness to Abraham and David, shown by the gift of John and Jesus?

St. Luke sums up John's childhood by saying he grew and became strong in spirit and was "in the wilderness" until the day of his manifestation to Israel. Now the wilderness was the desert area to the east of Jerusalem along the Jordan River and the Dead Sea. What would a boy being doing out there? How would he even survive? We don't know, but we do know that the Essenes ran a monastery on the north shore of the Dead Sea and took in boys to raise as future monks.[3] Did John the Baptist grow up that way? I suspect so but can't prove it.

The Nativity *(Luke 2:1–21)*

Now we turn to the birth of Jesus. God arranged the circumstances of Jesus' birth in such a way as to show us his connections with his forefather David. A Roman government census just happens to force Joseph to leave Nazareth to travel to Bethlehem for registration. Bethlehem was, of course, the birthplace of David and is located only a few miles from Jerusalem. Perhaps the census had brought unusually large numbers of people to Bethlehem, which was only a very small village to begin with, because St. Luke says "there was no place for them in the inn." Mary and Joseph take shelter with animals, probably in a cave, and when the baby is born, Mary wraps him in cloths and lays him in a "manger," a feeding trough. How appropriate this is: the baby who will become the bread of life, who will give himself to be eaten by others, is laid in a feeding trough in a town whose name, "Beth-lehem," means "the house of bread."

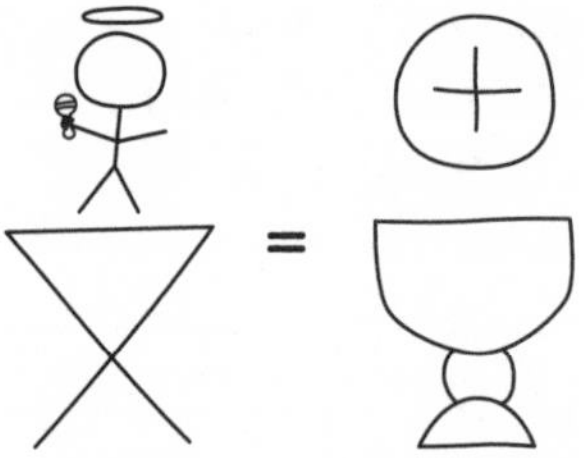

Baby in a feed trough = Eat my body ... Drink my blood

Bethlehem was also a shepherding village. David himself grew up as a shepherd, so it does not surprise us to find shepherds nearby. Angels appear to them, telling them of the birth of "the Anointed One, the Lord" in the village. Leaving their sheep, they go to find this babe and see him with their own eyes. As they gazed, some of them may have remembered the prophecies given about five hundred years before: "I will save my flock, they shall no longer be a prey. . . . And I will set up over them one shepherd, my servant David, and he shall feed them: he shall feed them and be their shepherd" (Ez 34:22–23). The baby in the feed trough is the new David who will feed the flock of Israel with his own body.

St. Luke indicates his source for the accounts of Jesus' childhood by mentioning that "Mary kept all these things, pondering them in her heart" (2:19). But Mary is more than a source for historical information; she is also a spiritual example because she teaches us how to meditate. When we pray the Joyful Mysteries of the Rosary, we, too, should "keep" all the mysteries and "ponder them" in our hearts, meditating on them and considering their deeper meaning. If we just mouth the words without really pondering the mysteries, we're not praying the Rosary as it should be.

God's law prescribed that at eight days, a male child should be circumcised as the mark of his entrance into the Abrahamic Covenant (see Gn 17:11–12).

Genesis 17:
Covenant of Circumcision

Jews also used this opportunity to officially bestow a name on the child. They name him "Salvation," in Hebrew *y'shua* and in English either "Joshua" or "Jesus." How profound that this baby, born as the very "seed of Abraham" through whom all the nations of the earth would be blessed (Gn 22:18), should now receive this ancient mark of Abraham's covenant. This first shedding of Jesus' blood looks forward to the ultimate shedding of his blood on the Cross when a stream of blood and water would flow out from his side, a sign of the Holy Spirit flowing from his body to bring blessing to all the nations and fulfill the promises to Abraham.

The Presentation *(Luke 2:22–38)*

The Law of Moses also specified a certain time of ritual cleansing for a mother after the birth of a baby boy, thirty-three days, after which she offered a sacrifice, was cleansed, and entered the sanctuary to worship (Lv 12). Mary and Joseph obey this law, even though it is likely that our Mother did not strictly require ritual cleansing due to the unique circumstances of Jesus' birth. They go up, with Jesus, to the Temple, in order to obey the law. They sacrifice an offering of the poor: two pigeons, the least expensive offering possible (Lv 12:8). So we see that the Holy Family was impoverished, and Jesus grew up in poverty, even though they were royalty, the bloodline of the kings of Israel.

There were elderly people who lived near the Temple and devoted the last years of their lives to prayer at the holy place. Two of these, a man named Simeon and a woman named Anna, recognize the child Jesus and prophesy about him. Simeon looks at the baby and says, *My eyes have seen your Salvation, your* y'shua! And then he identifies Jesus as the fulfillment of the prophecies of Isaiah: "A light for revelation to the Gentiles, and for glory to thy people Israel" (see Is 42:6, 49:6).

His words to Mary are more ominous: "This child is set for the fall and rising of many in Israel, and for a sign that is spoken against (and a sword shall pass through your own soul also)" (Lk 2:34–35).

Here Simeon predicts the *cosuffering* of Mary with Jesus, the pain that she will endure as a mother watching her only son be rejected, tortured, and executed. Mary will be united with Jesus in his passion, taking part with him in the redemption of the world. Every true Christian follows in Mary's footsteps, sharing Jesus' sufferings in some way.

In fact, Mary already suffers for the sake of Jesus some years later when Mary and Joseph traveled with Jesus to Jerusalem for the Passover. After the feast, they began the journey back to Nazareth together with their extended family and friends. People in the Near East live and travel in large, close-knit clans to this day.

But after a day had passed, Mary and Joseph noticed he was missing from the group and went back to Jerusalem to find him. Talk about an agonizing three-day search through that immense city! They finally find him in the Temple, and the Blessed Mother is distraught as she says, *Son, why have you done this to us? Your father and I were in pain, looking for you!* And Jesus replies in innocence, "How is it that you sought me? Did you not know that I must be in my Father's house? [or, about my father's business?]" (2:49).

What's going on here? Well, first of all, we should note that family life can be difficult. Misunderstandings arise even when both parents are saints and the child is divine! Second, the pattern of the prophet Samuel is helpful here. In different ways, Jesus has been compared to Samuel. Both are born to "grace-ful" mothers who sing similar songs about their births. Both are destined to be prophets and are connected to the Temple. Then we remember that Samuel, once he was old enough, was taken up to the Temple and left there to be raised by the priests (1 Sm 1:25–28). Surely that is no accidental similarity to Jesus' childhood. Perhaps the boy Jesus thought that, at age twelve, the end of boyhood in Judaism, his parents were taking him to Jerusalem to be left at the Temple, like Samuel of old. Surely the Blessed Mother had already spoken to him quietly of some of the special circumstances of his birth, which resembled that great prophet. In any event, St. Luke surely saw the similarity: he wraps up the story of Jesus' childhood with a line from Samuel's upbringing: "Jesus increased in wisdom and in stature, and in favor with God and man" (Lk 2:52, see 1 Sm 2:26).

Part 2 of Luke: Jesus' Early Ministry *(Luke 3–9)*

Luke's account of Jesus' early ministry covers similar ground to what we've already read in Matthew. In fact, this section of Luke is probably less unique than all the other sections of the gospel. So we won't rehearse the basic story again. We should, however, look at three stories in Luke that are unique compared to Matthew.

In Luke 3, we have a different genealogy of Jesus than the one given in Matthew 1. Matthew's genealogy flowed from Abraham down to Jesus, whereas Luke's goes backward from Jesus to Adam. Matthew shows Jesus as the savior of the Jews (the children of Abraham), whereas Luke shows Jesus as savior of the Gentiles (the children of Adam). But there's more: for long stretches, the two genealogies don't match, and they each list a different father for St. Joseph: "Jacob" in Matthew and "Heli" in Luke. Some think this is proof that one or both of the gospels is making things up and therefore the gospels can't be trusted.

However, it's not hard to explain why Matthew and Luke may have listed different fathers for St. Joseph. In ancient times, genealogies could follow either legal or biological descent or both.[4] Because of hard work, illness, and war, many fathers died young, and their sons were adopted by others. Because of adoption, it was not uncommon for a man to have both a biological and a legal father, especially in royal dynasties. For example, Augustus Caesar himself, the world emperor at the time of Jesus' birth, had no less than three fathers. His biological father was a certain Gaius Octavius, a Roman nobleman. But his father died when Augustus was four, and Augustus became the adopted stepson of his mother's new husband, Lucius Marcius Philippus. However, as a young soldier, Augustus greatly impressed his great-uncle Julius Caesar, and Julius adopted Augustus as his heir. Therefore, Roman law listed Augustus as the son of Julius Caesar, whom he succeeded as ruler of the Roman empire. But biologically, he was Julius's grandnephew.

Likewise, it's not hard to explain why St. Joseph would have two fathers. Tradition tells us that Mary was an only child. In Jewish law, the husband of an only daughter became her father's heir: for all intents and purposes, the son-in-law became the "son." So I suspect that Heli, listed as St. Joseph's father in Luke 3:23, is his father by marriage to the Blessed Virgin, and the line of descent given in Luke 3 is actually the biological line of Jesus through his mother, whereas Matthew 1 gives us St. Joseph's line through his natural father Jacob. I suspect this because St. Luke shows more interest in the Blessed Virgin, indicating her as his source twice, whereas St. Matthew shows more interest in St. Joseph. However, this is not Church dogma, and it could be the other way around. Or there may be yet a different reason St. Joseph had more than one father. The point is, it's not hard to explain why there could be two different genealogies.

In Luke 4:16–30, St. Luke tells us a story Matthew doesn't. Matthew simply says Jesus left Nazareth early in his ministry and relocated to Caphernaum (Mt 4:13). Luke explains why. After preaching and teaching throughout Galilee, Jesus returned to his hometown Nazareth to give his first sermon in his home synagogue. He chose as his text a collection of prophecies from the Book of Isaiah, especially Isaiah 61:

> The Spirit of the Lord GOD is upon me,

> because the LORD has anointed me
> to bring good tidings to the afflicted;
> he has sent me to bind up the brokenhearted,
> to proclaim liberty to the captives
> and the opening of the prison to those who are bound;
> to proclaim the year of the LORD's favor. (Is 61:1–2)

Now, the "year of the LORD's favor" was the Jubilee Year, a very ancient Israelite celebration every fifty years when all slaves were released, all sold property was returned to the owner, and everyone went home to their family property.

From the Dead Sea Scrolls, we have discovered that many Jews were expecting the mysterious priest-king Melchizedek (see Gn 14) to return at any time and announce the Jubilee Year of God, which would free people not of money debt but of the debt of sin. They believed Jesus' text from Isaiah 61 was describing this supernatural Melchizedek figure.[5]

Therefore, when Jesus sat down to begin to preach (because one preached from a chair in those days) and announced, "Today this scripture has been fulfilled in your hearing," the effect was electric. Here was this young rabbi, traveling around curing people and performing miracles, claiming to be the great Melchizedek returned to announce God's Jubilee Year!

And yet, the people of Nazareth were skeptical of this hometown boy: Isn't this just Jesus the son of Joseph the carpenter? We know his whole family, so how special can he be? Their lack of faith kept Jesus from performing any great miracles, and when Jesus pointed out that many of the great prophets performed their miracles of healing for Gentiles and not even for Jews, his townsfolk were incensed and tried to kill him! So that's one of the reasons Jesus relocated to Caphernaum, which was also a bigger city, located on a major highway.

In Luke 6:17–49, St. Luke records another sermon of our Lord, which sounds a lot like St. Matthew's Sermon on the Mount but also has significant differences. The wording is often different, and it takes place at a different location, a "level place" rather than a mountaintop. Therefore it's sometimes called the "Sermon on the Plain." Some think St. Luke has simply copied St. Matthew's Sermon on the Mount and changed the words around as well as the location. But it's unlikely that St. Luke's sense of honesty would allow him to put words in Jesus' mouth and concoct events for which he did not have sources. What's more likely is that both St. Matthew's "Sermon on the Mount" and St. Luke's "Sermon on the Plain" are variations on a standard sermon that Jesus preached wherever he went in Galilee.

Jesus was a traveling preacher. I know something about that, as I, too, used to travel around preaching, filling in for pastors who were sick or on vacation. I had one sermon that I preached wherever I went. (Why write a new one when no one had ever heard this one before?) However, I never preached it exactly the same twice. In every new location, there were different circumstances: the time of year was different, current events were different, and the congregations were different. So I adapted my message to the situation. If the congregation was all senior citizens, I would use different examples than if the congregation was all young families.

We can be certain that Jesus did not make up a completely new message for every city and village he visited. He had one basic message about the kingdom of God and how to get ready for it, which he probably preached hundreds if not thousands of times. People remembered his message, especially his disciples who traveled with him and heard it so often. They took notes, but there were many variations in

Jesus' basic message depending on the circumstances where he was preaching.

So what we have in Matthew 5–7 and Luke 6 are two versions of Jesus' basic message, given on two different occasions, that have been handed down to us. In either case, it only takes a few minutes to read Matthew 5–7 and even less to read Luke 6, but we know Jesus preached for the better part of a whole day. We are not getting a word-for-word recording of Jesus' preaching but a summary of his main points.

By the time we reach Luke 9, Jesus has preached much, performed many miracles, and told many parables. He has presented himself and his message to the people of Israel. Now, the mood of the gospel begins to change. Storm clouds blow in from the horizon as Jesus begins to predict his death multiple times (9:22, 44–45). The rest of the gospel records his final fateful journey to Jerusalem.

Part 3 of Luke: Jesus' Final Journey, the "Travel Narrative" *(Luke 10–19)*

The vast majority of Luke's gospel takes place during the last few months of Jesus' earthly life. Already in Luke 9:51 Jesus decides to journey to Jerusalem for the last time, knowing that death awaits him there. From chapters 10–19, he is on the journey, and chapters 20–24 recount what happened during his Passion Week.

Luke 9 is definitely the turning point. Jesus' ministry has been going well. Not only has he taught and worked miracles himself, but also he has trained twelve others to do so and sent them out on a successful missionary journey (9:1–11). Jesus is now alone in prayer one morning, and when he concludes his prayer, he asks his disciples a pointed question: "Who do you say that I am?" Peter responds, "The Christ ['Anointed One'] of God." That's who Jesus claimed to be from the time of his first sermon in Nazareth, when he read Isaiah's prophecy, "The Spirit of the Lord is upon me, because he has anointed me," and then said, "Today this scripture has been fulfilled in your hearing." So there is a sense of accomplishment with Peter's confession. The apostles understand and believe who Jesus is, at least in a basic way, and they've been trained to continue his ministry. That's a significant milestone. It remains for Jesus to usher in the New Covenant, but that will involve his death. He begins to speak openly of his death: "The Son of man must suffer many things . . . and be killed, and on the third day be raised" (Lk 9:22).

The Transfiguration is another turning point. About a week after predicting his death for the first time, Jesus climbs a mountain with his three closest disciples: Peter, James, and John. While in prayer at the top of the mountain, his appearance changes completely, and the disciples see him glorified: dressed in dazzling white, shining with the glory of God. The great prophets Moses and Elijah spoke to him about his "exodus" that he was soon to accomplish in Jerusalem (9:31). The disciples were sleeping while this was going on, and when they came to, they were completely overwhelmed at the vision of Jesus and the prophets. They really didn't know what to say. The vision ended with God's voice: "This is my son, my

Chosen; listen to him!" And then it was gone. Everything was quiet, and Jesus stood beside them in his normal clothes.

What is the meaning of the Transfiguration? One key to understanding this event is to pay attention to what Jesus was talking about with Moses and Elijah: literally, his "exodus," which English bibles translate as "death" or "departure" (9:31). But it's better to leave it as "exodus" because it is an important concept. Several of the prophets had predicted a "new" or "second exodus" at the end of time when God would regather his scattered people and save them (see Is 11:10–16). This "new exodus" would be led not by Moses again but by the royal Son of David (the "root of Jesse" in Is 11:10).

This helps us understand what Jesus is doing in Luke 9–19, the account of his final journey to Jerusalem. He is leading the new exodus! During his final trip to the Holy City, he gathers more and more disciples around him: the beginnings of the Church. By the time he arrives in Jerusalem, he has a mighty crowd, which celebrates around him during the triumphal entry (Lk 19:29–44). He then leads his disciples in a new Passover (the Eucharist, Lk 22) and delivers them from slavery to sin by his death on the Cross. This is the new exodus the prophets predicted, one that we continue to celebrate to this day, which is able to gather all of God's people, wherever they are scattered, out of the slavery of sin into a new life of freedom as the children of God.

Why were specifically Moses and Elijah at the Transfiguration? On the one hand, they represent the Law (Moses) and the prophets (Elijah), the two parts of the Israelite Bible, that is, the Old Testament. Jesus represents the New Testament, so it is almost as if scripture is having a conversation within itself. The Law and the prophets testify to Jesus. On the other hand, Jewish tradition held that Moses and Elijah were both assumed into heaven, unlike most Old Testament saints who awaited the resurrection in the place of the dead (Sheol). So Moses and Elijah are able to speak with the glorified Jesus because they already share in the heavenly glory.[6]

The Transfiguration, as strange as it may sound, is a foretaste of Calvary. These two mountains, the Mount of Transfiguration and Mt. Calvary, stand like pillars around Luke's account of Jesus' last few months. From Luke 9 to Luke 24 is a journey from one mountain to another.

From Glory to Glory

On the Mount of Transfiguration, Jesus is visibly glorified for his disciples. At Calvary, Jesus is also glorified, but it cannot be seen with physical eyes. You must look with the eyes of faith. And you must see that it is truly a great God whose love would lead him to lay aside his divine nature and submit to death in order to save his lowly creatures. What greater love is this? And what is greater than love? So the Cross of Calvary shows the glory of God's love for those with the faith to see it.

Shortly after the Transfiguration, St. Luke says this: "When the days drew near for him to be received up, he set his face to go to Jerusalem" (Lk 9:51). This is the formal start of Jesus' "death march" to the Holy City, what scholars call "the travel narrative." It's unique to Luke. No other gospel tells of this final journey in as much detail. Many special stories and teachings found only in Luke occur in this section: the

Good Samaritan (10:25–37), the Prodigal Son (15:11–32), and the Rich Man and Lazarus (16:19–31).

We can't discuss every story and teaching in this section, but we can sum up the main point. This last journey of Jesus is about the growth of the kingdom of God. As Jesus travels toward Jerusalem, he gathers more and more disciples around him. These are kingdom citizens, the beginnings of the Church. They form a great crowd by the time Jesus reaches Jerusalem (19:37–40). Many will fall away temporarily during his passion and death, but they will come back when the news of the resurrection bursts out.

Kingdom themes run through the travel narrative. The miracles that Jesus performs, such as exorcisms (10:17; 11:14–23) and healings (13:10–17; 14:1–6), are signs that God's kingdom is breaking into this world. In fact, Jesus teaches that very truth: after casting out a demon from a mute man, Jesus teaches the crowds, "If it is by the finger of God that I cast out demons, then the kingdom of God has come upon you" (Lk 11:20). Some had said that Jesus was casting out demons with Satan's own power, but Jesus points out how ridiculous that is: Why would Satan drive out his own servants? Rather, the exorcisms were signs that Satan's kingdom was crumbling before their eyes and God's kingdom was taking its place. Again, Jesus later teaches the crowds, "The kingdom of God is not coming with signs to be observed, nor will they say, 'Lo, here it is!' or 'There!' for behold, the kingdom of God is in the midst of you" (Lk 17:20–21). Jesus says this about himself: he is the King, and where the King is, there is the kingdom. The kingdom is already among the people, in Jesus' own person, but they don't recognize it.

Kingdom themes show up in the parables that Jesus teaches. Two favorite parables from this part of Luke are the Good Samaritan and the Prodigal Son.

Jesus tells the Parable of the Good Samaritan when an expert in religious law asks him the way to heaven. Jesus tells him to keep God's laws, especially the command "love your neighbor as yourself." That's a tall order; who of us can say we've loved our neighbor as ourselves? The man realizes how hard it is to live up to this, so he starts to quibble about terms: "And who is my neighbor?" (Lk 10:29).

Jesus tells a story. A Jewish man starts on the road from Jerusalem to Jericho. Now, this was a downhill stretch of several miles through barren country, dry and deserted like the parts of the American West. Like the Old West, it was also a lawless place full of bandits because it was easy to hide out there. So this was a very dangerous journey.

Sure enough, the man gets jumped by bandits, robbed, and left for dead. Two religious men, a priest and a Levite, pass by the victim. They probably feared that the man was already dead, and if they touched him, they would be contaminated and unable to perform duties in the Temple.

Finally, a Samaritan comes down the road. Jews despised Samaritans because Samaritans were part Gentile and part Israelite, descended from the ten unfaithful northern tribes of Israel that had broken off long ago and worshiped pagan gods. So Jews and Samaritans were distant "cousins," both from the tribes of Israel, but the Samaritans had wrong religious beliefs and worshiped at the wrong temple, not the one in Jerusalem. However, this Samaritan has compassion on the poor man, gives him first aid, takes him to an inn to recuperate, and pays his hotel fare.

Now Jesus says, "Who was a neighbor to the man who was robbed?" "The one who showed mercy," the expert replies. "Go and do likewise" (Lk 10:36–37). Jesus flips the man's question around. The man wanted to narrow down the definition of "neighbor" to a manageable number of people. But Jesus shifts the focus to becoming a good neighbor oneself. He also shows that neighborly love should spill over to people we normally despise and avoid: persons of different races, religions, and customs. Both the Samaritan and the Jewish traveler would ordinarily have stayed away from each other, not even touched each other. But in crisis, the barriers fall and the Samaritan shows love to his distant Jewish "cousin."

On another level, this parable is about the kingdom of God. The Old Testament kingdom of David had sadly split into two rival kingdoms, the kingdom of Israel in the north with ten tribes and the kingdom of Judah in the south with two tribes. The Jews descended from Judah, and the Samaritans from Israel. But the prophets had said, when the Messiah comes, he would reunite them in one kingdom: "They shall be no longer two nations, and no longer divided into two kingdoms" (Ez 37:22), but "David my servant shall be their prince," and "I will make an . . . everlasting covenant with them" (Ez 37:25–26). In the Parable of the Good Samaritan, a Samaritan from northern Israel and a Jew from southern Judah reconcile. It's like a rebel and a Yankee embracing, ending the "civil war" in God's kingdom. This is one of the things Jesus came to do.

Again, Jesus tells a parable about forgiveness. A man's younger son takes his inheritance and squanders it partying in a distant country. Out of money and close to starvation, he decides to come back home and ask his dad for a job. His father hugs him and throws a huge party to celebrate his return, but his older brother is steamed: Why throw a party for that good-for-nothing bum? His father has to come out and plead with the older brother to join the party.

That's the outline of the very familiar Parable of the Prodigal Son. We all know that it has a lot to do with God's forgiveness and the Sacrament of Reconciliation. But it is also a story of the kingdom of Israel. The younger son represents the northern kingdom of Israel, which rejected the Lord and went off to worship the gods of foreign countries. Israel was ruled by the tribe of Ephraim, the youngest son of Israel (actually, his youngest grandson, who was adopted as a full son). The older brother represents Judah, the southern kingdom that stayed closer to God through history and was still living around God's house, the Temple in Jerusalem. What about the anger of the older son when the younger son comes back? We will see that in the Book of Acts. There, the Judeans get angry and jealous when the apostles preach good news to the Samaritans (descendants of Israel) and even the Gentiles. The Judeans didn't think these groups should be reconciled to God. But let's remember that the parable ends with the father trying to get the older son to join the party. This is Jesus desire: for Jews and Samaritans to come together in God's kingdom, with Gentiles, too.

We see kingdom themes in Jesus' miracles and parables from the time Jesus leaves the Mount of Transfiguration (Lk 9) until he comes close to Mount Zion, the city of Jerusalem (Lk 19). As Jesus' journey comes to an end, the kingdom idea comes up several times: at Jericho, only a day's journey from Jerusalem, he cures a blind man who keeps calling to him, "Jesus, Son of David, have mercy on me! Son of David, have mercy on me!" "Son of David" was the title of the crown prince, the one to inherit the kingdom. The blind man can "see" what few others can: Jesus is the returning King!

While in Jericho, at the house of Zachaeus, he tells a parable about the kingdom of God in which a "nobleman" travels to a far country to be made king. He entrusts his wealth to his servants, to trade while he is gone. Upon his return, he rewards those servants who traded faithfully with the gifts he left them. Jesus is this nobleman who will go to a "far country" (heaven) to be made King (the Ascension) and will reward his servants (his disciples) upon his return.

Finally, Jesus enters Jerusalem (19:28–40), and his long march is over. He enters riding on a donkey's colt, as we saw in Matthew, with the crowds of his disciples shouting, "Blessed is the King who comes in the name of the Lord!" The King has entered the royal city to complete the sacrifice that will bring in the new kingdom.

Part 4 of Luke: Holy Week, the Passion Narrative *(Luke 20–24)*

Jesus' Passion Week unfolds in Luke in much the same way it did in Matthew, so we don't need to cover all the same ground again. We're already familiar with the cleansing of the Temple, Jesus' teaching and debating in the Temple courts, the prediction of the destruction of the Temple and of the world, and Judas's conspiracy to betray Jesus. Let's focus in on those places where St. Luke records unique and important information. One of those places is his account of the Last Supper, often called the "institution narrative" because it's where he *institutes* the Eucharist.

Luke tells us specifically that it was Peter and John who Jesus sent into Jerusalem to prepare the Passover. These two disciples are always hanging out together in Luke and Acts.

Jesus tells Peter and John to go into the city and look for a man carrying a jar of water. Now, water carrying was women's work, and most Jewish men would not have done it. However, the Jewish sect of the Essenes (ESS-seenz) practiced celibacy, and their celibate men had to carry their own water. Therefore, this man was probably an Essene, and the Essenes had their own liturgical calendar in which Passover always fell on a Tuesday.[7] We also know from archeology that the site of the Last Supper was in the Essene quarter of Jerusalem, that is, the neighborhood where all the Essenes lived together. All these facts together suggest that Jesus celebrated his last Passover with the Jewish Essene sect. Jesus and the disciples were not Essenes, of course, but they seemed to have gotten along well with them because the gospels do not record arguments between Jesus and the Essenes as they do with the Pharisees and Sadducees.

As in Matthew, Jesus speaks of not eating or drinking again until the coming of the kingdom of God. At the beginning of the Passover supper, he says, "I have earnestly desired to eat this passover with you before I suffer; for I tell you I shall not eat it until it is fulfilled in the kingdom of God" (Lk 22:15–16). What does Jesus mean? Is he not going to eat *this* Passover but merely serve it to the apostles? Will he not eat the Passover *again* until the coming of the kingdom? Or will he not eat *anything* until the kingdom comes? It's hard to make out the sense of our Lord's words beyond the fact that he speaks of not eating until the kingdom of God arrives. Likewise, he takes the cup just before the Last Supper, which would have been the second cup of the ancient Passover service. Over this cup he says, "Take this, and divide it among yourselves; for . . . from now on I shall not drink of the fruit of the vine until the kingdom of God comes" (vv. 17–18). This statement is clearer and indicates that, as we saw in Matthew, Jesus will not drink wine again until the kingdom has arrived.

Over the bread for the meal, Jesus says, "This is my body which is given for you. Do this in remembrance of me" (v. 19). By saying "this is my body given for you," Jesus not only transforms the bread into his body but also indicates that he is soon to die; he will soon "give his body" for the disciples in a sacrificial death. Let's not forget that Jesus knew exactly what he was doing. Many scholars nowadays say that Jesus' arrest and death took him by surprise. But all the gospels, as well as the writings of the apostle Paul, indicate that Jesus knew very well that he would suffer and die at the hands of the Jerusalem authorities. Scholars who say otherwise are simply ignoring all the historical testimony because they don't believe Jesus was really the Son of God and had prophetic knowledge.

After the meal, Jesus again takes a cup of wine, which would now be the third cup of the Passover service, and over it he says, "This cup [or 'chalice'] which is poured out for you is the new covenant in my blood" (v. 20). The words "in my blood" mean "consisting of my blood." Why would it make sense that the "new covenant" would consist of Jesus' blood? This makes sense because a covenant forms a family and families are related by blood. So we say, "He's blood to me," meaning, he's part of my extended family.

Jesus says that the cup is the "new covenant." When he says this, he draws a straight line back to Jeremiah 31:31, the only place anyone uses the phrase "new covenant" in the entire Old Testament. There, the prophet Jeremiah predicts, "Behold, the days are coming, says the LORD, when I will make a *new covenant* with the house of Israel and the house of Judah, not like the covenant which I made with their fathers when I took them by the hand to bring them out of the land of Egypt. . . . I will put my law within them, and I will write it upon their hearts" (Jer 31:31–33, emphasis added). Jeremiah contrasts the New Covenant with the old Mosaic Covenant.

This New Covenant will not be broken as was the old one, and the law will be written not on stone tablets but on the hearts of the people.

Notice that Jesus says the cup of his blood *is* the New Covenant. This fulfills the prophecies of Isaiah, where God said to his holy servant, "I have given you as a covenant to the people" (Is 42:6; 49:8). Jesus came not just to make a covenant but to *be* a covenant. That's what we see going on at the Last Supper. He calls his body and blood the "new covenant." Obviously, his body and blood are himself; therefore, he is *becoming* the New Covenant through the Eucharist.

Let's not miss that it's his eucharistic body and blood that Jesus calls the "new covenant." The Latin word for "covenant" is *testamentum*. "New Testament" means the same as "new covenant." But go ask any Christian in America what the "New Testament" is, and they'll point to the smaller second part of the Bible. The twenty-seven books and letters that make up the second part of the Bible are *not really the New Testament*. We should call them "the books we read when we celebrate the New Testament," or "the books that tell us about the New Testament" because that's what they really are. The New Testament itself *is the Eucharist*. To read the New Testament books without going to Mass is like looking at a menu without ever eating the meal or reading about swimming without ever jumping in the pool. The Bible says the "New Testament" is the Eucharist.

Let's go on reading Luke's account of the Last Supper. After the drinking of the third cup, a dispute arises among the disciples about who of them is greater than the others. Jesus had just told them that he was not going to drink wine again until the kingdom of God came. So, they must have expected the kingdom to arrive at any moment, and they were jockeying for positions of leadership. Jesus tells them this: "The kings of the Gentiles exercise lordship over them; and those in authority over them are called benefactors. But not so with you; rather let the greatest among you become as the youngest, and the leader as one who serves" (Lk 22:25–26). Jesus turns the worldly model of leadership upside down. We've said this before, but it bears repeating. The world thinks that service should flow up from the people to the ruler:

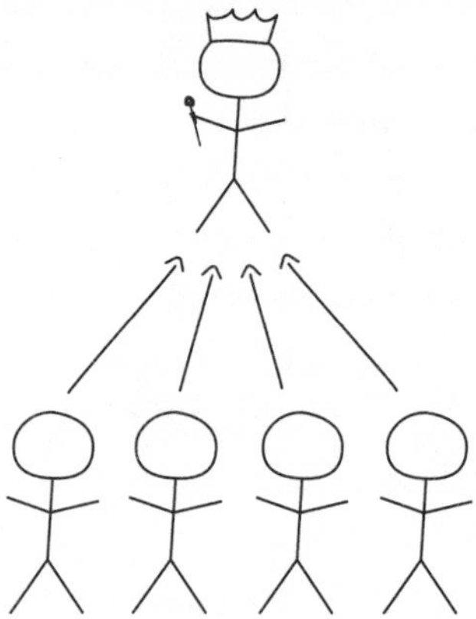

But Jesus says service should flow up from the ruler to the ruled:

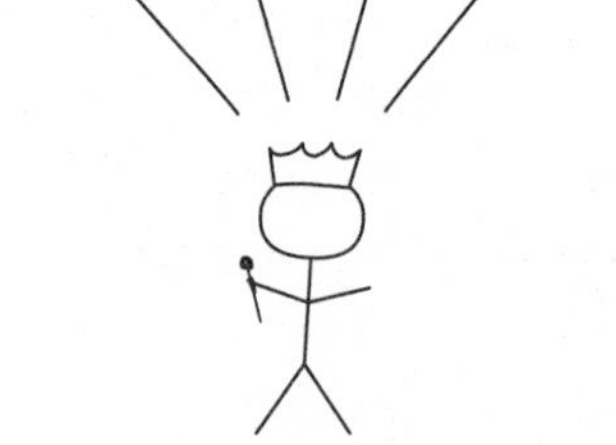

That doesn't mean the ruler doesn't have any authority. On the contrary, the ruler needs authority in order to serve.

Let's give some examples. My parish pastor lives to serve the people at our parish. He's there to serve us by making sure we have the sacraments we need to live a holy life: Baptism, Eucharist, Confession, and so forth. But in order for him to make sure we have the sacraments, he has to have the authority to set Mass and Confession times, to order repairs on the church building, to hire people to help out with ministry (secretaries, custodians, and teachers), and so on. How could he be effective if he didn't have any authority?

Likewise, our bishop lives to serve our diocese, to make sure we are all taken care of, spiritually first, but bodily, too, if needed. But to take care of us, he has to have the authority to manage the diocesan finances, build buildings or tear them down, assign priests to one place or another, and so on. Without that authority, decisions would never be made and things would all fall apart.

Finally, the pope lives to serve the whole Church. He has to make sure that around the world people have access to the sacraments and are taught the truth about Jesus without error. In order to do that, he has to have authority to teach the faith, appoint bishops and other leaders, and remove leaders who fall into sin or error.

One of the major ways that the pope serves the Church is by settling theological fights. If we didn't have someone who could settle arguments, the Church would tear itself apart with infighting. But in order to settle fights in the Church, the pope needs the authority. That's what we call papal infallibility. Papal infallibility means that when the pope settles an argument, it is settled for good because he's backed by God. If he wasn't infallible, no one would take his word as final, and the fights would never stop. So, for the sake of service to the Church, God gave Peter and his successors infallibility: "Whatever you bind on earth shall be bound in heaven" (Mt 16:19).

Because he is the Church's ultimate servant, one of the pope's titles is *servus servorum Dei*, "servant of the servants of God." That really does sum up the pope's role. He's there to serve us, and he has the authority to do so.

So, at the Last Supper, Jesus is really showing us how the Church should be run and what it means to be a leader in the kingdom of God. He goes on to say, "For which is the greater, one who sits at table, or one who serves? Is it not the one who sits at table? But I am among you as one who serves" (Lk 22:27). By bringing up the "table" image, Jesus shows that the Eucharist is where his leaders will show their leadership most of all. He, Jesus, is the one serving them their first eucharistic meal. After this, they will imitate him, leading the rest of the Church in the celebration of the Eucharist until the end of time. They will spend the rest of their lives "serving at the table."

To this day, our priests and bishops follow in the footsteps of the apostles and Jesus by "serving at table." At my parish, we use a Communion rail and kneel for Communion. We are like the disciples, and the Communion rail represents the table of the Last Supper. Our parish priests stand and walk around serving the Eucharist to all who have come to "recline" at the "table." Our priests are among us "as ones who serve." This is where their role of leadership in God's kingdom really shines.

Now let's read what Jesus says to the apostles after teaching them how to be leaders in the Church. I'm going to translate literally, which is slightly different from most English versions:

> You are those who have continued with me in my trials;

> So I *covenant diatithemi* to you, as my father *covenanted* to me, a kingdom;
> So that you may eat and drink at my table in my kingdom,
> And sit down [*kathemai*] on thrones judging the twelve tribes of Israel. (Lk 22:28–30)

Jesus uses the usual word for covenant-making (Greek *diatithemi*) to describe his gift of the kingdom to the apostles. Yet most English translations render it as "appoint" or something similar because translators don't think it makes sense to "covenant a kingdom." However, if you've been with me through the whole Old Testament in *Bible Basics for Catholics*, you know it makes a lot of sense to covenant a kingdom. There was only one kingdom in the Bible (and probably the world) that was founded on a covenant: the kingdom of David (2 Chr 13:5). Jesus is placing the kingdom of David, which has become the kingdom of God, upon the shoulders of the apostles.

The first privilege of the kingdom is to eat at the table of the King: "So that you may eat and drink at my table in my kingdom." Eating at the king's table meant being like "one of the king's sons" in olden times (see 2 Sm 9:11). The king was treating you as family. This is the eucharistic table, where the King is both host and food.

The second privilege of the kingdom is rulership: "You shall sit down [*kathemai*] on thrones judging the twelve tribes." Jesus is making the apostles into princes of the kingdom of David. In olden times, the royal princes sat on thrones judging law cases in Jerusalem: "There thrones for judgment were set, the thrones of the house of David" (Ps 122:5). Some think this promise to the apostles will only be fulfilled in heaven or in a future age when Christ returns to rule in Jerusalem. But the apostles begin to rule over the New Israel already in the Book of Acts, as we shall see. And their successors continue to "sit down on thrones" judging the tribes all over the world. Jesus says they shall "sit down," which is *kathemai* in Greek. A "seat" in Greek is a *kathedra*, and around a seat for an apostle we build a building called a *kathedral*. The Church has grown far beyond the original twelve tribes, and now there are successors of the apostles sitting down (*kathemai*) on *kathedras* in their *kathedrals* all over the world, judging the tribe of Steubenville (where I live), the tribe of Fort Wayne–South Bend (where this book is published), the tribe of Los Angeles, the tribe of Galveston-Houston, the tribe of New York, and so on.

Among these princes who will rule over the tribes of his kingdom, Jesus has appointed a leader, and at the Last Supper, he has special words for him: "Simon, Simon, look: Satan wanted to sift *y'all* like wheat, but I have prayed for *you* that your faith may not fail; and when you have come back, strengthen your brethren" (Lk 22:31–32). I've had to use English slang *y'all* to translate the Greek second-person plural, which we don't have in Standard English, but in the South it's *y'all* and where I live it's *yinz* (a contraction of "you ones"). The point is, Satan wanted *all* the apostles, but Jesus prayed specifically for Peter, that he would endure and bring the others back once he had recovered his senses.

Here again we see Peter's leadership of the apostles, a role that his successor, the pope, continues to play all through Church history. Times of trial throw the Church into distress, and sometimes even Peter's successor temporarily flees, as did Peter himself. But he recovers, turns back, and gathers the other brothers, his fellow bishops.

Well, after Jesus concludes the Last Supper and leaves the Upper Room with his disciples, the rest of his passion plays out much as it did in the Gospel of Matthew. Rather than rehearsing the well-known story again, let's fast-forward to a unique event that only Luke records: the walk to Emmaus (Lk 24:13–25).

It is Easter Sunday, and two disciples of Jesus, neither of whom were apostles, decide to leave Jerusalem and go to the quiet village of Emmaus, about a two-hour walk from the Holy City. They're depressed. They thought Jesus was the redeemer promised by the prophets of Israel. Now all their hopes are dashed.

As they walk along sharing their misery, Jesus slips in behind them unnoticed at first. After a while he butts into their conversation: *What are you talking about?* (I love the way Jesus plays dumb here, like the old police detective Columbo—or more recently Adrian Monk—who come across stupid at first, asking childish questions, until you begin to realize they know what they're doing.) *Are you the only visitor to Jerusalem who doesn't know these things?* Cleophas asks. In other words, *What's with you? Have you been living under a rock for the past week? Huh?* Jesus says, still acting dumb. *What are you talking about?*

So Cleophas explains to the "dumb Jesus" the whole story about how they had such high hopes for this Jesus of Nazareth guy and then the chief priests and elders connived to get him killed. Everything went to heck, and their womenfolk started acting crazy this morning, saying they had seen him at his tomb.

After Cleophas has spilled the whole story, Jesus can't contain himself any longer, and he drops the "ignorant" charade. This is like the conclusion of an episode of *Columbo* or *Monk*, when the detective gathers everybody and explains how the whole crime took place, when everyone else realizes they were following false leads. "O foolish men, and slow of heart to believe all that the prophets have spoken!" Jesus says, "Was it not necessary that the Christ should suffer these things and enter into his glory?" (Lk 24:25–26). And he launches into a lengthy explanation of the Old Testament scriptures that had spoken of the Messiah, his sufferings, and his glory: "Beginning with Moses and all the prophets, he interpreted to them in all the scriptures the things concerning himself" (v. 27).

Now, everyone is curious about what exactly Jesus said to them on the road to Emmaus, and I myself have done a lot of research on this question and believe I have reconstructed the events fairly accurately. It's now clear that along the Emmaus Road, about five miles from Jerusalem, there is a large flat dusty patch of ground on the north side of the road where Jesus took Cleophas and his friend aside and began to scratch the following figures in the dirt:

No, I'm kidding. I doubt Jesus drew the mountains and mediators of covenant history for them. But he probably did expand on the many of the themes and the texts of scripture that we have summarized with our mountains diagram.

Cleophas and his companion (perhaps St. Luke himself) gradually become aware that their unknown travelling partner seems to have a doctorate in biblical theology, so to speak. They enjoy his teaching so much that they beg him to stay the evening with them. Reluctantly, the Bible-expert friend joins them for dinner at the village where they've stopped. But when they sit down for dinner, he does a surprising thing. Rather than wait for one of them to serve, he begins to act as the host of the meal. He takes the bread himself, blesses it and breaks it, and gives it to them. As he's doing this, they have a sudden jolt of recognition: they've seen someone do this before. This guy is acting just like . . . no, wait, it's more than that . . . he actually *is* Jesus! "Their eyes were opened and they recognized him; and he vanished out of their sight" (24:31).

Cleophas and his buddy run back to Jerusalem in the dark to try to find the rest of the believers. They found the eleven remaining apostles gathered together with the other disciples, and they told "what had happened on the road, and how he was made known to them in the breaking of the bread" (24:35).

In the whole Emmaus Road episode, we can see the pattern of the Mass: first, the Liturgy of the Word, where the celebrant explains how the scriptures point to Jesus; and then the Liturgy of the Eucharist, when Jesus himself is revealed by the "breaking of bread."

While the two from Emmaus are explaining these things, Jesus himself appears to the Eleven, proving his identity by showing his hands and feet, and eating food in their presence. He commissions the apostles to be his "witnesses," literally, *martyrs* (Lk 24:48), who will preach the good news to all the nations, beginning from Jerusalem. Then, he blesses them and ascends to heaven, while they return to worship at the Temple. This ending of the Gospel of Luke sets up the beginning of his next book, Acts, which will open with a longer, more detailed account of the events summarized at the end of the gospel. The stage is set for the God's kingdom to spread rapidly out into the world starting from Jerusalem and the Temple.

Four

The Book of Acts

Luke

We now move on to the sequel to the Gospel of Luke: the Book of the Acts of the Apostles, or just "Acts." Acts is unique in the New Testament: it is the only book to tell us the history of the early Church. While we have four biographies of Jesus, we have only one of the infant Church. We should be grateful to St. Luke for recording for us the beautiful accounts of the Ascension (Acts 1:6–11), Pentecost (Acts 2:1–42), the Martyrdom of Stephen (Acts 7), the Calling of St. Paul (Acts 9:1–18), and so many other earthshaking events that shaped the Church and the history of the world.

It's not hard to figure out the theme of the Book of Acts. All you have to do is look at what Jesus is talking about with the apostles in the opening scene of the book: he appeared "to them during forty days . . . speaking of the *kingdom of God*" (Acts 1:3, emphasis added). Then, look at the last two verses of the Book of Acts, where Paul is under house arrest in Rome but is still "preaching the *kingdom of God* and teaching about the Lord Jesus Christ quite openly and unhindered" (Acts 28:31, emphasis added). When a book begins and ends on the same topic, scholars call it an *inclusio* (in-KLOOZ-ee-oh). It marks the theme. The theme of Acts is the *kingdom of God*. But you may know that many people say Acts is about the birth of the Church. So which is it: The kingdom of God or the Church? To this I say, yes! It's not an either/or because, as we have seen in the gospels, the Church is the beginning of the kingdom already on earth.

Acts can be divided into two basic sections: Acts 1–12 is the "Peter Channel" ("All Peter, all the time"), and Acts 13–28 is the "Paul Channel" ("All Paul, all the time").

That's a bit of a simplification, of course, because St. Paul makes an important appearance in Acts 9, and St. Peter makes an important appearance in Acts 15, and a few other characters get some major attention (such as St. Stephen in Acts 7). But it is true that Acts 1–12 basically follows the career of St. Peter from the Ascension of Jesus (Acts 1) till the martyrdom of St. James the Greater (Acts 12).

At that point, St. Peter goes into hiding due to persecution, and the action of Acts follows the career of St. Paul from his first missionary journey (Acts 13) to his imprisonment in Rome (Acts 28). The reason Paul gets more coverage (four more chapters) is that Luke was with Paul for some of his journeys and remembered the events in great detail (Acts

16, 20–21, 27). We can sketch the major divisions of Acts as follows:

Peter has the keys of the Kingdom (Mt 16:19). Paul has the sword of the Spirit (Eph 6:17) and a letter, since he was such a great letter-writer. Now that we have an idea of the theme and structure of Acts, let's plunge in!

The Forty Days and the Ascension *(Acts 1:1–11)*

Acts opens with Jesus spending time with the apostles over a period of forty days from Easter to the Ascension. We've already noted that during this time, he teaches them about the "kingdom of God" (Acts 1:3). Significantly, Jesus eats meals with the apostles during this time, as we can see from Acts 1:4, which says literally, "*While taking salt* [Greek *sunalizomenos*] with them, he charged them not to depart from Jerusalem." "Taking salt with" was a Greek phrase meaning "to eat with" because they served salt at every meal as a seasoning. Remember Jesus' words about not eating or drinking again until the kingdom of God comes? Here Jesus is eating and drinking with the apostles (see also Acts 10:41–42), so the kingdom has arrived, even if it is small like a mustard seed at this point.

The apostles want to know more about the kingdom: "Will you at this time restore the kingdom to Israel?" they ask. Jesus responds, “It is not for you to know times or seasons which the Father has fixed by his own authority. But you shall receive power . . . and you shall be my witnesses in Jerusalem and in all Judea and Samar’ia and to the end of the earth” (1:7–8).

Now, the usual interpretation of this is that Jesus is putting the disciples off. He’s telling them to forget about the kingdom and just preach the Gospel. I would like to suggest a different interpretation: the disciples ask *when*, but Jesus tells them *how*. They can’t know the matters of timing, but the “kingdom” will be “restored to Israel” through their preaching ministry. After all, the sequence Jerusalem–Judea–Samaria–“Ends of the Earth” is a theological map of the kingdom of David. Jerusalem was David’s capital. Judea was David’s own tribe. Samaria is northern Israel, David’s nation. The “ends of the earth” refers to the Gentiles, who were supposed to be David’s vassals: “Ask of me and I will make the nations your heritage, and the *ends of the earth* your possession” (Ps 2:8, emphasis added).

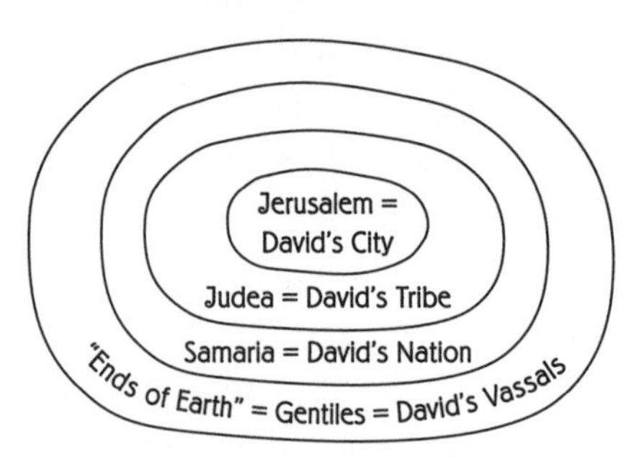

So Jesus’ words are a description of how the kingdom will spread to the whole world. Also, they indicate the structure of the Book of Acts, which will follow the sequence Jerusalem (Acts 1–7), Judea and Samaria (Acts 8), and “the ends of the earth” (Acts 9–28), that is, the mission to the Gentiles, beginning with the conversion of Paul, the apostle to the Gentiles in Acts 9, and ending with Paul preaching in Rome, the capital of the Gentile world, in Acts 28.

After commissioning the apostles as his royal emissaries, Jesus ascends into heaven where he sits enthroned at the right hand of God the Father (Mk 16:19; Eph 1:20; Acts 7:55–56). The Ascension is the beginning of Jesus' royal reign over all the earth through his body the Church. When you pray this mystery of the Rosary, a point of meditation can be, do I submit to Jesus' royal reign over every aspect of my life, including my work, entertainment, finances, and sexuality?

The Replacement of Judas by Matthias *(Acts 1:15–26)*

Angels tell the apostles to stop staring into heaven; Jesus will come back the same way. So they return to Jerusalem and get on with the business at hand. One of the first orders of business is the replacement of Judas the traitor. The apostles are down to Eleven, but since they mystically represent twelve new patriarchs of the twelve tribes of Israel, they must bring their number back up to twelve. Moreover, Peter finds a prophecy of this in the Psalms, for example, Psalm 109:8, which literally reads in both the Hebrew and Greek, "His office of oversight [Greek *episkopēn*] let another take." So they cast lots among two worthy candidates, and select Matthias to be enrolled among the Twelve in Judas's place.

This whole episode is of great, great importance for Catholic Christians. It demonstrates two important points: First, the apostles had a role or office (an *episkopēn*), which did not end with their death. Second, this role is described as an *episkopēn*, literally an "oversight," meaning a supervisory role. Calling the apostles' role an *episkopēn* shows the connection between the apostles and the later leaders of the Church, who are called *episkopoi*, or "bishops" (Acts 2:28; Phil 1:1; 1 Tm

3:2; Ti 1:7). The English word "bishop" is a corruption of the Greek *epi-skopos* ("over-seer" or "super-visor"): the syllable *bis* comes from *pis*, and the syllable *shop* comes from *skop*.

So, we see here the important principle of *apostolic succession*. That is, when death or another reason prevents an apostle from performing his duty, another is appointed to *succeed* him. Our leaders today (bishops and priests) were appointed by the previous generation of leaders, and they in turn by a previous generation, all the way back to the apostles, who appointed the Church's first generation of leaders during their own lifetimes. Thus, the bishops are successors of the apostles in the sense that they fulfill the apostles' role, which is one of leadership or *oversight* (*episkopēn*). This is a top-down system. There is no role in Christ's Church for those who simply appoint themselves as authorities or for groups that break off and make their own leaders unconnected to the chain of leadership going back to the apostles.

Pentecost *(Acts 2)*

Back up to their full number of twelve, the apostles are ready to receive the "power" that Jesus had promised them. They had already received the Spirit (Jn 20:22 and Lk 24:49a), but they need a special empowerment to "jump-start" the Church (Lk 24:49b; Acts 1:8).

It was the Feast of Pentecost in Jerusalem. "Pentecost" is a word from Greek meaning "fifty," so called because the festival was celebrated fifty days after Passover. This would fall at the beginning of the wheat harvest, but fifty days after Passover was also when the Israelites arrived at Mt. Sinai and received the Law of the Covenant, the Ten Commandments. So Pentecost was the great memorial of the giving of the Law at Sinai.

Pentecost is a new Sinai. At Sinai, God appeared in a frightening storm, with darkness, thunder, lightning, flame, smoke, and cloud.

Fearful Storm at Sinai

At Pentecost, there is also a storm, but it's not scary. There is a "mighty wind," and "tongues of fire" come to rest on the apostles and others.

Mt. Zion
Peaceful "Storm" of the Spirit

It is a peaceful storm of the Holy Spirit.

At Sinai, God gave a law written on tablets of stone. At Pentecost, he gives a law written on the human heart: the Holy Spirit poured into the hearts of the believers. Jeremiah had prophesied, "The days are coming . . . when I will make a new covenant . . . not like the covenant which I made with their fathers when I took them by the hand to bring them out of Egypt. . . . But this is the covenant which I will make with the house of Israel . . . I will put my law within them, and I will write it upon their hearts." (Jer 31:31–33). As St. Thomas Aquinas says, the law of the New Covenant is nothing other than the grace of the Holy Spirit.[1]

Pentecost was a pilgrimage feast, and "there were dwelling in Jerusalem Jews, devout men from every nation," St. Luke says (Acts 2:5), and goes on to list the various nations. As the Spirit falls on the apostles and they begin to preach in many different languages, the crowd is "bewildered," "amazed," and "perplexed" because *they can understand* the preaching. What we have here is a reverse of the Tower of Babel (Gn 11), where all the people were bewildered and perplexed because they *could not understand* what each one was saying. The power of the Holy Spirit erases the divisions in humanity that come from human sin.

Peter gets up to preach, addressing the whole crowd. St. Luke records a very brief summary of his sermon (Acts 2:14–36). St. Peter preaches that this miraculous outpouring of the Spirit fulfills the prophecies of the prophets, quoting a long passage from the prophet Joel (vv. 14–21). He continues to preach Jesus as the fulfillment of the Davidic Covenant, quoting several psalms of David because David was "prophet, and knowing that *God had sworn with an oath to him that he would set one of his* seed *upon his throne*, he foresaw and spoke of the resurrection of the Christ" (vv. 30–31, emphasis added). Peter points to the dramatic signs—the rushing wind, tongues of flame, and miraculous speaking in different languages—as proof that Jesus has been enthroned and has begun his royal reign. "Being therefore exalted at the right hand of God, and having received from the Father the promise of the Holy Spirit, he has poured out this which you see and hear" (Acts 2:33). The *visible* flames and the *audible* tongues prove that something has taken place in the *invisible* realm: Jesus has taken his throne.

When the crowds hear Peter's spirit-inspired preaching, they were "cut to the heart." This powerful phrase "cut to the heart" recalls prophecies of the "circumcision of the heart" from the Old Testament. Moses prophesied that, after many ups and downs in Israel's history, "the LORD your God will circumcise your heart . . . so that you will love the LORD your God with all your heart" (Dt 30:6). Ezekiel had said something similar: "A new heart I will give you, and a new spirit I will put within you; and I will take out of your flesh the heart of stone and give you a heart of flesh" (36:26).

Apparently God has done that since a stone heart can't be cut but these Israelites are "cut to the heart." "What shall we do?" the crowd asks the apostles. "Repent, and be baptized," Peter replies, "every one of you in the name of Jesus Christ for the forgiveness of your sins; and you shall receive the gift of the Holy Spirit" (2:37–38). So three thousand people, Jews and Gentile converts to Judaism from all the nations of the earth, get baptized on that first Pentecost and receive the Holy Spirit. This filling of the Holy Spirit in their hearts *is* the "circumcision" or cleansing of the heart that Moses predicted. Remember that circumcision was a covenant-making act. At Baptism, the outpouring of the Holy Spirit into our hearts makes the New Covenant between us and God.

What do the newly baptized do? They "devoted themselves to the apostles' teaching and fellowship, to the breaking of bread and the prayers" (Acts 2:42). And they "had all things in common" and "distributed . . . as any had need" (vv. 44–45). These are the basic elements of the Mass:

"The apostles' teaching": The Liturgy of the Word

"Fellowship": The passing of the peace

"The breaking of bread": The Liturgy of the Eucharist

"The prayers": The prayers throughout Mass

"Had all things in common": The collection of offerings

The "breaking of bread" is almost a technical term in Luke and Acts for the celebration of the Eucharist. That's what it was called in those early days. Those early Christians also practiced a kind of "charismatic communism" where they gave up personal possessions and "had all things in common." As the Church grew and spread all over the world, this proved impractical, so the Church switched to collecting people's excess wealth each Sunday at Mass. Then the bishop "distributed . . . as any had need." That's the origin of the collection at Mass. People in religious life, however, still usually "have all things in common" with their order, as did the early Christians. So what we see is that, after being baptized, the early Christians devote themselves to the celebration of the Eucharist and the other elements of what we now call "the Mass."

We can move more quickly over the events that take place after Pentecost. Sometime later, Peter and John heal a lame man while going to the Temple, and this becomes the occasion for Peter to preach another important sermon, this time emphasizing Jesus as fulfillment of the covenant with Abraham. He concludes his sermon saying, "You are the sons of the prophets and of the covenant which God gave to your fathers, saying to Abraham, 'And in your *seed* shall all the families of the earth be blessed'" (Acts 3:25). This is a quote of Genesis 22:18, God's oath to Abraham after the attempted sacrifice of Isaac, the "one and only" son of Abraham, laid on the wood of the altar at Mt. Moriah. Peter says Jesus is the "seed" of Abraham who will bless all the families of the earth. Jesus is the fulfillment of the covenant promises to Abraham:

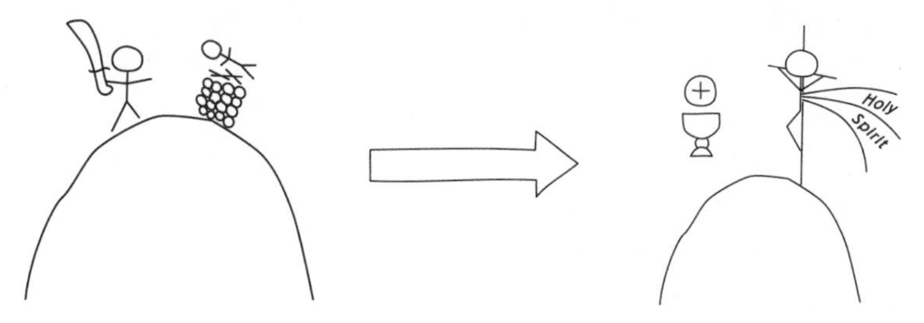

The Jewish council, called the "Sanhedrin," arrests Peter and John because they find their preaching annoying. But they have no legal case against them, so they end up threatening and releasing them. The whole experience just makes the Church bolder: they pray in the Spirit, and God blesses them with "signs and wonders."

The early Church was a restored Israel, composed of converts from all the different nations where the twelve tribes had been scattered (Acts 2:5–11). Jesus promised that the disciples would "sit on twelve thrones, judging the twelve tribes of Israel." While we don't see them sitting on physical thrones, we do see the apostles judging the restored "Twelve Tribes." St. Luke gives an example of their leadership: the believers had such respect for the authority of the apostles they would sell their houses and lands and put the money at the apostles' feet. A married couple, Ananias and Sapphira, decides to scam this system by only bring part of their proceeds (5:1–2). They lie to Peter that they are bringing the full amount, but Peter says, "You have not lied to men but to God" (v. 4). Notice how lying to the apostles, particularly Peter, is "lying to God." The apostles have authority from God. Both husband and wife fall dead in Peter's presence when the lie is revealed, only adding to the reverence people had for Peter and the apostles.

The Sanhedrin again calls in Peter and John, angry that they didn't stop preaching after the threats that were made the last time they were arrested (5:17–42). Peter's preaching about Jesus so infuriates the Jewish council that they almost lynch the two apostles on the spot. But calmer heads prevail, so the Sanhedrin contents itself with beating them and letting them go. This does nothing to stop the progress of the Church, however, so the leadership of the New Israel (the Twelve) is winning this contest with the leadership of the Old Israel (the Sanhedrin).

Not all is perfect in the kingdom of God, however. Greek-speaking Christian widows aren't getting enough food in the Church's daily distribution, probably because those passing out the food didn't speak Greek well and could not understand the widows' needs (6:1–6). The Greek-speaking

Jewish Christians complain to the apostles, and what the apostles do changes the structure of the Church forever.

"It is not right that we should give up preaching the word of God to serve tables," the apostles respond (6:2). That is, while works of mercy are good, they are not a higher priority than preaching the Gospel. As Jesus said in the desert, "Man shall not live by bread alone, but by every word that proceeds from the mouth of God" (Mt 4:4). And in another place Jesus says, "What does it profit a man if he gains the whole world and loses or forfeits himself?" (Lk 9:25). Likewise, what good would it do if the Church could feed every human being on the planet if they all rejected the Gospel and spent eternity separated from God? "Do not labor for food which perishes," Jesus says, "but for the food which endures to eternal life" (Jn 6:27). So the apostles, faced with a crisis of food distribution, don't want to give up the primary mission of the Church, which is teaching people the way to eternal life.

So the apostles say, "Pick out from among you seven men . . . whom we may appoint to this duty" (Acts 6:3). Luke lists the men chosen: Stephen, Philip, Prochorus, Nicanor, Timon, Parmenas, and Nicolaus. All of these men have Greek names, so they were probably Greek speakers. They would make sure the Greek-speaking widows got their food. We consider these men the first deacons. The Church sets them "before the apostles, and they prayed and laid their hands upon them" (6:6). This is what we now call "ordination." The laying on of hands transfers authority. The apostles are taking some of the authority given them by Jesus and placing it on these seven deacons for a specific task: managing the physical needs of the Church.

When I was a Protestant preacher, I used this text, Acts 6:1–6, to argue for a "democratic" form of Church government. See, I would say, the Church just chooses its own leaders and elects them. In hindsight, I realize I was wrong. The apostles are guiding this whole process. They are the ones who tell the congregation to put forward candidates for the diaconate. And then they "appoint" those men by praying and laying hands on them. The authority comes from the apostles. This is a top-down structure. Governed by Jesus the King and his royal princes the apostles, the Church is a monarchy, not a democracy.

With the seven newly appointed "deacons" managing the practical affairs of the Church, the apostles are freed up for more preaching. As a result, "the word of God increased; and the number of disciples multiplied greatly in Jerusalem, *and a great many of the priests were obedient to the faith*" (6:7, emphasis added).

This conversion of a large number of priests to become followers of Jesus is a fulfillment of God's promises in the Old Testament. The priests came from the tribe of Levi, and this tribe was special to God because of their zeal for him. God had made special promises to this tribe that they would always serve him as priests (see Jer 33:17–21). So this large gathering of Levite priests into the restored kingdom of Israel is a sign that God is keeping his promises. They do not lose their priesthood when they receive Jesus. Instead, they become part of the "royal priesthood," as St. Peter says (1 Pt 2:9). So the tribe of Levi enters the New Covenant and gains a share in the new priesthood.

The Martyrdom of Stephen *(Acts 7)*

You had to know the honeymoon couldn't last. There were people envious of the Church and how fast it was growing by the power of this new Gospel. So the growth of the Church leads to persecution, as it often does. In this case, the lightning rod for violence becomes Stephen, one of the new deacons. He's quite a good preacher and Bible teacher. His opponents get him arrested on false charges and drag him before the Jerusalem council. "This man never ceases to speak words against this holy place [the Temple] and the law," they say (6:13). "Is this so?" the high priest asks (7:1). And Stephen launches into his defense speech.

The speech is very long, most of Acts 7, and reads like comprehensive review of Bible history. What's your point, Stephen? Are you just stalling for time? Actually, there is a point to Stephen's speech. As he retells almost the whole history of Israel, he points out all the places and times that God appeared away from the Temple. He also points out how the true prophets were always rejected through salvation history. What are Stephen's take-home points? Number one: God can be worshiped anywhere, not just at this Temple. Number two: Jesus was a true prophet, and you folks have rejected him as you rejected all the true prophets before him.

Stephen's defense ends up being more of a hell-fire-and-brimstone sermon. Dale Carnegie wouldn't recommend ending a speech the way Stephen does if you want to "win friends and influence people": "You stiff-necked people . . . you always resist the Holy Spirit. Which of the prophets did not your fathers persecute? And . . . you have now betrayed and murdered [the Righteous One]" (Acts 7:51–52). Needless to say, the crowd wasn't too happy with this conclusion. They "ground their teeth against him" (v. 54). That's subtle body language that they are displeased. But Stephen said, "Behold, I see the heavens opened, and the Son of man standing at the right hand of God" (v. 56).

The Son of Man is Jesus, and the "right hand of God" is the position of authority. But shouldn't Jesus be "seated at the right hand" of God? (Lk 22:69). So why is he standing?

Before he "tastes death," Stephen sees
"the kingdom of God" (Luke 9:27)

Kings got up off their thrones and stood when they wished to show honor to someone who was coming into his throne room. So Solomon, for example, got up off his throne to greet his mother Bathsheba when she entered his court (1 Kgs 2:19). Jesus has risen from his throne and is standing to greet Stephen who is about to enter the throne room because the enraged crowd drags him out of the city and lynches him by stoning. "Lord Jesus, receive my spirit," he cries, and "Lord, do not hold this sin against them," dying with words very much like Jesus on the Cross (Acts 7:59–60; see Lk 23:34, 46), only Jesus had prayed to the *Father*, but Stephen prays to *Jesus*. Jesus and the Father are one (Jn 10:30). God parts the veil separating the visible from the invisible realm and gives Stephen a glimpse of invisible reality before his death.

The Outbreak of Persecution and the Spread of the Kingdom *(Acts 8)*

Stephen's death unleashes a wave of violence against the Christians, and all but the apostles themselves are driven out of Jerusalem into "Judea and Samaria." But this is in God's plan, for Jesus had said, "You shall be my witnesses [Greek, *martyrs*] in Jerusalem and *in all Judea and Samar'ia*" (Acts 1:8, emphasis added). So the kingdom of God is spreading out from David's capital to his tribe and his nation.

We hear about Saul (later Paul) for the first time now: he was a leader in the lynching of Stephen, and now he acts like the head of the religious secret police, going around rounding up Christians. But in time, he himself will become a "witness . . . to the end of the earth." Only not yet.

Meanwhile, Luke focuses on the ministry of Philip. Philip, like Stephen, is a deacon. Like Stephen, he's a powerful preacher. So we see that deacons can preach. That's true to this day in the church: the roles of the deacon include taking care of the material needs of the Church and preaching.

Philip goes to Samaria and preaches (8:4–25). The Samaritans are what's left of the ten northern tribes, the "House of Israel." Jeremiah promised, "The days are coming . . . when I will make a New Covenant with the *house of Israel and the house of Judah*" (31:31, emphasis added). So the Gospel has to be preached in Judea, the "house of Judah," and in Samaria, the "house of Israel." Many of these Samaritan Israelites accept the Good News of the kingdom of God and are baptized (Acts 8:12). Philip baptizes them. To this day, Baptism is one of the things deacons can do. But their baptism is not complete. They don't receive the fullness of the Holy Spirit. Peter and John, the apostles, have to come down and lay hands on them. Then they receive the Holy Spirit.

This is the origin of the Rite of Confirmation. Confirmation is a kind of sealing or completion of one's Baptism. It grants a fullness of the Holy Spirit, giving power to be a good witness to Jesus. Notice that the gift of the Holy Spirit is tied to the ministry of the apostles. In Acts, the Holy Spirit is poured out only by the hands of the apostles or in their presence or by someone authorized by them. St. Luke shows us the Spirit works with and through the "royal officers" of the Church, the apostles. This is why, as much as possible, the local bishop comes in person to confirm people. As with Peter and John coming to Samaria, the bishop comes as successor of the apostles to confirm the gift of the Spirit given in Baptism.

Jesus had told the apostles, "You shall be my witnesses . . . in all Judea and Samar'ia and to the ends of the earth" (Acts 1:8). The southern end of the earth, as folks thought in those days, was in the direction of Ethiopia. So it's striking that, after the good news of the kingdom has taken root in Samaria, Philip is led by God to the highway headed south to meet an Ethiopian royal official on his way home. The official was reading aloud in his chariot (because everyone read aloud in those days), and Philip could overhear him reading from the prophet Isaiah about God's servant who is like a sheep led to slaughter, who suffers in silence and is killed unjustly. "Do you understand what you are reading?" Philip asks (Acts 8:30). And the official responds, *Of course I do! I just pray to the Holy Spirit and God gives me instant understanding! The Bible is all I need!* Oh . . . actually, that's not what the official said. Instead, he says, "How can I, unless someone guides me?" (v. 31). This response teaches us something about the Bible and the Church. The Bible can be hard to understand. God never dropped us a book from heaven and expected us to figure it out on our own. At all times in history, there has been a people of God, God's family on earth, who treasured his Word and wrote it down. It's inside the people of God, the Church, that God's Word is properly understood. Philip is an officer and representative of the Church. As a deacon, he shares in Holy Orders and the responsibility to teach the truth of the Church's faith. Philip helping the official to understand the meaning of Isaiah is a great illustration of how the Church helps each one of us grasp the meaning of God's Word.

So Philip gets into the chariot and begins to explain how Isaiah speaks of Jesus of Nazareth, who suffered and died like a sacrificial lamb. The royal official is so moved he asks for Baptism right away. And Philip, one of the first deacons, baptizes him in some nearby water. As we noted above, to this day, deacons baptize as part of their role.

The Ethiopian official was overjoyed at his Baptism and continued down to Ethiopia in a festive mood. What did he do when he got home? He must have done some evangelism because Ethiopia is the first and oldest Christian country in Africa, where the Church has been present since apostolic times. That official was in for another surprise, too, as he rode home. You see, not only was he a non-Israelite foreigner, but also he was also a eunuch. And in the Mosaic Covenant, neither foreigners nor eunuchs could come into God's presence to worship him. Take your Bible and go back to Isaiah 53, the passage that Philip explained to the eunuch. Now, imagine the eunuch sitting in his chariot after his Baptism and moving on to read Isaiah 54, Isaiah 55, and Isaiah 56. Slow down on Isaiah 56 and look closely at verses 1–8. Imagine the Ethiopian eunuch reading this passage just an hour or so after his Baptism by Philip, and you can see why he was so enthusiastic by the time he got home that he helped his whole country become Christian.

So, the kingdom of God is growing. The Ethiopian eunuch will spread the kingdom to the southern "end of the earth," and in the next chapter of Acts we hear about the man who, more than any other, will be responsible for spreading the kingdom to the other "ends of the earth." Saul the Pharisee, not satisfied with arresting and abusing Christians in Jerusalem, heads off to Damascus in Syria to see if he can find Christians there to harm. On the way, a light flashes from heaven and knocks him from his horse. "Saul, Saul, why do you persecute me?" a voice asks. "Who are you, Lord?" "I am Jesus, whom you are persecuting" (Acts 9:4–5).

Notice he does not say, *I am Jesus, whose* followers *you are persecuting*. No, rather he says, "I am Jesus, whom you are persecuting." What is done to Christians is done to Christ. This is just like what Jesus said in Matthew, in the Parable of the Sheep and the Goats: "As you did it to one of the least of these my brethren, you did it to me" (Mt 25:40). Christians are so joined to Christ that they are one with him. Because of this, St. Joan of Arc could say at her trial, "About Jesus Christ and the Church, I simply know they are just one thing, and we shouldn't complicate the matter." Also, since Jesus is the King, and the kingdom-in-a-person, it follows that his Church, joined as one to him, is also the kingdom.

Well, Saul the Pharisee is struck blind for several days after his encounter with Jesus, until finally a Christian brother, Ananias, prays for him to regain his sight. Immediately, Saul begins preaching about the Jesus he once persecuted but that provokes a hostile reaction, and he has to flee for his life from Damascus. St. Luke then leaves off following St. Paul's career: he will be the focus of the second half of the book (Acts 13–28) and will carry the message of the kingdom of God to the ends of the earth. But for now, St. Luke wants to return to follow the career of St. Peter, who is the main focus of Acts 1–12.

St. Peter and the Gentiles *(Acts 9:32–10:18)*

St. Peter is so filled with the Holy Spirit that he can repeat the miracles of Jesus' own ministry. Just as Jesus healed a bedridden paralytic (Lk 5:17–26), so Peter heals a bedridden paralytic named Aeneas (Acts 9:32–35). Now, "Aeneas" is the name of the mythical founder of Rome, so this man may have been a Roman, and his healing points to St. Peter's role in opening up the Church to the Romans and other Gentiles.

Then, just as Jesus healed a dead girl by going into a house, sending all the mourners outside, taking her by the hand, and telling her to "arise" (Lk 8:49–56), so Peter heals the woman Tabitha, a Christian disciple in the coastal town of Joppa, using the same method as Jesus (Acts 9:36–43).

St. Luke tells us these stories of Peter's awesome Christ-like miracles in order to remind us that Peter's has the authority of Christ (Mt 16:18) and Peter continues Jesus' ministry. That's important because what Peter is about to do in Acts 10 was very, very controversial, and early Christians needed to be reminded that Peter had the authority to do it.

While staying near the seashore in Joppa at the home of a friend, St. Peter prays and falls into a trance. He sees a great sheet coming out of heaven with animals of many kinds, clean and unclean, kosher and not kosher. He hears God's voice: "Kill and eat." This happens three times. Then he comes out of his trance.

What was that all about? Well, in the Mosaic Covenant, after the people of Israel had sinned by worshiping the golden calf and going back to Gentile religion, God had given the people of Israel many laws to teach them to stay separate from the Gentiles and their unrighteous ways. God had given them laws about which animals were "clean" and could be eaten and which animals were not clean and could not be consumed. This was a teaching device. The clean animals symbolized the Israelites, and the unclean animals symbolized the Gentiles.

Also, since Israelites had to follow a different, restricted diet, they could not eat meals with Gentiles and basically had to stay separate from them almost all the time to avoid uncleanliness.

But God reveals to Peter that these laws have served their purpose, and now their time is over. Jews and Gentiles do not need to stay apart anymore. Under David and Solomon, the king of Israel had ruled over an international empire that included the surrounding Gentile nations. The Gentiles came up to Jerusalem to give tribute to the Davidic king and praise the God of Israel in the temple. David the king wrote of the Lord, “He subdued peoples under us, and nations under our feet” (Ps 47:3), and the leaders of the nations conquered by Israel would gather for worship: “God sits on his holy throne. The princes of the peoples gather as the people of the God of Abraham” (Ps 47:8–9).

Now, God is doing the same thing. Jesus is the Son of David, and in his kingdom he gathers all peoples to be the one people of God, the God of Abraham. Abraham’s covenant promised, “By your *seed* shall all the nations of the earth bless themselves.” Jew and Gentile are united in one kingdom-Church.

So, getting back to Peter. After his vision, in which God tells him that the food laws of Moses have to be retired, messengers come to St. Peter with a request: a Roman centurion (army captain) named Cornelius wants Peter to come and tell him the way of salvation. Peter goes and preaches the basic Gospel message of faith in Jesus (Acts 10:34–43). While he’s doing this, the Spirit falls on all the Gentiles present: Cornelius’s family and friends. They begin to speak in tongues, like the apostles themselves at Pentecost (Acts 2). In fact, we can call Acts 10 the “Gentile Pentecost.” They receive the Holy Spirit, even though they have not become Jews first by being circumcised. Peter commands them to be baptized. Truly, the kingdom is spreading “to the ends of the earth”!

But the Jews have been used to circumcision and keeping "kosher" for so long, it's hard to get used to the idea that someone could be a worshiper of God without doing those things. Not all the leaders of the mother church in Jerusalem are happy with what St. Peter is doing. But when St. Peter explains to the Jerusalem leadership what happened, there's nothing they can say except to praise God that even the Gentiles are gaining eternal life (Acts 11:1–18).

Christians spread everywhere to flee the persecutions in Jerusalem, and when they get to Antioch, more Gentiles come into the Church. For the first time, they're called Christians (Acts 11:19–26).

But the persecutions in Jerusalem just get worse (Acts 12:1–19). Finally, one of the apostles falls. Herod the Great's grandson, Herod Agrippa (ruled AD 41–44), executes James, son of Zebedee, usually the number two disciple after Peter in the gospels (Mt 17:1). Agrippa imprisons Peter. The Lord sends an angel to deliver Peter from prison, and Peter returns to the Upper Room, the place where the Lord had celebrated the Last Supper and that had served as the headquarters of the Church for several years. There, he lets everyone know of his miraculous escape and puts the other James in charge. This is James the son of Alphaeus, sometimes called "James the Less," who was a cousin of Jesus and wrote the epistle of James (according to tradition). This James would be leader of the Church in Jerusalem for the rest of his life. Why was Peter not this leader? Peter is now an outlaw. It's dangerous for him to appear in public. Peter exercises his ministry "underground" almost for the rest of his life. That's why we have so little record of Peter's comings and goings from here on. He's been mentioned fifty-four times from Acts 1 through 12 but will be mentioned only once again from here on out (at the "First Ecumenical Council of Jerusalem" in Acts 15:7).

It's not that Peter is no longer important. Rather, Peter may have still been alive when Luke finished Acts (Paul was still alive; see Acts 28:30–31), and it was dangerous to recount what he had done and where he had gone since escaping from arrest around AD 44. It could implicate people as traitors to the Roman government.

Instead, St. Luke switches here from the Peter Channel to the Paul Channel. St. Paul is first called "Paul" (previously his name was Saul) in Acts 13:9, and thereafter he's mentioned a total of 127 times from Acts 13 to 28. It's rather dramatic: St. Peter is mentioned 54 times in Acts 1–12 and "Paul" not once (he's called "Saul"). On the other hand, St. Paul is mentioned 127 times in Acts 13–28 and "Peter" only once (15:7). The focus clearly shifts from one apostle to the other at this point in the book.

Starting in Acts 13, St. Luke tells the stories of St. Paul's four missionary journeys:

1. Asia Minor (Turkey) in Acts 13–14;
2. Asia Minor and Greece in Acts 16–18;
3. Asia Minor and Greece and then Jerusalem in Acts 19–21; and
4. Jerusalem to Rome (27–28).

In between these journeys, St. Luke tells about the First Ecumenical Council of Jerusalem (Acts 15) and Paul's imprisonment and trials in Judea (Acts 22–26).

We can mark off the rest of Acts like this, rounding to the nearest chapters:

1. Paul's first missionary journey, to Asia Minor (Acts 13–14)

The First Church Council in Jerusalem (Acts 15)

2. Paul's second missionary journey, to Asia Minor and Greece (Acts 16–18)

3. Paul's third missionary journey, to Asia Minor, Greece, and Jerusalem (Acts 19–21)

Paul's Imprisonment and Trials in Judea (Acts 22–26)

4. Paul's fourth missionary journey, to Rome (Acts 27–28)

The theme throughout these chapters is Paul bringing the kingdom of God to all the ends of the earth.

St. Paul did a great deal of his ministry in a territory called "Asia Minor," roughly the area of modern-day Turkey. However, in Paul's day, Asia Minor was not settled by Turks. It was colonized by Greeks and was a major center of Greek-speaking culture.

St. Luke is at pains to point out that St. Peter and St. Paul are just alike and preach the same Gospel. There have always been attempts to split these apostles apart by claiming that St. Peter preached a "Jewish" Gospel and Paul a "Gentile" Gospel. In fact, scholars often accuse St. Paul of being the "true inventor of Christianity." This is not true. It was not Paul but Peter who first brought the Gospel of the kingdom to the Gentiles. Peter and Paul had their occasional differences, but Luke, who worked with them both, shows that they were really on the same page.

In fact, when we examine St. Paul's first recorded sermon, while he's traveling through Asia Minor (Acts 13:16–41), it sounds a lot like St. Peter's first sermons at Pentecost (Acts 2) and the healing of the lame man (Acts 3). As did Peter in Acts 4, Paul preaches that Jesus is the fulfillment of the promises made to their father Abraham (Acts 13:17, 26, 32). Imitating Peter in Acts 2, Paul preaches that Jesus fulfills the covenant given to David, that one of David's sons would rule over his kingdom (Acts 13:22–23, 32–33). Paul even repeats Peter's argument that David's prophecy about the "Holy One" who will not "see corruption" (Ps 16:10) has to be Jesus. This is the point: Peter and Paul preach the same Gospel. How appropriate it is that the Church celebrates their feast days together on June 29!

St. Luke shows that the Catholic Church was built up on the foundation of these two great apostles. He demonstrates that they both preached the same Gospel and shared the same Holy Spirit by showing a series of remarkable similarities between them. Examine the following table:

Both Peter and Paul . . .	Peter . . .	Paul . . .
. . . preach Jesus as the heir of the Davidic and Abrahamic covenants.	. . . in Acts 2 (Pentecost) and Acts 3 (Temple healing).	. . . in Acts 13 (Antioch of Pisidia).
. . . heal a lame man unable to walk.	. . . in the Temple courts (3:1–10).	. . . in Lystra in Asia (14:8–11).
. . . can heal people without even touching them.	. . . through his shadow (5:15).	. . . through handkerchiefs or other cloths (19:12).
. . . defeat a magician.	. . . converts Simon Magus (8:9–21).	. . . overcomes Elymas (13:8–12).
. . . confirm people with the Holy Spirit after Baptism.	. . . confirms Samaritans (8:17).	. . . confirms Ephesians (19:6).
. . . raise people from the dead.	. . . raises Tabitha (9:36–42).	. . . raises Eutychus (20:7–12).
. . . miraculously escape from prison.	. . . escapes in Jerusalem (12:6–9).	. . . escapes in Philippi of Macedonia (16:19–34).

The things that Peter does in Jerusalem, Judea, and Samaria Paul does in Gentile territories. So we see the whole world becoming the "Holy Land" where God can work. God's kingdom is spreading to the ends of the earth. This is St. Luke's point:

Together, Peter and Paul build up the kingdom of God.

Let's look closely at an example where Paul goes through a similar experience to Peter. Paul's first missionary journey, to Asia Minor (modern Turkey), makes a lot of Jewish communities mad (Acts 13–14). Many of the synagogues reject Paul's preaching, so he preaches to Gentiles instead. When he starts making large numbers of Gentile converts, the Jewish communities get jealous. Angry rabble-rousers basically follow Paul around Asia Minor, stirring up trouble for him wherever he stops.

However, just as Peter's preaching to Cornelius caused concern for some of the leaders in Jerusalem, so also Paul's journeys stir up a debate. Paul and Barnabas go up to Jerusalem and have to face those who insist everyone needs to become a Jew through circumcision before they can be full Christians (15:1–5). In the words of Yogi Berra: "It's like déjà vu all over again." Didn't we just have this discussion with Peter at the end of Acts 12?

But just like today, even though the Church has made official decisions, there are always dissenters around who try to reopen a closed issue. The apostles find it necessary to gather a council: "The apostles and elders were gathered together to consider this matter" (Acts 15:6). The Greek word for "elder" is *presbuteros*, and in English it got shortened to the word "priest." The modern-day equivalent of "apostles and elders" would be a gathering of "bishops and priests." What we have here is the first Church council. We can call it the "First Ecumenical Council of Jerusalem." The issue is not priestly celibacy, divorce and remarriage, the divinity of Christ, "salvation by faith alone," or any of the other hot-button issues of later centuries. The pressing issue here is: Can Gentiles become Christians without becoming Jews first?

After there was much discussion, St. Peter gets up and ends the debate: *You all know that God chose me to be the first to preach the Gospel to the Gentiles. They got the Spirit even without being circumcised. Why do you want to make them follow the Law of Moses, when even we Jews haven't been able to pull that off? We need to be saved by Jesus, just like they do* (my paraphrase, Acts 15:7–11).

After Peter speaks, there is no debate. But Paul gets up to support him, telling about all the works of the Spirit he had seen among the Gentiles. Finally, James the Less, the leader of the pro-circumcision party, gets up and gives a concession speech: *You all heard what Simon Peter said, how God has welcomed the Gentiles.* This is prophesied by Amos:

> After this I will return,
> and I will rebuild the dwelling of David. . . .
> I will rebuild its ruins,
> and I will set it up,
> that the rest of men may seek the Lord,
> and all the Gentiles who are called by my name."
> (Acts 15:16–17; see Am 9:11–12)

This is a very important prophecy for James to cite. The "dwelling of David" is a poetic way of talking about the *kingdom of David*. So follow this logic: when Peter speaks about the Gentiles coming into the Church, James says it fulfills the prophecies that God would rebuild David's kingdom, which included Gentiles. That makes so much sense, since we've been watching the "kingdom of God" expand through the concentric circles of the Davidic empire from the beginning of the book. So we see that the Apostles understood the Church as the fulfillment of God's covenant promises to David through Jesus.

Although this first Church council decides the Gentiles do not have to keep the whole Mosaic Law, for practical purposes, they rule that Gentile Christians should abstain from the more obvious behaviors that offend Jewish sensibilities: sacrificing food to idols, drinking animal blood, strangling animals, and sexual immorality. They send a letter, an "encyclical" if you will, to all the churches with this decision.

After relating the Council of Jerusalem, St. Luke recounts two more missionary journeys of Paul, his imprisonment, trials in Judea, and his final journey to Rome. He baptizes whole households, which would have included children, on various occasions (Acts 16:11–34). On two occasions, we see him celebrating the Eucharist, called the "breaking of bread," with the early Christian communities (Acts 20:7, 11; 27:35).

Throughout, we see that Paul's sufferings, especially his imprisonments and trials, actually provide him with the opportunity to evangelize government officials, the military, and royalty. It's such a paradox. If he hadn't been attacked and persecuted, he wouldn't have had the chance to preach to world leaders. As it is, the Book of Acts ends with Paul waiting to preach about the kingdom of God to Caesar himself, the civil ruler of the known world and thus to all the Gentiles who inhabit "the ends of the earth"!

So, Acts is about the growth of the kingdom, and we see that even within the lifetime of the first generation of Christians there was an amazing effort to get the Good News out to the whole world. But St. Luke has told the story in such a way that we Christian and Catholic readers may understand that we are still part of this story. The Good News is still going out, and the kingdom still growing, in our own day. We are still baptizing for forgiveness of sins and the gift of the Holy Spirit (Acts 2:38), still devoting ourselves to "the apostles' teaching and fellowship, to the breaking of bread and the prayers" (2:42) at every Mass. The successors of the apostles still come to lay on hands to appoint other men to share their leadership (Holy Orders, 6:6) and to complete the gift of the Holy Spirit to believers (Confirmation, 8:17). And we still suffer persecutions—in many places, every bit as severe as what the apostles themselves suffered. But those persecutions still create opportunities to preach the good news of the kingdom.

Let me close with a little story from more modern times. Vietnam is a country at the extreme southeast end of the continent of Asia. French Jesuits established the first churches there in the 1600s. In 1975, Francis Xavier Nguyen Van Thuan was appointed Coadjutor Archbishop of Saigon, seven days before the capital of South Vietnam was captured by the atheist communist forces of the north. The fall of South Vietnam seemed like an unmitigated disaster for the large numbers of Vietnamese Catholics, who had depended first on the French and then on the Americans to defend their religious freedom from Chinese-backed revolutionaries. As part of the communist suppression of the Church, Bishop Thuan was immediately arrested and sent to a "re-education camp" where he was kept in solitary confinement.

But Bishop Thuan did not despair. His only contacts with human beings were his prison guards. He befriended them. Finding out that they were uneducated, he began to teach them things, including foreign languages and the teachings of the Church. His communist guards would go off duty humming snatches of Latin chants. Some converted secretly. The prison officials became concerned. This prisoner was a dangerous influence on their guards! The officials began to rotate his guards frequently so that none would be exposed to the bishop for too long. But they still could not prevent him from winning the sympathy of the soldiers, some of whom smuggled him supplies to celebrate Mass and scribble messages to his flock.

After many years, Bishop Thuan was released and taken to Rome, where St. John Paul II made him a cardinal. He died in 2002, and his cause for sainthood is progressing. The Catholic Church in Vietnam is strong in faith and continues to grow.

In Cardinal Thuan, we see a true successor of the apostles, whose life was like St. Paul's: hostile imprisonments created chances to evangelize and spread the kingdom.

We are still living in the Book of Acts. We are still the witnesses (Greek, *martyrs*) "to the ends of the earth."

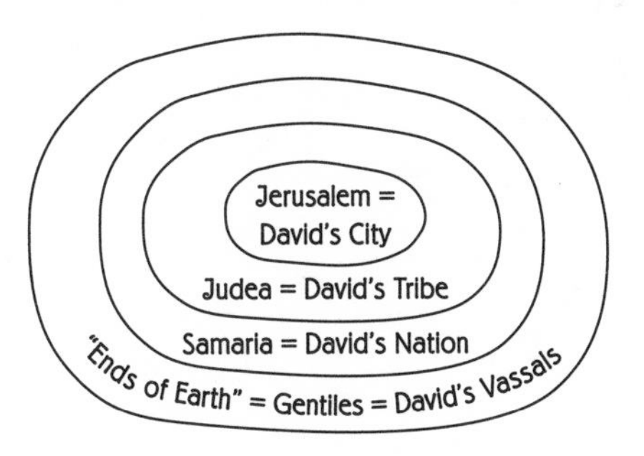

Part III
Living in the Kingdom!

Paul

Five

St. Paul and the Letter to the Romans

Now we move to St. Paul, who after Jesus Christ himself, was one of the most influential men in world history. St. Paul may have been the greatest missionary among the apostles, even though he was not one of the Twelve. Jesus appointed him separately, as a kind of "thirteenth" apostle sent especially to the Gentiles, whereas the Twelve were sent to regather the "tribes of Israel." St. Paul's letters make up a big portion of the New Testament—traditionally, the books from Romans to Hebrews—and scholars often think of St. Paul as the great theologian of the early Church. Big debates go on even today about how to interpret his writings. Pauline studies are almost a "sport" among Bible scholars. Many scholars have become famous (and sometimes wealthy) by writing books on St. Paul.

We've just read the Book of Acts, and so we know the basic biography of St. Paul. We know he was born in Tarsus, an important city on the southern coast of Asia Minor. At some point in his youth, he moved to Jerusalem to study the Law of Moses and Jewish Law from the great Pharisee Rabbi Gamaliel. Paul was basically trained as a Jewish religious lawyer, and that training can be seen everywhere in his writings. As Acts 7–9 recount, St. Paul hated the Christian movement at first and was its chief persecutor until he himself saw the risen Jesus Christ during a supernatural encounter while traveling to Damascus. To this day, we call a sudden, radical change in a person's beliefs a "Damascus Road experience." After his conversion, St. Paul began to preach the good news of Jesus vigorously and was sent out on several journeys through Asia Minor and Greece to plant churches. Acts ended with him under house arrest in Rome in the early AD 60s. Our information about him after that is unclear, but it seems that he was acquitted when his case first came before the Roman emperor and was released for a while to do further mission work before being rearrested and executed by the Emperor Nero around AD 66–68. St. Paul was a Roman citizen, so unlike other apostles and early martyrs, he was not crucified (illegal for Roman citizens) but beheaded. His body was buried in land owned by an early Christian outside the walls of the city of Rome, at the site that is now the Basilica of St. Paul Outside the Walls.

It's hard to overestimate the influence of St. Paul, especially the influence of his writings. Many of the great saints and Doctors of the Church were deeply influenced by meditating on St. Paul, including St. Augustine and St. Thomas Aquinas. Martin Luther believed he had found his doctrine of "salvation by faith alone" in the writings of St. Paul, setting off the Reformation and the breakup of Christian unity in Western civilization. The effects of Luther's interpretation of St. Paul are still very much with us. Many think of St. Paul as an early Protestant, whose teaching contradicts the Catholic Church. In many Protestant churches, the preaching is mostly from St. Paul rather than from the gospels. Even some Catholics are nervous that St. Paul's writings undermine the faith and shy away from studying him. They don't need to be nervous. St. Paul was and is thoroughly Catholic, and his writings are compatible with the Catholic faith because they shaped the Catholic faith.

Fourteen letters have been passed down in the Church as St. Paul's:

The Letter of St. Paul to the Romans

The First Letter of St. Paul to the Corinthians

The Second Letter of St. Paul to the Corinthians

The Letter of St. Paul to the Galatians

The Letter of St. Paul to the Ephesians

The Letter of St. Paul to the Philippians

The Letter of St. Paul to the Colossians

The First Letter of St. Paul to the Thessalonians

The Second Letter of St. Paul to the Thessalonians

The First Letter of St. Paul to Timothy

The Second Letter of St. Paul to Timothy

The Letter of St. Paul to Titus

The Letter of St. Paul to Philemon

The Letter to the Hebrews

These letters are arranged not by chronology but roughly by length, starting with St. Paul's longest letter (Romans) and proceeding to his shortest (Philemon). The letters to churches (Romans through 2 Thessalonians) precede letters to individuals (1 Timothy through Philemon). The Letter to the Hebrews is placed last since the author of the letter is unidentified, and the Church has never been completely sure it was from St. Paul. The theology of Hebrews has much in common with St. Paul, but the literary style is different. Perhaps it was written (or co-written) by a friend or disciple.[1]

This is how you can remember the letters of Paul. First, think "**R**oman **C**atholic **C**hurch." This will give you **R**omans, 1 **C**orinthians, and 2 **C**orinthians. Then, think "**G**eneral **E**lectric **P**ower **C**ompany." That gives you **G**alatians, **E**phesians, **P**hilippians, and **C**olossians. Third, think "Five teas need a lemon." All the *T*s are in a row, in alphabetical order: 1 **T**imothy, 2 **T**imothy, **T**itus, 1 **T**hessalonians, 2 **T**hessalonians, and Phi**L**emon. And if you don't like tea with lemon, what does Paul do? Why, *Hebrews* you some coffee.

Let's give a quick overview of these fourteen epistles of Paul:

The Letter to the Romans (AD 58) is probably Paul's greatest epistle.[2] He lays out his theology in greatest depth, emphasizing that the good news of Jesus Christ is the way of salvation for all human beings, whether they are Jews, Greeks, or barbarians (probably you and I would fall under "barbarians").

First Corinthians (AD 56) is a letter to the Church in Corinth to address problems in the local church and answer questions they had sent him concerning church unity, lawsuits, sexual morality, marriage, celibacy, idol worship, proper behavior at the Eucharist, spiritual gifts, and the resurrection of the body. Second Corinthians (AD 57) is a follow-up letter reinforcing his teachings on sexual morality and church discipline and defending Paul's authority as an apostle.

Galatians (AD 55) is Paul's angriest letter as he rebukes the Church in Galatia for telling people that they had to become circumcised and obey the laws of the Mosaic Covenant in order to be saved. Salvation is not by "works of the [Mosaic] law," St. Paul says, but by "faith in Jesus Christ" (Gal 2:16).

Ephesians (AD 59) was probably sent not only to Ephesus but to nearby churches as well. In it, Paul lays out Christian teaching on the Church and the Church's "mysterious" role in salvation. The Church is God's new temple, where Israelites and Gentiles live together. It's also the Body of Christ. The relationship of Christ and his Church is the model for Christian marriage and family life.

Philippians (AD 61/62) was written to thank the Christians of Philippi for their financial support of Paul during one of his imprisonments. It is Paul's most joyful letter, in which he gives a lot of practical advice on living the Christian life and staying joyful even when suffering.

Colossians (AD 59) seems like a shorter version of Ephesians. Paul writes to the Church in Colossae, summarizing what he said to the Ephesians and warning them about false teachers who would make them follow the Mosaic Law.

First and Second Thessalonians are some of Paul's earliest letters (AD 52–53). The Thessalonian Christians were very concerned about the end times, so Paul instructs them on the second coming of Christ, the resurrection of the dead, the final judgment, and the "Antichrist."[2] In the meantime, Christians should continue to work hard and lead holy lives.

Paul's last four letters are addressed to individuals. First and Second Timothy (AD 56, AD 60) and Titus (AD 58) are letters to highly trusted assistants of St. Paul who ruled the churches St. Paul couldn't get to, and each continued his ministry after his death. So in Paul's letters to them, we clearly see the principle of *apostolic succession*: the apostles invested other men with their apostolic authority to continue leading the Church on their behalf when they were gone (see 2 Tm 2:2). Timothy and Titus functioned as young bishops responsible for overseeing (Greek, *episcopein*) the congregations of Christians in a region. Paul first of all encourages them to keep their own faith strong and then instructs them on how to run the churches: how to identify and appoint leaders, how to handle different groups within the church, and so forth.

Philemon (AD 59), Paul's shortest letter, is a brief appeal to his friend Philemon, asking him to release his runaway slave Onesimus, whom Paul met in prison, so that Onesimus can become Paul's assistant in his ministry.

The anonymous Letter to the Hebrews comes at the end of Paul's epistles. Since the author does not clearly identify himself, the early Church was uncertain who wrote it. The ideas in the letter are often like those of St. Paul, but the Greek style is much more elegant than any of Paul's other letters. Perhaps Paul wrote it with the help of a Greek stylist such as St. Luke or else someone influenced by St. Paul wrote it. In any event, the Letter to the Hebrews is written to an all-Jewish Christian community where many are feeling the tug to go back to the old Mosaic Covenant. The author urges them to stay strong in the faith and recognize Jesus as superior to the angels, to Moses, and to the high priest in the Temple. Jesus has a better priesthood, covenant, sacrifice, and sanctuary than anything the Mosaic Covenant can offer.

That's our whirlwind tour of the letters of Paul. Now we are going to focus in-depth on just one of his letters, the one that I think best summarizes St. Paul's thoughts: Romans.

St. Paul's Letter to the Romans

To say the Letter to the Romans has had a big influence on Christian history is a lame understatement. To this day, some of the biggest divisions among Christians come down to the interpretation of what Paul says in this letter.

Let me give you a practical example. When I was training to be a Protestant pastor, I learned to preach the Gospel by reciting and explaining roughly six verses from Romans. This is a well-known method among American Protestants called the "Roman Road." Well, one day I was walking in a downtown neighborhood, getting trained in evangelism by an urban pastor. We knocked on the door of a woman who had visited his church a week or so before. She was home and invited us to her upstairs apartment, where my pastor friend began to talk to her about Jesus. He followed the "Roman Road" and asked her if she wanted to pray to "invite Jesus into her life." She said yes, and we prayed. And that was a good thing—as Catholics we would say she had made a "spiritual communion" with Jesus. But then something happened that was not so pleasant. My mentor began some basic faith instruction. He asked her, "Okay, so now you have prayed to receive Jesus. But if you went out and robbed a bank tomorrow, would you still be saved?"

"Umm . . . what do you mean?" she asked.

"Well, if you went out and did some really bad sins. What if a week from now, you got mad and shot someone. Would you still be saved?"

"Uh . . ." the woman hesitated, not knowing where this was going. "No?" she asked.

"*Yes*!" my friend replied, "you *would*!" And then he continued along these lines: "You've received Christ, and nothing you do can separate you from the love of God. Salvation is by faith alone. Your works don't matter. Once saved, always saved."

I sat there listening to this in a bit of shock. It's not that I would have disagreed with "salvation by faith alone," but I'd never heard it taught so crassly. I also had serious doubts that it was wise to start new Christians off by telling them they could go shoot people and still go to heaven. Even if that were true, it might not be the best way to open.

The woman never did become a member of our local church.

Over the next four or five years, I became an urban pastor myself and continued to do door-to-door evangelism. Occasionally, people would convert and join my church. But even within the few years I pastored, I lived to see people I had evangelized turn from a Christian life back to lives of open sin. And when I confronted them about it, sometimes they would tell me, "I'm saved by faith alone. I know what I'm doing is wrong, but I'll still go to heaven." That was also a shock to me. I hadn't run into people who took the idea of "salvation by faith alone" to that extreme before. But I've come to believe it happens frequently in American Christianity. There are also many in America who have become atheists or at least rejected Christianity because they see "salvation by faith alone" as a crude form of hypocrisy: "Christians think that they can do whatever they want and still go to heaven because they 'believe in Jesus,' while the rest of us can do as much good as we want but are going to hell because we believe the wrong thing." To such people, Christians look as if they are using belief in Jesus as a "get out of jail free card" to avoid having to answer for their actions.

All these issues flow out of a misinterpretation of the Letter to the Romans that can be traced back to Martin Luther. We'll sort it out in the pages to follow.

* * *

Many hold Romans to be St. Paul's greatest epistle. Certainly, it is his longest. It's played a huge role in world history. Romans played an important part in the conversion of St. Augustine to Christianity. After a long spiritual battle, St. Augustine was sitting outside one day with his friend Alypius, almost in despair over what to do with his life. He heard a child singing next door, "Take up and read! Take up and read!" So he picked up a copy of Romans that he had with him and read the first passage he found: "Let us conduct ourselves properly as in the day, not in reveling and drunkenness, not in debauchery and licentiousness, not in quarreling and jealousy. But put on the Lord Jesus Christ, and make no provision for the desires of the flesh" (Rom 13:13–14). He took this as God speaking to him, to leave off his partying lifestyle and give his life to Jesus. St. Augustine went on to become the most influential Church father in the Catholic tradition.

As I mentioned above, for better or for worse, Martin Luther would find his doctrine of "salvation by faith alone" while reading Romans and go on to spark the Reformation, changing Europe and world history forever. John Wesley, founder of the Methodist movement, was converted when his heart was "strangely warmed" while listening to a commentary on Romans.

Romans has probably led to countless other conversions of people less famous. Mountains of commentaries have been written on it, people have come to blows over how to interpret it, and it's changed the course of history forever on more than one occasion. What is this book? Why did Paul write it? What does it mean?

Well, Romans is, of course, a letter that Paul wrote to the Christian community in Rome while he was in Corinth. The letter-like features are especially clear in chapter 1 and chapters 15–16. Much of the rest of Romans seems more like a sermon or a theological lecture.

Why was Paul writing? He wrote this letter for several reasons. Most pressing was a practical issue. Paul planned to travel to Spain to do mission work. He was going to have to stop in Rome on the way, and he wanted to introduce himself to the Christians there so that they would be ready to help him get the rest of the way to Spain.

But there were other reasons, too. Paul genuinely felt God had given him insight into the meaning of the Gospel, the Good News. Paul had come to understand how the Good News had already been predicted in the Old Testament. The prophets of Israel had spoken of a time to come when some of the laws of Moses would pass away and both Israelites and Gentiles would be saved by God. That time had come, St. Paul was convinced. He wanted to share with the Church in Rome the insights he had on how the Old Covenant related to the New and how Jews and Gentiles could now live together as one people of God, the Church.

A Mental Map of Romans

Before we jump into reading Romans closely, let's "zoom out" as in Google Maps and get a bird's-eye view of the route we're going to travel through the book. The beginning (1:1–15) and the ending (15:14–16:27) of the book are taken up with the greetings and other polite things you say in letters as well as other practical matters.

St. Paul begins the body of his letter by stating a thesis: "I am not ashamed of the gospel: it is the power of God for salvation to every one who has faith, to the Jew first and also to the Greek. For in it the righteousness of God is revealed through faith for faith; as it is written, 'He who through faith is righteous shall live'" (Rom 1:16–17). This is what St. Paul seeks to prove: the Gospel, the Good News about Jesus, is the way of salvation for everyone in the world. There are not two ways to salvation: Moses for the Jews and Jesus for the Gentiles. No, Jesus is for everyone. And another thing is that the Good News is a way to be right with God (the "righteousness of God") that starts with trust and continues by trusting God every step of the way ("through faith for faith").

After stating that the Good News is the way to be saved for everyone, St. Paul has to show that everyone *needs* to be saved. So his next step is to present the "bad news" that all human beings have sinned, turned away from God, and need to repent. Both Gentiles (1:18–32) and Jews (2:1–3:20) need salvation, even though the Jews already have the laws of Moses.

After showing that everyone needs to be saved, St. Paul will restate his thesis: the only way to become right with God is through faith in Jesus Christ, not by keeping the laws of Moses (3:21–30).

St. Paul then answers three objections to his thesis that he expects Jewish Christians will probably raise:

Objection number one: St. Paul, your thesis basically overthrows the whole Old Testament (Rom 3:31). On the contrary, St. Paul says, the Old Testament itself shows that salvation is a matter of faith, not simply keeping the laws of Moses (4:1–5:21).

Objection number two: St. Paul, your thesis implies we can keep on sinning since we don't have to obey the laws (6:1). On the contrary, St. Paul says, in Jesus we died to sin and have begun to live a new life (6:1–7:6).

Objection number three: St. Paul, your thesis implies that God's law in the Old Testament was an evil thing (7:7). On the contrary, St. Paul says, God's law in the Old Testament was fine; it just wasn't enough to save us (7:7–25).

After answering these three objections, St. Paul is ready to summarize his whole message in Romans 8, the most important chapter in the whole epistle. There Paul explains that the Mosaic Law told us what was right and wrong but did not give us the power to do it. Now, Jesus has taken the punishment for our sins by his death on the Cross and given us the Holy Spirit so that we have the power to keep God's law. Provided we live by the Spirit and not by our old nature, we will be saved.

What about ethnic Israelites now that the New Covenant has come? What is to become of them? This is Paul's topic for the next three chapters, Romans 9–11, where he argues that God has not forgotten the ethnic people of Israel, and in the end, "all Israel will be saved" (11:25–26).

If all this is true, how should we live? Paul takes up this question at the beginning of Romans 12. For the next few chapters, he discourses on humility, love, patience, meekness, kindness, and the other virtues that should describe the Christian life.

Finally, Paul concludes the letter, beginning in Romans 15:14, with a laundry list of final instructions, greetings, and blessings.

We can outline the Letter to the Romans as follows:

I. Opening greeting (1:1–7)

II. Doctrinal section (chapters 1–11)

A. Thesis: The Gospel is the way of salvation by faith for everyone, Jew and Gentile (1:16–17).

B. Support: Both Gentiles and Jews have sinned and need salvation (1:18–3:20).

C. Restating the thesis: The Gospel is the way of salvation for everyone, apart from the Mosaic Law (3:21–31).

D. Objections and responses (chapters 4–7):

1. *Paul, you are throwing out the Old Testament.* No, the Law actually contains the Gospel (chapters 4–5).
2. *Your Gospel implies we can keep on sinning.* No, we died to sin and can't live in it any longer (chapters 6–7).

3. *Your Gospel implies that the law is bad.* No, but our sinful nature makes bad use of the law (chapter 7).

E. Summary: We live now according to the Holy Spirit, not the flesh (chapter 8).

F. Digression: *What about ethnic Israel now that the New Covenant has arrived?* God still has a role for his people (chapters 9–11).

III. Practical section (chapters 12–15)

A. Practice love, humility, meekness, self-sacrifice, and the other virtues of holiness.

IV. Closing instructions, greetings, and blessings (15:14 to end)

Now let's dive into Romans more closely.

Paul's Opening Greeting *(Romans 1:1–7)*

> Paul, a servant of Jesus Christ, called to be an apostle, set apart for the gospel of God which he promised beforehand through his prophets in the holy scriptures, the gospel concerning his Son, who was descended from David according to the flesh and designated Son of God in power according to the Spirit of holiness by his resurrection from the dead, Jesus Christ our Lord, through whom we have received grace and apostleship to bring about the obedience of faith for the sake of his name among all the nations, including yourselves who are called to belong to Jesus Christ;
>
> To all God's beloved in Rome, who are called to be saints:
>
> Grace to you and peace from God our Father and the Lord Jesus Christ. (Rom 1:1–7)

Paul begins his letter to the Romans first by greeting them and then by thanking God for them. That's standard practice in most of Paul's letters.

Paul's greeting in Romans is elaborate and flowery. When he introduces himself, he gives a full background on what it means to be an apostle of Jesus. He basically summarizes the Gospel message just in his own self-introduction. In the process, he makes several important points. First, the "gospel . . . [was] promised beforehand . . . in the holy scriptures." The "holy scriptures" for St. Paul are what we would call the Old Testament because the New Testament books have not been written yet. It is very important to St. Paul that the Good News of Jesus was *predicted* and *foreshadowed* already by the Old Testament prophets.

Second, this "gospel" is about God's "son, who was descended from David." Although St. Paul does not make a big deal about kingdom language in Romans, in the background of his thought is always the restored kingdom of David, which includes both Israel and the Gentiles.

Third, this Jesus, the "son . . . descended from David," has appointed Paul as his royal messenger, his "apostle," to bring about the "obedience of faith . . . among all the nations." That is, St. Paul is sent to the Gentiles to make them obedient to the Davidic King, Jesus. Now, there is a dispute between Catholics and some Protestants over what "obedience of faith" means. This dispute is at the heart of the story I told at the beginning of the chapter. You see, my evangelism trainer, along with many Protestants, understood "obedience of faith" to mean "an obedience that consists only in believing." That is, the only "obedience" that God expects is that you believe, that you "have faith." The Catholic Church, on the other hand, understands "obedience of faith" to mean a true change in behavior that comes from having faith in Jesus. I think it's going to become clear, though, as we work through Romans that "obedience of faith" really does mean a transformed life and changed behavior that comes from having faith in Jesus Christ.

After his long introduction of himself, St. Paul greets the Romans with "grace and peace to you from God our Father and the Lord Jesus Christ." "Grace" (Greek, *charis*) is the typical Greek greeting. "Peace" (Hebrew, *shalom*) is the typical Jewish greeting. Paul is combining the two, as he writes to the Church, a new community of God's people made up of Jews and Greeks together. And by "Greeks," we mean Greek-speaking Gentiles. Greek was the international language, spoken by every educated person in the Roman Empire. Oftentimes "Greek" means the same as "Gentile" in Paul's writings.

After the greeting, Paul thanks God for the Romans. "Your faith is proclaimed in all the world," Paul says (Rom 1:8). The Roman Church was famous for its faithfulness to the Gospel from the beginning. The Church in Rome would eventually become the mother church of Christianity, especially because both Peter and Paul were martyred there, leaving their bones and their successors in the city. Since Rome has such a great influence on the Church around the world, Paul has been eager to get there, to explain his insight on how Jews and Gentiles should get along in the New Covenant.

Thesis *(Romans 1:16–17)*

Preliminaries done, St. Paul now states the main point of his letter: "For I am not ashamed of the gospel: it is the power of God for salvation to every one who has faith, to the Jew first and also to the Greek. For in it the righteousness of God is revealed through faith for faith; as it is written, 'He who through faith is righteous shall live'" (1:16–17). "Gospel," as you know, is literally the "good news" (in Greek, *eu-angelion*, from *eu*, "good"; and *angelion*, "message"). The "good news" about Jesus is the way of salvation for everyone. There is not one way for Jews and a different way for Greeks (here meaning "Gentiles"). No, Jesus is the good news for everyone, and the way of salvation Jesus teaches is the way of faith, that is, trusting in God.

Catholics disagree with some Protestants about what this "righteousness of God . . . through faith for faith" actually is. Some Protestants think it means a "righteousness" that consists only in having "faith." That is, you believe in Jesus, and God counts it as righteousness. The Catholic Church understands it as a true righteousness, a true change in behavior, that comes by trusting in Jesus. Which view is correct? We will have to keep reading Romans to see.

This is St. Paul's "good news": God has revealed a way to be saved for everyone that comes through faith in Jesus. But in order to appreciate the "good news," people need to understand the "bad news," which is that everyone needs salvation. If people don't think they need to be saved from anything, then the "good news" is not very significant. "Who cares if I can be 'saved' by faith in Jesus?" someone might say. "I don't need to be saved at all!" So in the next section of Paul's letter, he sets out to explain the "bad news": human beings are under the judgment of God.

Support: The Bad News *(Romans 1:18–3:20)*

This is the bad news: "For the wrath of God is revealed from heaven against all ungodliness and wickedness of men who by their wickedness suppress the truth" (v. 18). All humanity is experiencing the "wrath" of God. What is the "wrath" of God? St. Paul will explain in what follows.

There is enough evidence in the world, St. Paul explains, for every human being to know that there is a God and to know the basics about him. "What can be known about God is plain to them," St. Paul says, because God's "invisible nature" can be "clearly perceived in the things that have been made" (1:19–20). Why then is there such unbelief in the world? Because people "suppress the truth" (v. 18).

With St. Paul, the Catholic Church teaches that people can *know* God by reason, even without faith. Sometimes I tell my students, "I don't believe in God anymore." They look at me puzzled while I let that statement sink in. Then I say, "I *know* God exists." When you work through the evidence and arguments that demonstrate that there *must* be a God, God's existence becomes a matter of *knowledge*, not just *faith*.

The evidence of God's existence is just as strong today as it was in St. Paul's day, or ever has been, because the way things are has not changed. Because we know more about the world today, we can prove God's existence now in ways that are more powerful and precise than in St. Paul's day or even a hundred years ago.

One of the most powerful proofs for God's existence is what philosophers and scientists call the "fine-tuning of the universe." "Fine-tuning" refers to the fact that all the primary forces of the universe seem to have been adjusted by some intelligence to exactly the values necessary to produce intelligent life.

Let me explain. The operation of the universe appears to be governed by forces we call the physical constants. Some examples of the physical constants are as follows:

- The speed of light
- The force of gravity
- The rate at which the universe is expanding
- The ratio of protons to electrons in the universe

And there are many, many others.

Now, you may remember from high school science class that there is a number associated with each of these constants.

For example, the speed of light is about 186,000 miles per second, and the force of gravity at the earth's surface causes objects to accelerate toward the earth at the rate of thirty-two feet per second.

Advances in modern science have proven that all the physical constants are set with great precision, such that if any one of them were off by the smallest percentage, the universe could not support life.

For example, if the ratio of the number of protons to electrons in the universe were off by even one part in a trillion trillion, the force of electromagnetism in the universe would overpower gravity, and no stars, planets, or life would ever form.

To give another example, Stephen Hawking points out that "if the rate of expansion of the universe one second after the Big Bang had been smaller by even one part in a hundred thousand million million, the universe would have already recollapsed before it reached its present size"; in other words, before human life appeared on earth.[4]

Imagine you had a universe-making machine with some forty or more dials on it that control the basic laws of nature. To make a universe in which life could exist, each dial would have to be set at exactly the right number, always to an accuracy of more than thirty decimal places.

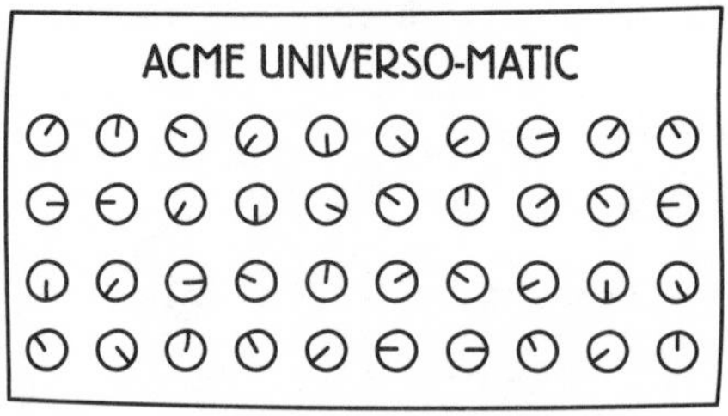

ACME UNIVERSO-MATIC

Every dial must be set exactly!

What is the chance that all this could happen by accident? About one chance in ten followed by 229 zeros. In other words, if you piled dimes in the state of Texas to the height of the moon and painted one red, a blindfolded man would have a better chance of finding your red dime in one attempt than the universe would have appearing randomly with all its forces properly set to allow life.

Even atheists admit this seems to point to God. Atheist astronomer Sir Fred Hoyle admits, "A commonsense interpretation of the facts suggests that a super-intellect has monkeyed with the laws of physics."[5]

Atheist Stephen Hawking agrees: "The remarkable fact is that the values of these numbers (i.e., the constants of physics) seem to have been very finely adjusted to make possible the development of life," and he concedes that one could accept this as evidence of "a divine purpose in Creation and the choice of the laws of science."[6]

The reality of cosmic "fine-tuning" has only been recognized within the last one hundred years due to advances in science. It's an irrefutable fact, recognized by atheist and theist alike, and it's one of the strongest evidences of a powerful, creative intelligence—a God—as the source of the universe.[7] However, when I ask the students in my classes how many have heard of cosmic fine-tuning, hardly any have. These are fairly well-educated Catholic young people from around America. Why haven't they heard these facts? Why are they also ignorant of:

- the amazing complexity of even the simplest life forms;
- the sudden, inexplicable explosions of new forms of life in the fossil record;[8]
- the incredible nature of the "Big Bang"; and
- other scientific evidence that points to a creator?

Because, as St. Paul says, "men . . . by their wickedness suppress the truth" (Rom 1:18). Our culture is based on atheism, and it would overturn our social-political system if people knew that there were strong scientific and philosophical reasons to believe in a creator God. I am a professional scholar with an earned doctorate and have worked in academic circles for the past twenty years. I can attest that there is strong social and political pressure in academic circles to withhold information from students that would point to the existence of God, especially in state schools but also in many Protestant and Catholic institutions. The scholar who presents this information risks making his or her colleagues mad and ultimately endangering their own employment.

So what St. Paul says in Romans 1:18 is still very true. Perhaps never in human history have we been able to construct such precise and compelling arguments for God's existence as we can now. But now more than ever the information does not get out because it is too politically incorrect.

St. Paul says humanity knows about God because there is enough evidence in the creation to recognize his existence. But humanity does not worship God, "for although they knew God they did not honor him as God or give thanks to him, but they became futile in their thinking and their senseless minds were darkened. Claiming to be wise, they became fools, and exchanged the glory of the immortal God for images resembling mortal man or birds or animals or reptiles" (1:21–23). St. Paul here describes ancient religion, which was focused on the worship of idols that were supposed to represent various gods. These gods were personifications of things people wanted: they worshiped Venus the goddess of sexuality, Dionysius the god of wine, Mars the god of violence, and Pluto the god of wealth. They worshiped these "gods" to get the things the gods represented.

Modern society is not that different. The idols are gone, but through their music, their parties, their work, and their lifestyle, people still worship sexuality, drugs, violence, and wealth.

How does God respond to people's rejection of him? Well, he gives them what they want. After describing humanity's rejection of God, St. Paul goes on to describe three stages of "punishment" that God places on human society. At each stage, God "gives them up" to their desires.

At the first stage, God "gives them up in the lusts of their hearts to impurity" (1:24). This means unrestricted sexuality outside of marriage. People who reject God start pursuing sex for pleasure rather than love. Why is this? We were made for a loving relationship with God. When we reject God, there is a God-shaped vacuum in our lives that is painful and wants to be filled. People try pushing sex into the vacuum because sex provides an illusion of a loving relationship—if not with God, at least with another person. But of course, without lifelong commitment—that is, without marriage—sex isn't really about love; it just gives the illusion of love. As Tina Turner famously said about sex, "What's love got to do with it?"

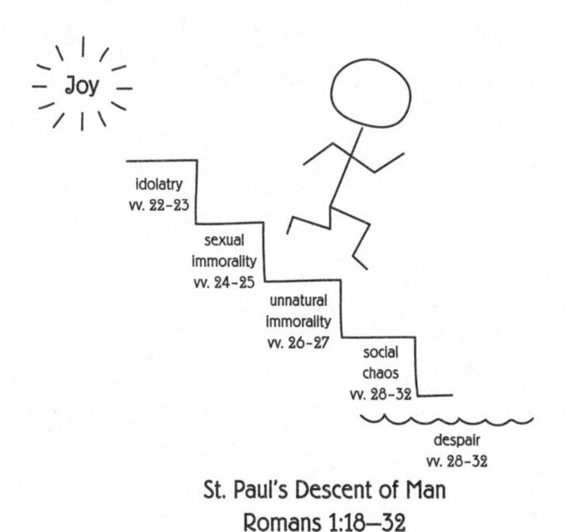

St. Paul's Descent of Man
Romans 1:18–32

So when people get tired of pushing sex into the God-shaped void of their lives, we reach the next stage of God's "punishment" of those who reject him: "For this reason God gave them up to dishonorable passions. Their women exchanged natural relations for unnatural, and the men likewise" (1:26–27). At this second stage, people become frustrated with normal sex, which does not provide them the satisfaction for which they hunger. They begin to experiment with other forms of sexuality that do not follow God's design of our bodies, hoping that these more exotic experiences will provide satisfaction for their souls. But since what we truly desire is God himself, this does not satisfy either but is ultimately harmful for both body and soul.

Then we reach the final stage of God's punishment, when God gives "them up to a base mind and to improper conduct" (1:28). I call this stage "social chaos." St. Paul paints it as no pretty picture: "They were filled with all manner of wickedness, evil, covetousness, malice. Full of envy, murder, strife, deceit, malignity, they are gossips, slanderers, haters of God, insolent, haughty, boastful, inventors of evil, disobedient to parents, foolish, faithless, heartless, ruthless" (1:29–31). Basically, society has broken down, and love is no more. Why is this? In a large part, society disintegrates because all of the sex outside of marriage in the first two stages breaks up the family unit and produces many children outside of wedlock. In ancient times, many of these children were killed as infants, and nowadays we kill them before birth in large numbers, about 1.5 million a year in America alone. But many others survive and grow up without a married father and mother who love them and are committed to them for life. Growing up with a lack of love and a lack of guidance, many never learn right from wrong and act out of their pain by inflicting pain on others.

What St. Paul has described is a cycle that begins with rejection of God and ends with chaos among human beings. Paul described it as God's "wrath" being revealed against men, but we have seen that God's "wrath" means giving people what they want. When we desire what is *not* God, the punishment is built in. This cycle from rejection of God to chaos is repeated throughout history in persons, families, cultures, and nations. It's a sad cycle, but it's not inevitable. There is an alternative: to turn to God, whose love is shown through Jesus Christ.

Now, while Paul is describing how things go from bad to worse among the Gentiles, there are Jewish believers listening in who think what he is saying doesn't apply to them. They are probably nodding in agreement, thinking to themselves, *You tell 'em, Paul! Preach, brother! Those Gentiles sure are wicked, and they deserve what they get!* But in Romans 2, St. Paul turns on these self-righteous folks and calls them out for hypocrisy: "Therefore you have no excuse, O man, whoever you are, when you judge another; for in passing judgment upon him you condemn yourself, because you, the judge, are doing the very same things" (2:1).

There are some among St. Paul's Jewish audience who are very judgmental about the Gentiles for breaking God's laws but who, at the same time, are disobeying God's law themselves. St. Paul warns them: "Do you suppose, O man, that when you judge those who do such things and yet do them yourself, you will escape the judgment of God?" (2:3). For God "will render to every man *according to his works*" (2:6, emphasis added). That is a strange thing for St. Paul to say in a letter that many Protestants believe teaches "salvation by faith alone," not by works. But as we will see, St. Paul and Romans have been badly misunderstood. St. Paul clearly teaches that what we actually *do* plays an important role in our eternal destiny: "There will be tribulation and distress for every human being who does evil . . . but glory and honor and peace for every one who does good" (2:9–10). When we are judged at the last day, God will take into account how much knowledge of him we had. "All who have sinned without the law will also perish without the law, and all who have sinned under the law will be judged by the law" (2:12). Here, "the law" refers to the scriptures. God will be more lenient on those who did not have the scriptures and more demanding on those who did. There are Gentiles, for example, who "do by nature what the law requires" and show that "what the law requires is written on their hearts" (2:14–15). These are people who do not know the scriptures but follow the natural sense of right and wrong that is quietly written into human nature. These persons may be "excused" by God at the final judgment.

But the simple fact that Jewish persons have heard and know the law of God and have been circumcised according to the Old Testament requirement will not help them at the final judgment if they "break the law." For "he is a Jew who is one inwardly, and real circumcision is a matter of the heart, spiritual and not literal" (2:29). By saying true circumcision is spiritual, St. Paul is not overturning Judaism. He is getting this idea from Moses himself, who promised that one day God would circumcise the hearts of his people (Dt 30:6). This recalls the Israelites who were "cut to the heart" when they heard Peter preach (Acts 2:37) and received Baptism and the Holy Spirit.

However, the circumcision of the heart is not some hidden reality that has no effect on one's behavior. No, but as St. Paul says earlier, "it is not the hearers of the law . . . but the *doers of the law* who will be justified" (Rom 2:13, emphasis added). Again, this is a strange thing for Paul to say in a document where he is supposed to be teaching the doctrine of "salvation by faith alone." But as we will see, St. Paul never teaches "salvation by faith alone." He certainly teaches "salvation by faith," but that *faith* transforms our lives, including what we actually *do*.

Well, if it's not just *hearing* the law and performing ceremonies such as circumcision that make a person right with God, is there anything special about being a Jew rather than a Gentile? Paul takes up that question in Romans 3. Paul answers that, in a sense, Jews have an advantage, and in a sense they don't.

On the one hand, they have an advantage because they have been given the scriptures. God spoke to them in a way he did not with any other people. That is a blessing, even if many Jews through history have ignored God's word (Rom 3:1–8).

On the other hand, Jews are no better off because they have sinned against God like everyone else. St. Paul quotes a large number of scriptures from the Old Testament that speaks of the sins of God's people Israel (3:10–20). The scriptures themselves make clear that both Israel and the Gentiles have offended God and need salvation.

Restating the Thesis: Salvation by Faith, not Works of the Law *(Romans 3:21–31)*

Okay, St. Paul is done stating the "bad news" that both Jews and Gentiles have sinned and are under God's "wrath." Now Paul sums up his thesis once more, and it's worth moving carefully through what Paul says because he is often misunderstood.

"No human being will be justified in [God's] sight by works of the law, since through the law comes knowledge of sin" (3:20). The phrase "works of the law" was a technical term in Judaism that referred to the different cleanliness and purity regulations of the Law of Moses. The Essenes, for example, used the term "works of the law" to refer to many issues of ritual cleanliness: how to handle leather, dogs, unclean liquids, grain handled by Gentiles, and so forth.[9] "Works of the law" did not refer to what we would think of as "works of mercy" or "good deeds." Jews did and still do believe that morally good actions are necessary *for every human being*, including Gentiles, and are not unique to the Law of Moses. "Works of the law" were ceremonial issues that were *unique* to the Law of Moses. Good works were required of all.

When St. Paul says, "No human being will be justified . . . by works of the law," his primary meaning is that keeping the ceremonies of the Law of Moses, especially circumcision, will not save you.

Okay, Paul, but if circumcision and the other ceremonies Moses commanded don't make us right with God, what does? "But now the righteousness of God has been manifested apart from law, although the law and the prophets bear witness to it, the righteousness of God through faith in Jesus Christ for all who believe," Paul says (3:21–22). There's a different way. This way is apart from the Law of Moses, with all its ceremonies. However, "the law and the prophets" (the Jewish way of talking about the Old Testament) prophesy about this different way. This way involves receiving God's righteousness (the Holy Spirit) by having faith in Jesus.

"For there is no distinction; since all have sinned and fall short of the glory of God" (3:22–23). This is a very famous verse. Many Protestants have it memorized. I memorized it when I was a pastor and used to quote it when doing door-to-door evangelism. I used to take the verse as proof that every human being has sinned and needs a savior. Now, that's certainly true, with the exception of Our Lord and the Blessed Mother. However, when Paul says "all have sinned," he doesn't *primarily* mean each and every human being. In context, he means there is no distinction (between Jews and Gentiles) since *all* (both Jews and Gentiles) have sinned and fall short of the glory of God.

St. Paul continues, "They are justified by his grace as a gift, through the redemption which is in Christ Jesus, whom God put forward as an expiation by his blood, to be received by faith" (3:24–25). Although we have sinned, if we put our trust in Jesus, he will give us his grace, which is the Holy Spirit, and we will be made right with God.

Finally, St. Paul summarizes once again: "We hold that a man is justified by faith apart from the works of the law" (3:28). In other words, it is through faith that you receive the Holy Spirit, and the Holy Spirit makes you right with God inside ("justified"). The works of the Law of Moses, such as circumcision and food laws, cannot give you the Holy Spirit.

Let's remember:

The Mosaic Covenant began like this:

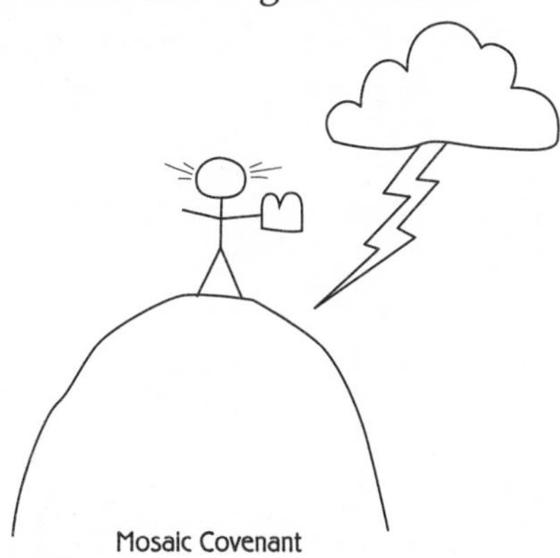

But then more laws had to be added after the people's sin. These were the "works of the law":

Then even more extra laws, more "works of the law," were added in Deuteronomy, when Moses was angry with the hard-heartedness of God's people:

This covenant, with its laws for people who are hard of heart"(Mt 19:8), is no longer fitting for people who have God's love in their hearts (Rom 5:5).

Now Paul has to answer three objections that he knows his Jewish readers are going to raise:

Objection 1: Paul, You Are Throwing Out the Old Testament *(Romans 4–5)*

Many of Paul's Jewish readers would understandably object to what he is saying. If circumcision and the other works of the Law are not necessary for salvation, then Paul is undermining the authority of the Law or Torah, the five Books of Moses, the heart of the Old Testament. Now, Jews called the Old Testament "the Law and the Prophets." The "Law" was the first five books, the Books of Moses, and consisted of Genesis through Deuteronomy. The "Prophets" were all the rest. So when Paul asks in 3:31, "Do we then overthrow the law by this faith?" he has in view the Torah, the Law in the sense of the Books of Moses.

"By no means!" Paul answers. And he proceeds in the next two chapters (Romans 4–5) to show places from the Law of Moses, especially Genesis, that point to salvation by faith in God rather than by external ceremonies.

For example, in Genesis 15:6, Abraham puts his trust in God, and the Bible says it was "reckoned . . . to him as righteousness." So Abraham was right with God because of his faith or trust *long before he was circumcised* since the command of circumcision was not given until two chapters and many years later in Genesis 17. If Abraham could be "righteous" in God's eyes without circumcision or any of the other ritual works of the Law that Moses commanded long afterward, then it stands to reason that such things are not absolutely necessary to be right with God (Rom 4:1–2). That's Paul's argument in Romans 4:1–12.

In the next section (Rom 4:13–25), Paul makes another argument for salvation by faith based on the life of Abraham. He points out that when God gave Abraham the commandment to circumcise himself and his sons as a sign of the covenant (Gn 17), at the very same time, God promised to Abraham that he would become the "father of many nations," which can also mean "father of many Gentiles." This has to refer to spiritual fatherhood since Abraham was not physically the father of many Gentile nations.

There is an unspoken argument in this passage. St. Paul perhaps assumes it's obvious to his readers, but we no longer pick up on it. It goes like this: As Gentiles join the Church, they share Abraham's faith, and he becomes their spiritual father. However, if all the Gentiles become Jews first by accepting circumcision and other Jewish laws, then Abraham would only be the spiritual father of *Jews* and *the prophecy would not be fulfilled that Abraham becomes a father of many nations*. Therefore, the Gentiles have to *stay* Gentiles when they enter the Church so that Abraham will truly become the "father of many Gentiles" as St. Paul states twice (vv. 17–18).

After praising God for his great love for us, that even while we were sinners, he sent his son to die for us (Rom 5:1–11), Paul returns to the Law, the Books of Moses, to continue explaining the Gospel (5:12–21). This time, he moves earlier in human history from Abraham, to compare Jesus with Adam, the first man and father of the human race.

This is Paul's argument (5:12–21): Adam sinned, and his sinful nature was passed on to his descendants before they had done good or bad. Jesus is a New Adam. His righteous nature is passed to us by faith before we have done good or bad. You didn't have to do anything to receive a sinful nature from your father Adam. In the same way, you don't have to do anything to receive the grace of God from Jesus; just trust him and accept it. But let's remember that the "grace of God" is not just forgiveness of our sins. It is the Holy Spirit himself, who changes who and what we are. As St. Paul said earlier, "God's love has been poured into our hearts through the Holy Spirit who has been given to us" (Rom 5:5).

To recap to this point, St. Paul responds to the objection that he is overthrowing the Law, that is, the Books of Moses, by going to the first book of Moses, Genesis, and looking at the figures of Abraham and Adam. Abraham was right in God's eyes even before any of the laws of Moses were given. Further, God predicted that he would be the "father of many Gentiles," which is happening as Gentiles join the Church.

Adam is a contrasting image with Jesus. Adam "freely" gave his sinful nature to the rest of us. Jesus freely offers his righteous nature to us. So, the Books of Moses (the Law) show us images of salvation by faith through Jesus Christ.

Objection 2: Your Gospel Implies We Can Keep On Sinning *(Romans 6–7)*

Heavens, no! Paul responds, using three metaphors: death, slavery, and marriage.

First, Paul says, we can't live in sin any longer because we've died to sin (6:1–14).

RIP

Death

In Baptism, we share Jesus' death and resurrection. Going down into the water is being buried with Jesus. Coming up out of the water is being raised with him. Our old, sinful nature that we got from Adam gets killed in the process. Like Jesus, we have begun a new life: "We were buried with him by baptism . . . so that as Christ was raised from the dead, . . . we too might walk in newness of life" (Rom 6:4).

Second, Paul says, we can't live in sin any longer, because we are no longer slaves of sin but "slaves of God"! Don't you know that slaves have to do what their master tells them? Well, before we came to Jesus, we were all slaves of sin. But now we have gotten rid of that master and gotten a much different and better one: God.

Slavery

"You have been set free from sin and have become slaves of God" (6:22). This is a much better employment situation, because "the wages of sin is death, but the free gift of God is eternal life in Christ Jesus our Lord" (6:23).

Third, Paul says, we can't keep sinning, because we are not "married" to sin any longer.

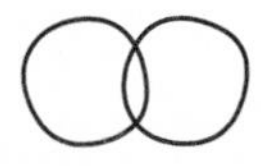

Marriage

Before we came to Christ, it was as if we were married to our sinfulness and couldn't get away from it. But now, through Baptism, we have died to all that. Just as death ends a marriage and allows the surviving partner to marry again, so our death in Baptism frees us to marry Christ, our bridegroom. Now we are joined to Jesus and live a "new life of the Spirit" (7:6).

Objection 3: Your Gospel Implies That the Law Is Bad *(Romans 7)*

Heavens, no! Paul again responds. He explains that it's not God's *law* that's bad; rather, it's our sinful nature, or what he calls "sin which dwells within me" (7:17), that is bad.

Let's summarize what St. Paul says in Romans 7: Every human being has the experience of doing things that we know are wrong. It's odd; we know something is wrong, and inside we are objecting to it, even as we watch ourselves do it. We experience a force for evil and a force for good within ourselves. This "force for evil" Paul calls "a law of sin" that lives in us (7:23).

Now, God's law is good. It tells us right from wrong, and it is good to know what is right and what is wrong. But sometimes when we hear God's laws, we get a desire to break them, just to find out what we are missing (7:7–8). It's like being a kid and having someone tell you not to lick the flagpole in front of the school in the wintertime because your tongue will stick to it. That made you want to lick the flagpole just to see if it would really happen. Rules sometimes tempt us to break them out of unhealthy curiosity.

Even though God's laws are good, their *effect* on us can be bad because we get tempted to break them just to find out what happens. In fact, without God's power working in our lives, we can get ourselves into a pretty pitiful state. We have a tendency to do what is wrong, even though we know it is wrong, and then get stuck in a pattern of evil (7:15–20). Nowadays we call this "addiction," and every one of us has a tendency toward addiction to things that we know are unhealthy for body, mind, and spirit: drugs, sex, TV, sports, alcohol, novels, video games, social media, and many other things. St. Paul experienced it himself and describes it as being "captive to the law of sin which dwells in my members. Wretched man that I am! Who will deliver me from this body of death? Thanks be to God through Jesus Christ our Lord!" (7:23–25). Jesus can give us freedom from this pattern of sin through the Holy Spirit.

Summary: Life in the Spirit: The Heart of St. Paul's Good News *(Romans 8)*

Now we get to the heart of this letter to the Romans and the heart of St. Paul's gospel. This is found in Romans 8, the central chapter of the whole epistle. Here Paul explains the difference between the Mosaic Covenant and the New Covenant. He calls the Mosaic the "law of sin and death" and the New the "law of the Spirit of life in Christ Jesus." Now the Mosaic Covenant, the Law, was fine so far as it goes; it taught what was right and wrong, but its major limitation was that it did not give people the power to do what was right. That is the big difference between the Old Covenant and the New Covenant: the pouring out of the Spirit, which gives us the power to keep God's law. God sent Jesus to take on himself all the punishment for sin that was required in the older covenants in salvation history and to pour out the Holy Spirit so that his disciples could actually live lives pleasing to God. This is taught in Romans 8:3–4: "For God has done what the law, weakened by the flesh, could not do: sending his own Son in the likeness of sinful flesh and for sin, he condemned sin in the flesh, in order that the just requirement of the law might be fulfilled in us, who walk not according to the flesh but according to the Spirit."

The "Heart" of St. Paul's Gospel:
"God's love has been poured into our hearts through the Holy Spirit" (Rom 5:5).

God sent Jesus to pay the price for sin and give us the Spirit so that we can keep "the just requirement" of the law. What is the "just requirement"? It's to love God above all things and our neighbor as ourselves. As Paul will teach later, "Love is the fulfilling of the law" (Rom 13:10).

So Paul is certainly not teaching that we are saved just by believing some truths about Jesus. Nor is he teaching that we can just receive the Holy Spirit and then go on our merry way, doing whatever we like. Once we get the Spirit through faith in Jesus, we have to live by God's Spirit. There are practical things we need to do.

First, we need to "set [our minds] on the Spirit," not on the things of the flesh, because "to set the mind on the flesh is death, but to set the mind on the Spirit is life and peace" (8:6). To "set one's mind" on something means to focus one's thoughts and desires on it, and "the flesh" here means physical pleasure and possessions. So, if we focus our thoughts and desires on physical pleasures and possessions then we are going to die spiritually. But if we focus our thoughts and desires on the things of the Spirit, then we will live with God forever. What are the things of the Spirit? Elsewhere Paul lists the "fruit of the Spirit" as love, joy, peace, patience, goodness, kindness, gentleness, faithfulness, and self-control (Gal 5:22–23). Our thoughts and desires should focus on these virtues.

Second, we need to live according to the Spirit, which means "putting to death the deeds of the body" through the Spirit. "For if you live according to the flesh you will die, but if by the Spirit you put to death the deeds of the body you will live" (8:13). Note again that Paul is not teaching "salvation by faith alone" as that is usually understood. No one who "lives according to the flesh" is going to gain eternal life, even if they believe all the right facts about Jesus (v. 13). Our faith in Jesus has to be lived out by the power of the Holy Spirit. Now, "putting to death" in Latin comes out as "mortification," from the roots *mortis*, death, and *facio*, "to do or make." This is where we get the idea of "mortifications" in the Catholic spiritual tradition. We have to mortify (put to death) the deeds of the body. And the deeds of the body refer to all the selfish physical pleasures we like to indulge in, pleasures that do not help us to love God or anyone else. We can't live like that anymore. A life focused on making ourselves feel good is just a form of self-love. But God's love is self-giving, not selfish. God the Father is always giving himself to the Son, and the Son is always giving himself to the Father, and the Self that they give is the Holy Spirit. They also give us the Holy Spirit through faith in Jesus so that we can be part of the circle of self-giving love. But that's completely against a lifestyle focused just on making ourselves feel good. We have to practice self-denial if we really want to love God and love others. And every act of self-denial involves a little "death" of ourselves—a "mortification." This involves suffering, but suffering is a necessary part of living as a child of God. God's own Son Jesus came to suffer in order to prove his love for us. If we share Jesus' Spirit, our lives will follow the same pattern. "You have received the spirit of sonship," St. Paul says. So we are "fellow heirs with Christ, *provided we suffer with him* in order that we may also be glorified with him" (8:15, 17, emphasis added).

Why do we need to suffer with him? We need to suffer with Christ so that our love may be proven and purified. You see, love and suffering are inseparable. Until you suffer for the sake of what you love, it is not clear that you really love. For example, young couples often think they are "in love." Are they really? Who knows? When you are young, healthy, and wealthy, what is there not to like? Who would not like to be around another person who's attractive and in the bloom of life? Whether the young couple really loves each other will not become clear until there is sickness, children, exhaustion, stress, and aging. If they are still faithful to each other in those times, then we can say they are "in love." So the proof of love is not putting on a fabulous wedding. Anyone with enough money can do that. The proof of love is staying faithful "till death do us part."

So it is with God and us. God proved his love for us in this: while we were unlovable, he sent his Son to suffer and die for us (Rom 5:8). And now, he permits various sufferings in our lives, so that we have the privilege and opportunity of proving our love in return.

I've heard a good friend of mine phrase it like this: "Suffering without love is unbearable; love without suffering is impossible."

Not that the Christian life is all suffering and gloom! While suffering is certainly necessary and unavoidable, St. Paul reminds of several reasons for hope and joy:

First: "The sufferings of this present time are not worth comparing with the glory that is to be revealed to us" (8:18). In other words, heaven will be so good it will make this world seem like a bad dream from which we have awoken. Not just our souls but also our bodies and even the whole creation will be renewed one day.

Second: During this time of waiting, we have the Holy Spirit. He "helps us in our weakness" and prays for us "with sighs too deep for words" (8:26). What a comfort it is to know that God's spirit lives in us and inspires our prayers!

Third: God works in everything for our good. This is the way Paul phrases it: "We know that in everything God works for good with those who love him" (8:28). In the Catholic tradition, this verse is often summarized by the Latin phrase *Omnia in bonum*, meaning "all things for the good." Note that St. Paul does *not* say, "Everything that happens *is* good."

Indeed, a lot that happens is bad. But God can bring good out of it, for those who love him, just as he brought the greatest good—our salvation—out of the greatest evil act in world history: the murder of the innocent Son of God.

Fourth: Nothing can separate us from the love of God. The same God who sent his son for our salvation will be our judge on the last day: How could we ask for a judge who is more "on our side" than that? Nothing in this life can keep him from loving us. Even sufferings, such as "tribulation, or distress, or persecution, or famine, or nakedness, or peril, or sword" (8:35), don't break the bond of love; instead, they become opportunities for us to return his love. "No, in all these things we are more than conquerors through him who loved us. For I am sure that neither death, nor life, nor angels, nor principalities, nor things present, nor things to come, nor powers, nor height, nor depth, nor anything else in all creation, will be able to separate us from the love of God in Christ Jesus our Lord" (8:37–39). The only major thing St. Paul does *not* mention is sin. Sin can separate us from the love of God, because sin is our choice to deliberately turn away from God. God respects our choices. But outside of our own free will, there is nothing in the entire universe that can keep us from God's love.

Digression: The Role of Israel in the New Covenant Era *(Romans 9–11)*

By the end of Romans 8, St. Paul has accomplished his main objective. He has explained his gospel, which is "through faith for faith" (Rom 1:17). No one is made right with God simply by performing the ceremonies of Moses's covenant, the "works of the law." Instead, you become right with God when you place your trust in Jesus and receive from him, through Baptism, the Holy Spirit, who cleans and heals your inner person. Once we have the Holy Spirit, we are actually able to keep the heart of God's law, which is to love God and our neighbors as ourselves. We can do it because we have the love of God living in us, empowering us. Love leads to suffering, of course, because it is only through suffering that love proves itself genuine. But suffering is temporary and can never separate us from God's love.

This is not enough:

We need this:

Now, St. Paul turns his attention to three other matters before concluding his letter. First, what about Israel now that salvation is not through the Law of Moses? Second, how should we live if this Gospel is true? And finally, what are Paul's immediate instructions for the Roman Christians?

In Romans 9–11, St. Paul takes up the difficult question of the role of the ethnic people of Israel who have not accepted Jesus as the Christ and entered the New Covenant. This causes Paul great sadness. As an Israelite himself, from the tribe of Benjamin, his deepest desire is that all the ethnic descendants of Israel would recognize Jesus as the Messiah promised by the prophets and enter into his kingdom.

St. Paul's discussion of this issue is often complex, and he digresses into related theological problems in these three chapters. But we can summarize the main points he makes about the old covenant people of God:

1. Biological or ethnic identity alone has never been enough to guarantee a right relationship with God. Throughout the Old Testament, we see examples of one brother who embraces the covenant and another who rejects it. "It is not the children of the flesh who are the children of God, but the children of the promise are reckoned as descendants" (Rom 9:8). In many periods of history, the majority of ethnic Israel rejected God's covenant, and only a minority held fast. So we shouldn't be surprised that a similar thing is happening now that the New Covenant has arrived.
2. In fact, the prophets themselves predicted that the majority of God's chosen nation would reject his salvation: "Isaiah cries out concerning Israel: 'Though the number of the sons of Israel be as the sand of the sea, only a remnant of them will be saved'" (9:27); and "'All day long I have held out my hands to a disobedient and contrary people'" (10:21).
3. Despite all that, God has not rejected his people. There is a remnant of Israelites who have accepted Jesus, including Paul himself, not to mention the apostles, the Blessed Mother, and many others. This is just like earlier times in

Israel's history, such as the days of Elijah, when only a few thousand in Israel stayed faithful (11:2–5).

4. Finally, God still waits with open arms for any of Israel who wish to come to him. The Church can be compared to an olive tree whose trunk is Israelite (Jesus, Mary, the apostles, and the early Christians) but many of whose branches are Gentiles "grafted" in (11:17–24). If God can graft Gentile branches onto the olive tree of Israel in order to create the Church, he can surely graft back in the broken branches of Israelites onto their own tree. God's heart is always tender toward the people of Israel because "they are beloved for the sake of their forefathers. For the gifts and the call of God are irrevocable" (11:28–29).

In fact, St. Paul sees God working, in a mysterious way, to save all Israel: "I want you to understand this mystery, brethren: a hardening has come upon part of Israel, until the full number of the Gentiles come in, and so all Israel will be saved" (11:25–26). Many wonder what it can mean that the Gentiles coming in will be the way that "all Israel" is saved. Perhaps St. Paul is referring to the way that most of Israel—the ten northern tribes, sometimes called the "lost tribes"—were scattered among the Gentiles way back in the 700s BC. Now that Gentiles are coming to God, among them are the descendants of those "forgotten" tribes. In God's mystery, all the tribes are again coming to God.

Practical Section: Living the New Life in Christ *(Romans 12–15)*

Most of St. Paul's letters divide into two major sections, the first doctrinal and the second practical. Romans is no exception. The doctrinal teaching is finished (chapters 1–11), and now St. Paul makes applications (chapters 12–15).

St. Paul's guidelines for Christian living all surround the central command of love. The heart of his message is found in Romans 13:8–10: "Owe no one anything, except to love one another; for he who loves his neighbor has fulfilled the law. The commandments, 'You shall not commit adultery, You shall not kill, You shall not steal, You shall not covet,' and any other commandment, are summed up in this sentence, 'You shall love your neighbor as yourself.' Love does no wrong to a neighbor; therefore love is the fulfilling of the law." We need to combine his instruction here with his teaching from earlier: "God's love has been poured into our hearts through the Holy Spirit which has been given to us" (Rom 5:5).

That gives us the full picture of St. Paul's view of the Christian life. We don't do good to earn our way to heaven. We trust in Jesus, and Jesus gives us the Spirit. The Spirit fills us with love and changes the way we live. That's it in a nutshell.

In this section (chapters 12–15), St. Paul makes various applications of the principle of love:

Out of love, we should "present [our] bodies as a living sacrifice, holy and acceptable to God, which is [our] spiritual worship" (12:1). This is how we love God, the first commandment. Offering sacrifice is a priestly duty; we are all priests.

The Church calls this the "common priesthood" (*CCC* 1591–92) or "royal priesthood" (*CCC* 1174, 1322).

Priesthood of the Christian

The sacrifice we offer is our "bodies," which means our whole lives. This is why all Catholics should start their day by praying a "morning offering," such as the following: "O my Jesus, through the immaculate heart of Mary, I offer to you all my prayers, works, joys, and sufferings of this day, for all the intentions of your Sacred Heart, in union with the Holy Sacrifice of the Mass around the world, in reparation for my sins, for the intentions of all my relatives and friends, and especially for the intentions of the Holy Father." By offering all the realities of our day as a sacrifice to God, we obey St. Paul in Romans 12:1 by performing our priestly duty in the New Covenant. This offering of all the "raw material" of our lives is symbolized in the Mass, when the laypeople bring forward the unblessed bread and wine to the priest. He takes it, prays for the Holy Spirit, and offers it to God as the Body and Blood of Christ. This shows how the *ministerial priesthood* of our pastors works together with the *common priesthood* of us laypeople. We need each other, and together we offer the

Eucharist, Christ's own sacrifice, to God. We are his people and his body.

Paul makes other applications of the principle of love:

Christians should be *humble* (12:3–8), using whatever gifts God has given them to love others, recognizing that no one's gifts are more important or more necessary than anyone else's. We all have something to share in Christ's body, so we should not be proud of our own gifts, nor threatened by others'.

Christians should show special love *to fellow Christians*, their brothers and sisters in Christ, by encouraging them and helping them in every spiritual and physical need (12:9–13).

But Christians should also show love to *their enemies*, praying for those who persecute and returning love for hatred, good for evil, and kindness for abuse (12:14–21).

A life of love involves *respect for authorities*, recognizing that the government has a good purpose and is supposed to serve God by rewarding the good and punishing the evil (13:1–7).

We should also *love our weak brother*, an important topic for St. Paul (14:1–15:6). The "weak brother" is someone who can easily be led into sin. We have to be careful, in living with other believers, not to do things that seem sinful or would encourage others to sin.

In St. Paul's day, many Christians were really bothered by the idea of eating food that had been sacrificed to idols. Pagan temples were almost like slaughterhouses in those days. Many animals were sacrificed to the gods daily, and the extra meat was sold in the marketplace. Now, these pagan gods were really demons, and many Christians just couldn't eat such sacrificial meat without feeling like they were supporting a demonic cult. On the other hand, there was nothing actually wrong with the meat itself, so other Christians felt okay eating it. St. Paul counsels the believers not to fight about this issue but also not to do things that upset fellow believers or lead them to do something they feel is wrong.

In our day, if you go out to eat with a Christian man who is recovering from alcoholism, you don't want to order a big beer and drink it in front of him. You would be tempting him to do something that would be spiritually dangerous for him. Likewise, we want to be modest in our dress, careful not to cause attractions in our brothers and sisters that would be inappropriate or lead them to sin. Our lifestyle should encourage our fellow Christians in their faith.

Many PSs: Paul's Long End to His Letter *(Romans 15:14 to end)*

Although it contains a lot of heavy theology, Romans is still a letter, and letters have to end with greetings, blessings, farewells, last thoughts, and PSs. The last two chapters of Romans (from 15:14 to 16:27) have all of these and more. Paul explains that he feels he's done enough evangelism from Jerusalem all the way to the Balkans, and now he wants to move on to fresh territory. He hopes to go to Spain and to pass through Rome on the way. Hopefully the Roman Christians will give him a hand when he arrives and help him raise the funds and resources he needs to get to Spain. But first, Paul is journeying to Jerusalem to bring the Jewish church there a large sum of money that he had raised from Gentile Christians in Greece. He plans to travel to Rome afterward. As we know from Acts, all things did not work out smoothly. He was arrested in Jerusalem and spent two years in prison before being sent to Rome in chains.

Rome was the center and capital of the empire, so there was a lot of traffic to and from the city. St. Paul knows a large number of people from Rome and others whom he met elsewhere and who have now settled there. Most of chapter 16 is taken up saying "Hi" to all his friends and acquaintances. These verses remind us that the Christian faith is not just a philosophy or set of teachings but also always involves real, living human beings and a community we call "the Church" that has been alive for two thousand years. Finally, St. Paul ends with a beautiful doxology praising God: "Now to him who is able to strengthen you according to my gospel and the preaching of Jesus Christ, according to the revelation of the mystery which was kept secret for long ages but is now disclosed and through the prophetic writings is made known to all nations, according to the command of the eternal God, to bring about the obedience of faith—to the only wise God be glory for evermore through Jesus Christ! Amen" (16:25–27). Notice he returns to the idea of "obedience of faith," which he first mentioned at the start of the letter (1:5). What does it mean? It means we receive the Holy Spirit from God through *faith* in Jesus and then have the power to *obey* God's commandment of love. That's Paul's gospel. Faith makes it possible to love.

Part IV

The Kingdom Perfected!

John

Six

The Gospel of John

Welcome at last to the high point of the New Testament, the writings of the apostle John. The Church Fathers regarded John as the "eagle" because his theological insight soared to the heights of divine love.

Christian tradition holds John to be the author of five books of the New Testament: the Gospel of John, three epistles of John, and the Book of Revelation.[1] We are going to deal with the first and last of these, the Gospel and Revelation. We'll start with the Gospel.

What we're about to study is the greatest piece of world literature, period. This is the most influential, the most widely distributed, and the most historically significant book in human history.

I can demonstrate that. Think about it with me for a moment. What's the world's perennial number one best seller worldwide? It's not the Qu'ran, it's not *The Hobbit*, and it's not Harry Potter. It's always the Bible. And of the entire Bible, what part has pride of place? What do we stand up for in Mass? We stand for the four gospels. And of these four, is there any one that was singled out by the Church, by the Fathers, as *soaring above the rest*? It's the Gospel of John.

The Gospel of John is the best of the best, the cream of the cream of the world's most popular book. Harry Potter was a one-hit wonder by comparison. Twenty years from now the fad books of today will be forgotten, but we'll still be talking about the Gospel of John.

And what we're going to find out in the next few pages is that the Gospel of John is actually a book about the Catholic sacraments. I invite you to ponder that: the world's most popular book, the world's most widely read book, is actually a book about the sacraments of the Catholic Church.

Many regard John's picture of Jesus as being much different from the other gospels, but the Church really hasn't seen it that way. If the Church had perceived John's picture of Jesus as different from Jesus in the other gospels, the Church would not have embraced this gospel. Whether Jesus in John is truly different from Jesus in Matthew, Mark, and Luke depends a great deal on interpretation. If you want the pictures to conflict, you can make them conflict. If you see the pictures as complementary—that is, as completing each other and filling each other out—you can get a richer portrait of Jesus by reading all four gospels together. In fact, a patristic tradition recounts that John was asked, near the end of his long life, to write down his memories of the Lord, and the result was his gospel. Indeed, the Gospel of John seems to be the last of all the gospels, intended to fill out their picture of Jesus. John avoids telling you the same stories you've already heard three times, although he assumes you know about them. Instead, he goes deep on a select few events, which he often calls "signs."

In fact, the Gospel of John is structured, in part, around a sequence of seven miraculous "signs." These signs give the book its backbone:

- The changing of the water to wine at the wedding at Cana (2:1–11)
- The healing the official's son at Cana (4:46–54)
- The healing of the paralytic at Bethesda (5:1–18)
- The feeding of the five thousand (6:1–15)
- The healing of the man born blind (chapter 9)
- The raising of Lazarus from the dead (chapter 11), and
- Finally, the dead and resurrection of Jesus (chapters 19–20)

These miracles are called "signs" because they point beyond themselves. We don't want to get attached to the signs themselves. We want to see the one the signs point to. Jesus rebukes people who get fixated on the miracles, who want to see Jesus do "another one" as if they were watching a fireworks show or a magician. He criticizes thrill seeking that gets attached to the miracles because these miracles are signs. They point to something (or someone) else.

When I drive home to Steubenville from somewhere out west, the first sign I see for Steubenville is about twenty miles north of here on Ohio Route 7. But I don't stop at the first sign, get out, hug it, and say, "I'm home! I'm home!" The sign is just a pointer to help me find my way to the real thing.

A major theme in the Gospel of John is that Jesus' power in the *signs* still touches us through the *sacraments*. When I was a kid, my parents used to read to me from the gospels, and I used to love to hear these great stories of Jesus' miracles. I often thought, *I wish I could have lived back then, could have reached out and touched the hem of his garment. If only I could have contacted Jesus and could experience his power.*

The Gospel of John is written precisely to address this kind of longing. The apostle tells the stories of Jesus' life in such a way that we can see that the sacraments were already present in what Jesus was doing, and his ministry continues through the sacraments. We don't have to read these stories and say, "Oh I wish I could go back and touch Jesus," because we *can* touch him now, through the bread and wine of the Eucharist, the waters of Baptism, the words of the priests in the confessional, and the other sacraments as well. John tells the miracles of Jesus' life in such a way that we can see the connection and say, "Ah ha! The same thing that Jesus is doing the Church continues to do, and I can still touch Jesus."

* * *

As we move through the Gospel of John, we're going to make a link between each of the seven signs of John and the seven sacraments of the Church.

The First Sign: The Changing of the Water to Wine at the Wedding at Cana *(John 2:1–11)*

> On the third day there was a marriage at Cana in Galilee, and the mother of Jesus was there; Jesus also was invited to the marriage, with his disciples. When the wine failed, the mother of Jesus said to him, "They have no wine." And Jesus said to her, "O woman, what have you to do with me? My hour has not yet come." His mother said to the servants, "Do whatever he tells you." Now six stone jars were standing there, for the Jewish rites of purification, each holding twenty or thirty gallons. Jesus said to them, "Fill the jars with water." And they filled them up to the brim. He said to them, "Now draw some out, and take it to the steward of the feast." So they took it. When the steward of the feast tasted the water now become wine, and did not know where it came from (though the servants who had drawn the water knew), the steward of the feast called the bridegroom and said to him, "Every man serves the good wine first; and when men have drunk freely, then the poor wine; but you have kept the good wine until now." This, the first of his signs, Jesus did at Cana in Galilee, and manifested his glory; and his disciples believed in him. (Jn 2:1–11)

The first thing that we want to note is when this sign took place. Verse 1 says "On the third day there was a marriage." That immediately raises the question, "Third day from what?"

To find out, let's go all the way back to the first verse of the gospel: "In the beginning was the Word, and the Word was with God, and the Word was God."

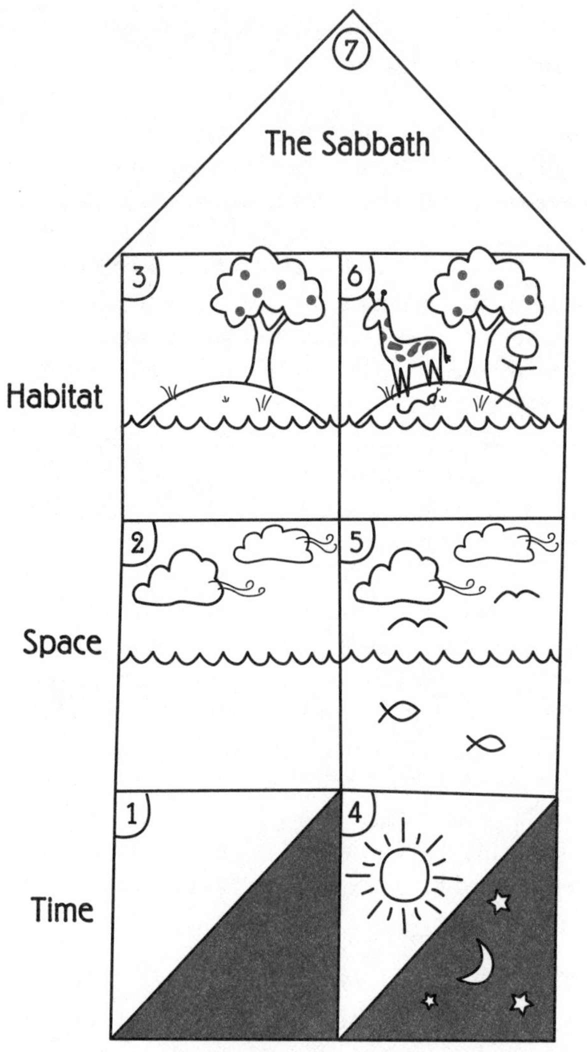

There's only one other Bible book that begins with "In the beginning": the very first, Genesis. The apostle John draws a connection between his gospel and the Book of Genesis, in effect saying, *The coming of Jesus is so momentous, it's like a new beginning to world history. It's a new Genesis. It's a new creation.*

St. Paul says the same thing in 2 Corinthians 5:17, one of my favorite verses in the Bible. St. Paul says, "If anyone is in Christ, he is a new creation." You start all over when you encounter Jesus.

The Gospel of John continues with more connections to the Book of Genesis: "In the beginning was the Word, and the Word was with God, and the Word was God. He was in the beginning with God; all things were made through him, and without him was not anything made that was made. In him was life, and the life was the light of men. The light shines in the darkness, and the darkness has not overcome it" (Jn 1:1–5). John begins speaking of light and darkness. When did light and darkness come on the scene of history? Obviously, on day one of the creation story: "And God said, 'Let there be light'" (Gn 1:3). So we are in day one of John's "new Genesis" of Jesus.

As we continue reading John 1, we encounter John the Baptist, the "man sent from God" who is not "the Christ" but a "voice crying in the wilderness." Suddenly, we read, "*The next day* he saw Jesus coming toward him, and said, 'Behold, the Lamb of God, who takes away the sin of the world!'" (1:6, 20, 29; emphasis added).

So apparently we are counting days. Everything that came before this must be in day one. Now we're onto the next day, so that's got to be day two, starting with verse 29. This pattern continues. If you scan through the rest of John 1, you'll see that the phrase "the next day" recurs in verses 35 and 43 as well. If you count up the days, you'll find that by the end of chapter 1, four days have elapsed in the gospel, and chapter 2 begins "on the third day" counting from the previous chapter, giving us a total of *seven days*.

This is the creation weeks of the new creation in Jesus. In Genesis, Adam is made on the sixth day, falls into a deep sleep, God takes his rib, makes Eve, wakes Adam, and brings

Eve to him. When Adam wakes up, you'd assume that would be the morning of the seventh day. And that's when Eve is introduced to him for the first time. The first time woman comes into human history is on the seventh day.

Likewise, in the Gospel of John, it is on the seventh day of the gospel that a woman is first mentioned: "There was a marriage at Cana in Galilee, and the mother of Jesus was there" (2:1). Mary is the New Eve.

Jesus is also invited to the marriage. He is the New Adam. Obviously, it's not Jesus' marriage, but it is a marriage, and the only identified people at this marriage are Jesus and his mother. So they stand to the forefront as the New Eve and the New Adam, the man and the woman who are going to bring forth a new human race through their cooperation.

So let's read a little into this account. Verse 3 says, "When the wine failed . . ." Now apparently it fails on the first day. That's a really bad party. In these ancient times the wedding feast was supposed to last seven days, and you're supposed to have seven days' worth of wine, stored up for all your family and friends. This wine runs out on the first day—"epic fail," as kids say these days.

"When the wine failed, the mother of Jesus said to him, 'They have no wine'" (2:3). Mary teaches us a little secret about prayer here. Look at how she approaches her divine Son. She comes to Jesus and says, "They have no wine." She doesn't twist his arm to manipulate: *You ought to do this, I want you to help them out, they're friends of mine, and I need you to make more wine.* There's none of that. What does she do? She just lets the Lord know her problem. I'm convinced she's showing us how to pray: just let your needs be known to the Lord. You don't have to manipulate; you don't have to give him five suggestions about how he can solve your problems. Just leave it in his hands.

Jesus responds, "O woman, what have you to do with me? My hour has not yet come" (2:4). That's full of meaning. Note that he does not say, *I haven't come to provide wine* but rather says, "My hour has not yet come." This implies, *I have come to provide wine but not yet.* When does Jesus ever provide drink elsewhere in this gospel? We see this only at the Cross, when "blood and water" flow from his side (19:34). That is the eucharistic wine of his blood. But that is three years down the road. Here Jesus is asking his mother, *Do you want to start the ball rolling down towards the cross, where I'm truly going to provide wine? It's a little early to start heading down that path!*

Mary just says to the servants, "Do whatever he tells you," and walks off (2:5). Now we've got six servants standing around looking at Jesus. Mary hasn't manipulated, argued, pleaded, or whined. She just leaves the ball in Jesus' court. This is an example for us in prayer: leave your problems in Jesus' hands and get a good night's sleep.

"Now six stone jars were standing there, for the Jewish purity rituals, each holding twenty or thirty gallons. Jesus said to them, 'Fill the jars with water.' And they filled them up to the brim" (2:6). So that's about 120 to 180 gallons of water. They take it out, bring it to the MC of the wedding reception (something like the best man) and let him taste it. Immediately, he calls the bridegroom over (2:9). And that is very important, folks. Take note: he assumes that the bridegroom provided the wine. In those days, that was his duty, just as in our culture the father of the bride pays for the wedding and the father of the groom pays for the rehearsal dinner.

This is the point: our Lord has just performed the duty of the bridegroom, and he's done it a lot better than the guy whose party it really was. The steward (best man) calls him over: "Every man serves the good wine first; and when men have drunk freely, then the poor wine; but you have kept the good wine until now" (2:10). That sounds nice and calm and formal in our English translation. But you can be sure in real life it was more like this: *Dude! What's your problem? Don't you know how to throw a party? Why did you lead with your bottom-shelf stuff when you had* this *stashed away!?*

I know just a little bit about buying wine. When you go to the grocery store, on the bottom of the wine shelf are things sold in huge jugs or in boxes. Note to self: if it's sold in a box or in sizes larger than a half-gallon, it's not good wine. Now, as you work your way up the shelves, there is more and more foreign language on the bottles. That language is French. No one can understand French because the way it is pronounced has no relationship to how it is spelled. The French like it this way because then Americans and British can't tell what they're saying. Anyway, when you get to the top of the shelf, the bottles are smaller and all in French and you can't tell what it is you're buying—you're just assuming it's wine, and it better be good because you're paying twenty dollars or more for less than a quart.

Now, Jesus makes 180 *gallons* of fine French import! A sea of the good stuff sold in little bottles. Jesus does everything big in the Gospel of John. He is the abundant bridegroom. A key verse in the gospel is 10:10 (emphasis added): "I came that they may have life . . ."—just enough life to squeak by? No! The verse continues—". . . and have it *ABUNDANTLY*!" Likewise, near the start of the gospel, John exclaims, "From his *abundance* we have all received grace upon grace" (1:16).

This theme of abundance is going to run through the gospel as Jesus does everything in a big way: an enormous amount of bread and fish for the five thousand (chapter 6), a ludicrous amount of spices poured on his body at his burial (chapter 19), and an absurdly large catch of fish in the Sea of

Galilee (chapter 21). Jesus is our bridegroom who has come to satisfy us to the full.

In this sign that Jesus performs at Cana, we obviously see a relationship to the Sacrament of Matrimony. Jesus is the true bridegroom of every single one of us. Even when we get married, what we're doing is entering into a relationship with another man or another woman, and that man or woman is going to show us the love of Jesus through themselves.

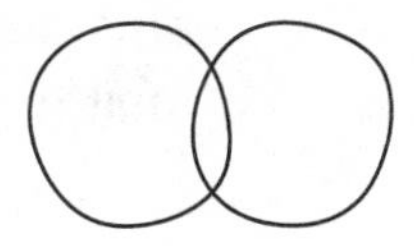

Our spouse becomes Jesus to us, or in other words, the love of Jesus is supposed to embrace us through our spouse.

* * *

Jesus is the bridegroom of our souls, and when we enter into marriage, he funnels all that abundant grace—symbolized by the 180 gallons of wine here—to us through our spouse. That's part of the theology of the Sacrament of Matrimony.

By being present at this wedding, blessing it with a miracle, and using it to start his ministry, Jesus shows how much he endorses this Sacrament of Matrimony and how important the idea and the beauty of marriage are to his plan of salvation.

Marriage is not something that we humans invented. God designed marriage and put it in place at the beginning of creation. And God designed that husband and wife relationship to reflect the covenant relationship between himself and his people. The covenant relationship between himself and his people comes first, and God designed marriage to reflect it.

So marriage is something God sets in place: it's an icon of Christ and his Church, which is why we can't change the rules about it. Just as two plus two equals four and that's a fact of reality that no one can change, so one man and one woman forever equals a marriage. Obviously, people can vote to call other relationships "marriage," and courts can insist that other relationships are given the same rights as marriage. But this doesn't change reality. The Supreme Court could rule that two plus two will now equal five and force everyone legally to say that it does. But that won't make it true. God established one man, one woman, open to children, and forever to reflect the divine relationship between God and his people. And it's unalterable.

* * *

Now the sign that Jesus performs also points to the Eucharist. The early Christians who read the Gospel of John realized very well that if Jesus had the power to turn water into wine he also had the power to turn wine into his blood.

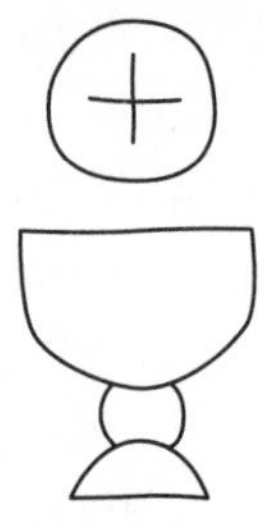

Not only that but from early times the Eucharist has been called "the Wedding Feast of the Lamb." So there's a close relationship between marriage and Eucharist: in the Sacrament of Matrimony, you embrace your spouse; in the Sacrament of the Eucharist, we come forward for Communion and embrace the body of our bridegroom in the Host. The Mass is communion between God and the Church. Matrimony is communion between husband and wife. So there's a strong parallel between these sacraments.

The following story that we're going to take a look at is not a sign but we want to examine it quickly because it's going to set us up for the seventh sign. After the wedding at Cana, Jesus goes up to Jerusalem and cleanses the Temple:

> The Passover of the Jews was at hand, and Jesus went up to Jerusalem. In the temple he found those who were selling oxen and sheep and pigeons, and the money-changers at their business. And making a whip of cords, he drove them all, with the sheep and oxen, out of the temple; and he poured out the coins of the money-changers and overturned their tables. And he told those who sold the pigeons, "Take these things away; you shall not make my Father's house a house of trade." His disciples remembered that it was written, "Zeal for thy house will consume me." The Jews then said to him, "What *sign* have you to show us for doing this?" Jesus answered them, "Destroy this temple, and in three days I will raise it up." The Jews then said, "It has taken forty-six years to build this temple." (Jn 2:13–20, emphasis added)

Actually, the Jews weren't finished building the Temple. This conversation is taking place around AD 26. They had been working on it for forty-six years and wouldn't finish it for another thirty-eight to thirty-nine years, in AD 66.[2] Then it stood for four years until the Romans burned it to the ground in AD 70.

But Jesus wasn't talking about the stone Temple: "He spoke of the temple of *his body*" (2:21, emphasis added). The *sign* that Jesus will show them to demonstrate he has the authority to cleanse the Temple is the raising up of his temple-body after they have destroyed it. So here, near the beginning of the Gospel of John, we already get a forecast of what the seventh and final sign is going to be: the death and resurrection of Jesus.

So the Gospel of John is setting us up to see that. That's important because when we get to the end of the Gospel of John there's going to be no verses in chapters 19 or 21 calling the death and the resurrection a sign. But we don't need any verses back that far to tell us because we've already been warned up front to expect that as the last sign.

The theme of Jesus as bridegroom that we saw at the wedding at Cana continues into John 3, where Jesus discusses with Nicodemus how a man needs to be "born anew" by "water and the Spirit" in order to "enter the kingdom of God" (Jn 3:3–5).

This is a follow-up from the wedding at Cana. How are the New Adam and the New Eve we saw at the wedding going to give birth to children? In no natural way, but "by water and the Spirit," that is, through Baptism. But Nicodemus cannot comprehend this yet.

Jesus leaves to go throughout Judea, preaching and letting his disciples baptize. John the Baptist hears of Jesus' ministry, which is now attracting more followers than his own. But John is not jealous; he calls Jesus "the bridegroom" and compares himself to a best man (3:29). The best man is happy for the bridegroom and ready to step into the background.

Bridegroom themes continue into the next chapter, where Jesus encounters a woman from Samaria. While traveling through that country, he sits down by a well. As soon as he does so, we know a woman is going to show up because that is what always seems to happen in the Old Testament: Isaac,

Jacob, and Moses all met their future wives at a well (see Gn 24, 29; Ex 2). And sure enough, one does!

Jesus proceeds to ask her for a drink. That reminds us of Genesis 24, where Abraham's servant asked Rebekah for a drink in order to tell if God intended her as a bride for Isaac. The Samaritan woman shows surprise that Jesus, a Jew, has asked her for a drink, and the two get into a conversation. At some point Jesus promises that he can provide "living water" for the woman. This reminds us of Jacob, who provided water for all Rachel's flock when he first met her at the well. In fact, the watering hole where Jesus and the woman were talking was known as "Jacob's well." Then Jesus brings up the subject of marriage explicitly by telling the woman to go get her husband. This brings up the woman's personal history—which is checkered—and after a bit of theological discussion, Jesus flabbergasts the woman by claiming to be the Messiah. Floored, she wanders back into town and calls the townspeople to come out and meet this astounding Jewish prophet. The townspeople do, and listen to Jesus' teaching. After two days, they are won over and come to believe he truly *is* the Messiah (Jn 4:1–41).

The point of this story in John 4 is not that there was a romantic relationship between Jesus and the Samaritan woman. Rather, this woman was a symbol of the Samaritan people as a whole. The Samaritans were the last surviving descendants of the ten northern tribes of Israel. These tribes were the "wife" of God according to the prophet Hosea. And although they had been unfaithful to their husband God and had intermarried with five pagan peoples and worshipped their gods (2 Kgs 17:24–41), still Hosea had promised that God would return and "marry" them once again (Hos 2:4–23). Jesus is God, returning to the last descendants of Israel and inviting them to "marry" him again, to return to him in love.

The Second Sign: The Healing of the Official's Son at Cana *(John 4:46–54)*

As we move on to the end of John chapter 4, we get the account of the second sign. Once again, the sign occurs in Cana, a town that lies on the shores of the Sea of Galilee. An official from that town comes out to find Jesus and pleads with Jesus to heal his deathly ill son. Jesus says, "Go, your son will live." The official returns home to discover that his son had recovered at the very moment Jesus had spoken the word of healing, so "he himself believed, and all his household. This was now the second sign that Jesus did when he had come from Judea to Galilee" (Jn 4:50, 53–54).

Here we see a connection to the Sacrament of the Anointing of the Sick, formerly called "Last Rites" or "Extreme Unction" (Latin for "last anointing").

For a long time in Church history, it was only given when a person was near death. But in recent years, we have recovered the notion that this is appropriate any time you're gravely ill because the Sacrament not only heals the soul for eternal life but can heal the body as well.

Note the parallels between this sign and the Sacrament of the Anointing of the Sick. The official's child is gravely ill. He says to Jesus, "Come down before my child dies" (4:49). And this is the usual condition when a person calls for the Sacrament of the Anointing of the Sick. And then the word of Jesus restores the son to health. So what we're seeing is the power of Jesus to restore those who are approaching the point of death—and that's the fundamental connection with the Sacrament of Anointing. The Sacrament of Anointing aims to unleash this same power of Jesus for the healing of a person's soul and body. It's not a perfect comparison because the Sacrament involves anointing and Jesus does not use oil in this miracle. But our point is not that Jesus establishes the exact form of each sacrament in his various signs. It's that the *essential powers* of Jesus in his signs carry over into one or more of the sacraments.

The exact form of the Sacrament of Anointing began to take shape very early in Church history. St. James makes reference to how the early Church dispensed Jesus' power for the sick: "Is any among you sick? Let him call for the elders [Greek, *presbuteros*] of the church, and let them pray over him, anointing him with oil in the name of the Lord; and the prayer of faith will save the sick man, and the Lord will raise him up; and if he has committed sins, he will be forgiven" (Jas 5:14–15). So anointing is a very biblical practice, when we call the *priest* (a contraction of *presbuteros*) for anointing, prayer, and forgiveness of sins. This is the way the Church continued to pass on Jesus' power to heal those near death, a power we see in his second sign in John 4.

The Third Sign: The Healing of the Paralytic at Bethesda *(John 5:1–18)*

The third sign follows immediately after in John 5. We have the account of the healing of the paralytic at the pool of Bethesda (or Beth-za'tha). The pool was thought to have healing powers, so many ill and handicapped gathered around it. An angel stirred the waters, and the first one in afterward was healed. Jesus went there and came across a man who had been waiting by the pool for thirty-eight years for healing. "Do you want to be healed?" Jesus asked. The man doesn't give a straight answer: "I have no man to put me into the pool," he says. Jesus commands, "Take up your pallet, and walk" (Jn 5:6–8). The man does and is healed. Later, Jesus finds him and warns him: "See, you are well! Sin no more, that nothing worse befall you" (v. 14).

Jesus asked this man a very profound question: "Do you want to be healed?" And at first we think, *Well, the answer is obvious, right? Why else would the guy be waiting by the miraculous pool? Of course he wants to be healed.* But then we begin to ponder a little bit more deeply: *Hey, why has he been there for thirty-eight years and never once managed to get into the water first? Is there some kind of problem? Is there a lack of motivation here?* Because, after all, you can get used to living with your illnesses. I don't just mean this in a physical sense; it's true in a psychological and spiritual sense as well.

This man's illness is a sign of our sin. We are like the blind, the lame, and the paralyzed who are lying by this pool. Our sins blind us, make us lame, and paralyze us spiritually. In fact, we get used to our sins and dysfunctions and don't want to change. Sometimes we find ourselves going back again and again to the Sacrament of Confession, always confessing the same things. The problem isn't that there's no power in the Sacrament. The problem can be a lack of desire on our part; we don't want to be healed.

So when Jesus approaches the man and says, "Do you want to be healed?" it's a realistic question. Maybe the man had grown to like his condition: he gets to lay out in the sun all day by the pool, people have pity on him, they throw money in his cup, and he doesn't have to work. Maybe he's gotten used to it just as we get used to our dysfunctions; we get comfortable with them: *This is the way I am, I don't want things to change, I don't want a radical holiness, I don't want to become like a saint. Holiness is hard, the saints were always suffering for Christ. That's scary. Just let me live with my sins and dysfunctions.*

"Do you want to be healed?" Jesus asks us. The sign that Jesus performs for this man calls to mind the Sacrament of Reconciliation. Note some of the parallels here: first, it's not necessary for the man to enter the water again, which would be like a form of Baptism.

Instead, it's just the word of Jesus that heals. This is like Reconciliation, which the Church Fathers called a "second Baptism," but doesn't require us to enter the water once more. Second, at the end of the account, Jesus says, "See, you are well! Sin no more, that nothing worse befall you," indicating that sin was at the root of this man's illness, and his sins had now been forgiven. Sin isn't usually the direct cause of illness (9:2–3), but sometimes it can be (5:14).

Acting as Jesus, the priest in the confessional forgives our sin and urges us to "go and sin no more." We confess, and he gives us counsel about how to avoid sin. We make our act of contrition, he gives the absolution, and then we walk out upright, healed. The same power of Jesus that healed this paralyzed man is still available to us in the confessional.

The Fourth Sign: The Feeding of the Five Thousand *(John 6:1–15)*

After healing the man in Jerusalem, Jesus returned to the north, to the shores of the Sea of Galilee, where crowds came to hear him teach, and the occasion arose for another "sign." All the people gathered on the mountainside to hear Jesus teaching seemed hungry. Jesus posed a question to the apostle Philip: "How are we to buy bread, so that these people may eat?" Philip answered, "Two hundred denarii would not buy enough bread for each of them to get a little" (Jn 6:5–7).

A denarius is a day's wage at minimum wage levels, so nowadays perhaps sixty dollars, or whatever an entry-level person would make doing manual labor. And then two hundred times sixty dollars equals twelve thousand dollars; we're talking about a lot of money, a lot of people. I've adapted the standard translation to reflect the vividness of the original language.

> One of his disciples, Andrew, Simon Peter's brother, said to him, "There is a lad here who has five barley loaves and two fish; but what are they among so many?" Jesus said, "Make the people lie down." Now there was much grass in the place; so the men lay down, in number about five thousand. Jesus then took the loaves, and when he had given thanks, he distributed them to those who were reclining; so also the fish, *as much as they wanted. And when they were filled up*, he told his disciples, "Gather up the fragments left over, that nothing may be lost." So they gathered them up and filled twelve baskets with fragments from the five barley loaves, *left in abundance by those who ate*. When the people saw the sign which he had done, they said, "This is indeed the prophet who is to come into the world!" (Jn 6:8–14; emphasis added)

With so many people to feed at a picnic, we expect Jesus and the apostles to practice what they call "portion control" in the food service industry: line everyone up, give them all one of those foam plates with the three compartments, and run them through the buffet: a piece of fish, a little roll, maybe two tablespoons of coleslaw, and a six-ounce cup of weak red punch, and out they go! That'll hold 'em till they stumble back home.

But that's not how it is. Just as at the wedding at Cana where we had 180 gallons of fine French Cabernet Sauvignon, here also Jesus overdoes it. It's an all-you-can-eat fish fry for five thousand (or more, with women and kids)! The people come through the line, and the apostles are heaping deep-fried filets and Kaiser rolls till the plates won't hold more. Jesus made "as much as they wanted" until they were "filled up" or "satiated." We've got five thousand people lying on the grass, looking at the sky, and moaning, *Oh man, I can't eat another bite. I don't even want to see another piece of fish for a week. I can't even move. Just let me take a nap.*

Even after feeding upward of five thousand with all-you-can-eat fish and rolls, the disciples go around collecting the leftovers and come up with not twelve little foam boxes but twelve big *baskets* full of fish and bread.

The point is, "I have come that they may have life, and have it *ABUNDANTLY*" (Jn 10:10, emphasis added). Jesus didn't come so that we could lead mediocre lives, hoping to squeak into purgatory by a hair at the end. No, Jesus wants abundance, lives full of joy, full of attraction, full of children, and overflowing with grace and love, inviting other people to come into the party. The Catholic life should be a party, a party of the sacraments. We are a partying people; that's why we "celebrate" Mass and every few days have a "feast" for a saint.

The apostle John has told this miracle in such a way that every early Christian would unmistakably make the connection to the Last Supper recounted in Matthew, Mark, and Luke, where Jesus established the Eucharist. Scholars point out that John uses five Greek words or phrases that also show up in the Last Supper accounts: "take," "loaves," "give thanks," "break," "distribute," and "recline."

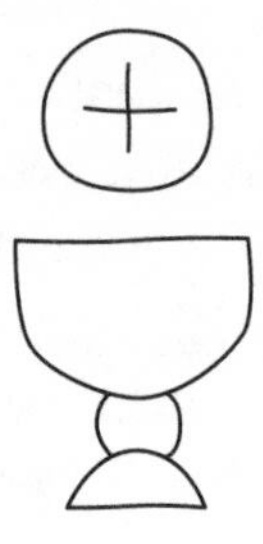

At the Last Supper, Jesus *takes loaves, gives thanks, breaks* them, and *distributes* them to the disciples *reclining* at the table. In John 6, Jesus *takes loaves, gives thanks, distributes* the loaves and fish to the *reclining* crowds, and then has the "*breakings*" ("fragments") picked up.

Imagine the early Christians, meeting in a cave or in a forest in secret for Mass on a Sunday morning, maybe around the year AD 95. And they've just gotten a copy of the apostle John's last memoirs of the life of Jesus. The man in charge—the *episkopos*—begins to read aloud, and he gets to the account of Jesus multiplying the loves. All the Christians gathered hear those words: "take," "loaves," "give thanks," "breakings," and "gave to those who were reclining." What are they going to think? They're going to think this: *Oh, that's just like what we do every week. That's just what we do with the bread and wine of the Eucharist. Jesus started these customs already in his ministry of miracles*. There is absolutely no way the early Christians would *not* have made the connection between this miracle and their Eucharist. John knew they would make the connection and *wanted* them to make the connection.

The following day, the crowds searched Jesus out again because they wanted another free lunch. Jesus preached to them instead, a famous sermon we call the "Bread of Life Discourse." In this sermon, Jesus compares his body to certain kinds of miraculous food from the Old Testament, such as the manna that fell from heaven in the wilderness. The crowds were shocked that he would compare himself to the manna: "The Jews then murmured at him, because he said, 'I am the bread which came down from heaven'" (Jn 6:41). The Greek word being used here is the same word used in the Old Testament about the Israelites traveling through the desert, and they "murmur" against Moses because they don't have enough food (eg. Ex 15:24; 16:2, 7, etc.). John is doing this in a beautiful way so we can hear echoes of the past. It's just as if history is repeating itself. They're murmuring again, and he's talking to them now about a new bread from heaven, a new manna, which is himself. Remember, the manna was supernatural food, and you had to eat it to stay alive. That's important because Jesus is going to stress the need to eat his body, as in this passage: "Truly, truly, I say to you, he who believes has eternal life. I am the bread of life. Your fathers ate the manna in the wilderness, and they died. This is the bread which comes down from heaven, that a man may eat of it and not die. I am the living bread which came down from heaven; if any one eats of this bread, he will live for ever; and the bread which I shall give for the life of the world is my flesh" (Jn 6:47–51). Now he says a couple of times that the one who eats his flesh will not die. Only one kind of food in all the Bible had the power of eternal life: the fruit of the tree of life, which we have not had access to since our first parents were kicked out of the Garden of Eden.

Tree of Life

So remember how we saw that the beginning of this gospel presented a "new creation week." Why is the coming of Jesus like starting creation all over again? Because he gives us the tree of life back. We've been restored to a situation where we can reach out and eat of a food that promises eternal life. And that's like being back in the Garden of Eden.

But remember, the fruit of the tree of life had to be eaten.

New Tree of Life

And as Jesus continues in the Bread of Life Discourse, he becomes very emphatic about the need to eat his flesh and blood. In fact, when talking about his body and blood, he switches from the usual word "to eat" (Greek, *esthio* [es-thee'-o] or *phego* [phago]) to the word for "chew" or "munch" (Greek, *trogo* [tro'-go]).

> So Jesus said to them, "Truly, truly, I say to you, unless you eat the flesh of the Son of man and drink his blood, you have no life in you; he who *munches* my flesh and drinks my blood has eternal life, and I will raise him up at the last day. For my flesh is food indeed, and my blood is drink indeed. He who *munches* my flesh and drinks my blood abides in me, and I in him. As the living Father sent me, and I live because of the Father, so he who *munches* me will live because of me. This is the bread which came down from heaven, not such as the fathers ate and died; he who eats this bread will live for ever." (Jn 6:53–58)

So it's very graphic: crunching up Jesus' body with your teeth! Jesus doesn't get more symbolic as his sermon moves along. Instead, he begins with abstract things and gets more *physical* and *concrete* as the sermon progresses.

I was a Protestant pastor for years, and if anyone had asked me what John 6 meant, I would have told them, "Well, it's all symbolic. 'Eating me' means having faith in me." The problem with that interpretation is that in the Old Testament, the symbolic meaning of "eating me" is always hostile. Eating another person is used as a metaphor for military defeat and devastating somebody's land or destroying their country. It always has negative connotations and is not a phrase that Jesus would have used with his fellow Jews to speak about something positive like having faith. No, it's the plain sense of "eating my flesh" that Jesus is after.

Some say Jesus cannot mean this literally because "drinking blood" was forbidden in the Old Testament. That's true: the Old Testament forbade drinking animal blood because "the life is its blood" (Lv 17:14), and God did not want the

Israelites to share in animal life. However, *divine life* is in the veins of Jesus, and God *does* want us to share in divine life. So the same principle—"the life is its blood"—is the reason animal blood is forbidden but Jesus' blood is commanded: "Unless you . . . drink his *blood*, you have no *life* in you" (Jn 6:53, emphasis added). The very fact that Jesus brings up the topic of drinking blood shows that he is speaking about the Eucharist. If you go back and read through Jesus' discourse here, you'll see that abruptly at verse 53 he brings in the idea of "drinking blood," whereas up to this point the entire discussion had just been about bread. Why introduce this idea of blood drinking? Where is he going with this? It's clear where he's going: the Eucharist.

Others say Jesus cannot actually be commanding us to eat his flesh and blood because in verse 63 he says, "It is the spirit that gives life, the flesh is of no avail." That's a clever argument, but note that Jesus says "*the* flesh" is of no avail, not "*my* flesh" is of no avail.

"The flesh" is a term that both St. John and St. Paul use to describe fallen human nature without God's help. We read in John 8:15, "You judge according to *the flesh*, I judge no one" (emphasis added). But "the flesh" is different than "my flesh." Jesus says, "The bread which I shall give for the life of the world is *my flesh*" (Jn 6:51, emphasis added). Who has the courage to walk up to Jesus and tell him, *Sorry, Jesus, but giving your flesh for the life of the world is wasted effort; your flesh is of no avail*? Or again, John 1:14 says, "The Word became *flesh* and dwelt among us" (emphasis added). Does that mean that Christmas was pointless because "the flesh" is of no avail? Of course not.

Human nature (the flesh) has no power in itself. But *Jesus' flesh*, which he has taken on and united to his divine person, has great power. This is the flesh that people touch and they get healed. This is the flesh that we touch in the sacraments, and it heals us from our sins and leads us to holiness.

Sadly, many, many Christians read John 6 today and can't see the obvious connection between this chapter and the Eucharist. But none of the first Christians would have missed the point. From historical records, we know that the most distinctive practice of early Christians was that they gathered on the first day of the week and reenacted the Last Supper, repeating Jesus' words over the bread and wine: "This is my body. This is my blood." They gathered early while it was still dark in secret places for fear of the Roman authorities. There is *no way* that they would have read Jesus' words, "unless you eat the flesh of the son of man and drink his blood, you have no life in you," and not seen the connection with the ritual they performed every Sunday morning. And the earliest pastors of the Church taught that Jesus meant exactly what he said in this passage. For example, St. Ignatius, pastor of the Church in Antioch, wrote the following words while traveling to his martyrdom about AD 106, ten years after the death of the apostle John: "Now note well those who hold heretical opinions about the grace of Jesus Christ. . . . They abstain from Eucharist and prayer, because they refuse to acknowledge that *the Eucharist is the flesh of our savior Jesus Christ*, which suffered for our sins and which the Father by his goodness raised up."[3] I was thirty years old when I first read this passage, and it converted me to the Catholic Church.

I had two graduate degrees in theology under my belt and had been a pastor for four years. For all that, I had never read the earliest Church Fathers in my life. When I read Ignatius of Antioch, it finally dawned on me that the earliest Christians had believed in the real presence of Jesus in the Eucharist, and only later did Protestants such as myself give up on this basic teaching. It also dawned on me that the real presence was the literal teaching of the New Testament. How could I, a Bible-believing Christian, reject the plain teaching of the New Testament and the faith of the earliest Christians?

To sum up, the fourth sign, the feeding of the five thousand, clearly points to the Sacrament of the Eucharist.

The Fifth Sign: The Healing of the Man Born Blind *(John 9)*

The fifth sign is the healing of the man born blind in John 9. The events of John 7–9, including this miracle, take place during or after the Jewish Feast of Tabernacles. It would be helpful to know a little bit about the Feast of Tabernacles in order to fully appreciate the healing of the man born blind.

The Jewish Feast of Tabernacles celebrated God's dwelling with the people of Israel in various holy sanctuaries through history—past, present, and future: the Tabernacle in the wilderness built by Moses; the present Temple built in Jerusalem; and the miraculous future temple that the Messiah would build.

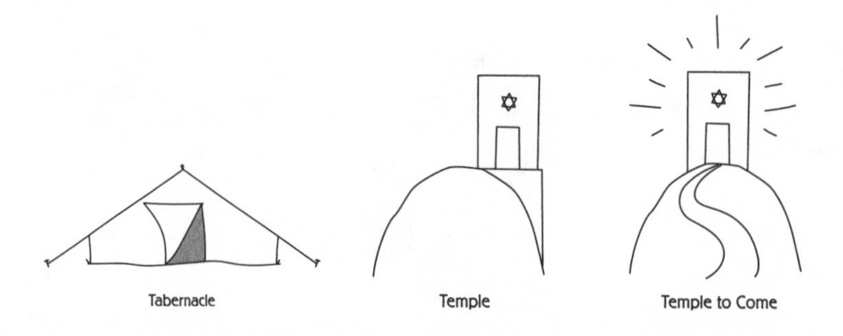

Various Old Testament prophecies said that the Temple to come would be a source of light and water for the whole nation (Ez 47:1–12; Jl 3:18; Zec 14:6–8). So the Jews put on light and water ceremonies during the weeklong Feast of Tabernacles. For a week, they lighted huge candelabras (menorahs) in the Temple courts that were so big they had to be lit by young priests climbing up ladders. Then, during the night, the priests would come with torches and perform fire dances. It was so bright that people said, "There is no shadow in Jerusalem during the Feast of Tabernacles." This symbolized that the Temple was—or at least would be—the source of light for the whole world.

At the last day of the Feast of Tabernacles, the priests would go down to the Pool of Siloam—the main source of water for the city of Jerusalem—and fill a golden pitcher with water. Then they would carry it up to the Temple and pour it out on the steps of the altar, making a little artificial stream flowing from the center of the Temple. This was to act out the prophecies that in the future, a stream of fresh water would flow out of the Temple bringing life to the land (Ez 47:1–12).

In the course of John 7–9, Jesus speaks of himself as both light and water. In John 7, on the last day of the Feast of Tabernacles, Jesus stands up on the very day when they made the artificial stream coming from the Temple, and says, "If any one thirst, let him come to me, and let him drink who believes in me. As the scripture has said, 'Out of his heart shall flow rivers of living water'" (Jn 7:37–38).[4] It's not the stone Temple but Jesus himself who is the source of the life-giving stream of God. Jesus' body is the new Temple, and at his crucifixion, we will see a stream of blood and water flowing from his temple-body.

Jesus, the Temple to Come

Again, in John 8, Jesus proclaims, "I am the light of the world; he who follows me will not walk in darkness, but will have the light of life" (v. 12). Again, it's not the stone Temple but Jesus himself who will illuminate the whole world.

When we get to John 9, Jesus performs a miracle, a "sign," where he uses *water* to bring *light* to a man who was born blind. Jesus becomes the miraculous new Temple for this poor man. Here's the account:

> As he passed by, he saw a man blind from his birth. And his disciples asked him, "Rabbi, who sinned, this man or his parents, that he was born blind?" Jesus answered, "It was not that this man sinned, or his parents, but that the works of God might be made manifest in him. We must work the works of him who sent me, while it is day; night comes, when no one can work. As long as I am in the world, I am the light of the world." As he said this, he spat on the ground and made clay of the spittle and anointed the man's eyes with the clay, saying to him, "Go, wash in the pool of Silo'am" (which means Sent). So he went and washed and came back seeing. The neighbors and those who had seen him before as a beggar, said, "Is not this the man who used to sit and beg?" Some said, "It is he"; others said, "No, but he is like him." He said,

> "I am the man." They said to him, "Then how were your eyes opened?" He answered, "The man called Jesus made clay and anointed my eyes and said to me, 'Go to Silo'am and wash'; so I went and washed and received my sight." They said to him, "Where is he?" He said, "I do not know." (Jn 9:1–12)

Now this whole sign is a beautiful catechesis on the Sacrament of Baptism. As with this man, each one of us is born in the darkness of original sin. It wasn't this man's fault that he was blind; it was something he was born with, but he still needed healing. That's parallel to original sin. Original sin is a lack of God's life in our soul, lost by Adam and Eve. In other words, our first parents lost the Holy Spirit, and we only get it back through Baptism.

Everyone is curious why Jesus bothers to spit and make mud. Apparently, the Jews of Jesus' day had a certain way of imagining how God created the first man. Genesis says, "The LORD God formed man of dust from the ground" (2:7), but dust doesn't naturally stick together, does it? You need a little moisture. So where are you going to get that moisture? Jewish tradition (reflected in the Dead Sea Scrolls) thought of God spitting on the dust to make clay and forming the body of a man.[5]

Jesus spitting and making clay for this man is a powerful symbol. Jesus is reenacting the creation of Adam. New creation has been a theme from the first verse of this gospel. Here again, Jesus re-creates this man. Just as God's first creative act was the creation of light, so Jesus pours light into this man's world by opening his eyes.

Baptism is a re-creation. The classic form of Baptism is to be plunged under the water and pulled back out. And that's like the earth as a whole, which began under water (Gn 1:2) and then emerged as dry land through the power of God's "wind" or "Spirit."

Later, Noah and his family experienced a "new creation" when they went through the waters of the flood and then saw the dry land emerge once more when God sent out his "Spirit."

Likewise, the Israelites were re-created when they plunged into the Red Sea and came back out as a new people the other side. A generation later, their children would plunge into the Jordan and emerge as a new people on the other side in the Promised Land.

All these events—the creation, the flood, crossing the red sea, and crossing the Jordan—are applied to you when you're baptized. The Sacrament makes you a part of the story.

Many children's stories and movies have been developed around the idea of a magic book—a book that sucks you into its narrative when you begin reading it. The Bible is like the ultimate "magic book," if you will—better, it is the miraculous book. And the way that we become part of the story line is by receiving the sacraments—the sacraments make the biblical story become *our personal* story.

It's not just the mud that heals the man's eyes. Jesus sends him to wash in the Pool of Siloam, and that's very significant. The Pool of Siloam was where the priests took the water to pour on the altar on the last day of the Feast of Tabernacles. The Pool of Siloam caught the waters of the Gihon—the one constantly flowing spring that provided water for the city of Jerusalem. The Gihon was named after one of the rivers that flowed out of the Garden of Eden. In Jewish tradition, it was virtually a sacred river flowing with the waters of creation. It passed through a half-mile tunnel carved by King Hezekiah and out into the Pool of Siloam, which Herod had rebuilt into a beautiful, paved, Olympic-sized pool where all the people of Jerusalem could get water to drink or wash.

The water of Siloam was symbolically the water of Eden. And the name "Siloam" means "sent," which has two senses with respect to Baptism. First of all, to be baptized is to wash in Jesus, who is the "Sent One," the one sent by the Father into the world. Second, when we wash in Baptism, we ourselves are sent. Everybody who is baptized is on a mission. God commissions every one of us to share with others the Good News about Jesus.

When the man comes back from washing, he can see! His old neighbors don't know what to make of it. They argue; some say he's the same man, but others say he's someone else who just looks like the old blind man who used to hang around there. The man's own response is ambiguous: "I am" he says. Most English translations have him saying "I am the man," but the original language of the gospel just reads, "I am." His old acquaintances must have been confused: *You are who? The same guy or a different guy that just looks the same?* Yes! the man probably would have replied.

You see, in a sense he is both. Yes, he's the same guy who used to sit here and beg. On the other hand, he is a completely new creation, a new man who just *resembles* the old man who used to be here. And that's a parallel with Baptism because after our Baptism we both *are* and *are not* the same person that entered the baptistery.

In my case, after my Baptism I was, in one sense, still John Bergsma, fifth child of Herbert and Luella Bergsma. But in another sense, I was a completely new creation, a creature changed in his very nature by the reception of the Holy Spirit. I was a new person who just *looked like* the child who existed before the waters of Baptism were poured on me. As St. Paul says, "If any one is in Christ, he is a new creation" (2 Cor 5:17).

This is also the only place in the Gospel of John where anyone except Jesus uses the phrase "I am." This is the name of God that the Lord revealed to Moses in Exodus 3:14: "Say this to the people of Israel, 'I AM has sent me to you.'" After Baptism, we can truly say "I am" for the first time because now we share in the divine nature and have the Spirit of the great "I AM." We *truly* begin to exist for the first time because only *God's* life is *true* life!

This whole miracle story in John 9 is a beautiful, beautiful catechesis on the Sacrament of Baptism, and that's why we read it in the lectionary each year on the Fourth Sunday (Laetare Sunday) of Lent as catechumens are preparing for Baptism.

The Sixth Sign: The Raising of Lazarus from the Dead *(John 11)*

Some time after the healing of the man born blind, Jesus was called back to Bethany, on the outskirts of Jerusalem, to attend to his friend Lazarus:

> Now a certain man was ill, Laz'arus of Bethany, the village of Mary and her sister Martha. It was Mary who anointed the Lord with ointment and wiped his feet with her hair, whose brother Laz'arus was ill. So the sisters sent to him, saying, "Lord, he whom you love is ill." But when Jesus heard it he said, "This illness is not unto death; it is for the glory of God, so that the Son of God may be glorified by means of it."

> Now Jesus loved Martha and her sister and Laz'arus. So when he heard that he was ill, he stayed two days longer in the place where he was. (Jn 11:1–6)

That's surprising. We expect to read, *He heard that he was ill, so he departed immediately to attend to him.* But instead we get, "He stayed two days longer." But there's a reason Jesus does this. He plans his return to Bethany so that Lazarus will have been dead four days by the time he gets there. That is important because the Jews believed that for the first three days after death, your soul hung around the body and you were just "mostly dead." After three days you were "all dead."

Those who've seen the classic movie *The Princess Bride* know that "there's a big difference between 'mostly dead' and 'all dead,'" in the words of Miracle Max, the hilarious healer played by Billy Crystal. But the point in John 11 is that by the time Jesus arrives, Lazarus is certainly "all dead." There was no hope of resuscitation. "Then Jesus, deeply moved again, came to the tomb; it was a cave, and a stone lay upon it. Jesus said, 'Take away the stone.' Martha, the sister of the dead man, said to him, 'Lord, by this time there will be an odor, for he has been dead four days'" (Jn 11:38–39). You have to love Martha. She's one of these obsessive housekeepers who is always reminding people to put the mayonnaise back in the fridge right away and be sure to use hand sanitizer after you blow your nose. In this case, she doesn't hesitate to remind the Savior of Israel, the Son of David, the Son of God, the rabbi and miracle worker, *There's going to be a bad smell if you open the tomb.* Of course! Jesus must have forgotten about that. "Jesus said to her, 'Did I not tell you that if you would believe you would see the glory of God?' So they took away the stone. And Jesus . . . cried with a loud voice, 'Laz'arus, come out.' The dead man came out, his hands and feet bound with bandages, and his face wrapped with a cloth" (Jn 11:40–41, 43–44).

Lazarus was almost mummified, so when he comes walking out of the tomb, it's like a freaky scene from a zombie movie. "Jesus said to them, 'Unbind him, and let him go'" (Jn 11:44).

We've seen so far that the signs in John's gospel have parallels and elements in common with the sacraments, and this is no exception. The raising of Lazarus resembles the Sacrament of Confession because you enter the confessional in a state of spiritual death (if you've committed a mortal sin), then you hear the word of the priest speaking on behalf of Christ, and you exit the confessional spiritually "raised from the dead."

Reginald Garrigou-Lagrange, a great theologian and one of St. John Paul II's teachers, wrote about this: "Even the raising of the dead to life, the miracle by which a corpse is reanimated with its natural life, is almost nothing in comparison with the resurrection of a soul, which has been lying spiritually dead in sin and has now been raised to the essentially supernatural life of grace."[6] But we also note some parallels from the raising of Lazarus to the Sacrament of Confirmation. This sign follows right after the "Baptism" imagery in John 9. And there are many similarities between these two signs: in both cases, the man is moved from darkness to light, the darkness of the tomb to the light of the outside—moved from a state of uncreation or death to a state of life. Baptism and Confirmation are closely linked; so are the "signs" in John 9 and 11.

Another strong and important connection that we can draw between Confirmation and the raising of Lazarus is the gift of an extra grace to witness powerfully for Christ, even in the face of opposition. Sometimes Confirmation is called the "spiritual warfare" sacrament because it strengthens us for courageous spiritual combat while witnessing to Christ.

That's exactly what Lazarus does following this sign: "When the great crowd of the Jews learned that he was there, they came, not only on account of Jesus but also to see Laz'arus, whom he had raised from the dead. So the chief priests planned to put Laz'arus also to death, because on account of him many of the Jews were going away and believing in Jesus" (Jn 12:9–11). Lazarus witnesses to Jesus so powerfully that he now shares with Jesus the threat of persecution and death. There's a bit of dark humor in this, too: Isn't it a little bit comical that the chief priests are plotting to kill this man that rose from the dead? *Hey, you! Get back in the grave! Can't you see you're causing a disturbance?* If his first death didn't get rid of him, why do they think killing him a second time will work?

As with the other signs, the raising of Lazarus points strongly to Jesus' divinity. In fact, Lazarus's resurrection connects specifically to a famous prophecy of Ezekiel, a prophecy he uttered after his famous vision of a valley of dry bones coming back to life as an enormous army: "Thus says the Lord GOD: Behold, I will open your graves, and raise you from your graves, O my people; and I will bring you home into the land of Israel. And you shall know that I am the LORD, when I open your graves, and raise you from your graves, O my people" (Ez 37:12–13). Appropriately, this is the first reading on the Fifth Sunday of Lent, when we read John 11 as the gospel. Note the statement, "You shall know that I am the LORD, when I . . . raise you from your graves." In this way, we *know that Jesus is the Lord, the God of Israel,* when he opens Lazarus's grave and raises him to life. That's divine power for all to see.

The Seventh Sign: The Death and Resurrection of Jesus *(John 19–20)*

So far we've seen six signs in the Gospel of John and observed connections with Matrimony, Confession, Anointing of the Sick, Eucharist, Baptism, and Confirmation. The final, seventh sign, the death and resurrection, relates to all the sacraments. Every sacrament is rooted in Jesus' death and resurrection. Baptism is a sharing in Jesus' dying and rising. In Matrimony, we give our body to our spouse as Jesus gave his body on the cross. The Eucharist makes present once more the sacrifice of Christ's crucified body. We could go on. However, since none of the previous signs offered a connection to Holy Orders, as we look at Jesus' death and resurrection, we will draw the connecting lines to this Sacrament.

Let's begin in John 19:17–24:

> So they took Jesus, and he went out, bearing his own cross, to the place called the place of a skull, which is called in Hebrew Gol'gotha. There they crucified him, and with him two others, one on either side, and Jesus between them. . . .
>
> When the soldiers had crucified Jesus they took his garments and made four parts, one for each soldier; also his tunic. But the tunic was without seam, woven from top to bottom; so they said to one another, "Let us not tear it, but cast lots for it to see whose it shall be." This was to fulfill the scripture,
>
> "They parted my garments among them,
> and for my clothing they cast lots."

Why does John bother to mention that Jesus' tunic was seamless? At first, that seems to be a meaningless, "throwaway" detail. But actually it's not. Outside of the Gospel of John, there's only one seamless garment that we know about from ancient literature. The Jewish historian Josephus, whose lifetime overlapped with the apostle Paul, records the following about the way the Jewish high priest used to be dressed: "The high priest is indeed adorned with a vestment of blue color. This is a long robe reaching to his feet. . . . Now this vestment was *not composed of two pieces, nor was it sewed together upon the shoulders and the sides, but it was one long vestment*, so woven as to have an opening for the neck."[7]

The point is, Jesus was wearing a garment appropriate for the high priest. When Jesus goes to the cross, this is a priestly act. Jesus is both priest and sacrifice when he goes to the cross. This is not the only connection with priesthood that we see during Jesus' passion. As we saw, the tunic was not torn, and they cast lots for it. Surprisingly, "it just so happens" that the Law of Moses forbade the high priest from ever tearing his clothes (Lv 21:10). (Incidentally, the high priest who condemned Jesus broke this law [Mk 14:63].)

After our Lord has died and his body is taken down from the cross, Joseph of Arimathea and Nicodemus bring ointment and the finest spices, included liquid myrrh, and they spread one hundred pounds of it, which is an enormous amount of extremely expensive perfume, all over the body of Jesus. Imagine some fine fragrance for men, some imported *eau de toilette pour homme* that costs sixty dollars for 1.7 ounces at the duty-free shop in the airport. Now imagine a twelve-gallon keg of that cologne poured all over Jesus' body, and you get some idea of the expense and extravagance they lavished on Jesus.

That one hundred pounds of ointment that they spread over his body is just like the twelve baskets full of bread and fish; it's just like the 180 gallons of wine. It's abundance. It's showing Jesus is everything big, and his going to the Cross is a priestly act; he is being anointed with perfumed oil that befits a high priest because the Law of Moses (Ex 30:22–33) insisted that the high priest be anointed with an oil of the finest of spices, including myrrh, for his ordination.

After being taken down from the cross, Joseph of Arimathea and Nicodemus wrapped Jesus' body in linen, the only cloth appropriate for the clothing of the high priest. As Moses commanded, "He shall put on the holy linen coat, and shall have the linen breeches on his body, be girded with the linen girdle, and wear the linen turban; these are the holy garments" (Lv 16:4).

"Now in the place where he was crucified there was a garden, and in the garden a new tomb where no one had ever been laid. So because of the Jewish day of Preparation, as the tomb was close at hand, they laid Jesus there" (Jn 19:41–42). Why does John point out that it was a tomb "where no one had ever been laid"?

It's because the tomb of Jesus, which receives his body, is an image of the bride of Christ, the Church. And the Church is a virgin bride. Likewise, the high priest was commanded to take a virgin bride: "The priest who is chief among his brethren . . . shall take a wife in her virginity" (Lv 21:10, 13).

So throughout the account of Jesus' passion, death, and burial, there are signs of Jesus' high priestly role. We'll see how Jesus transfers his priestly role to the apostles in a moment.

Right now, I want to call attention to what I think is one of the most powerful verses in scripture, John 19:34–35: "But one of the soldiers pierced his side with a spear, and at once there came out blood and water. He who saw it has borne witness—his testimony is true, and he knows that he tells the truth—that you also may believe." So why is the flow from the side of Christ so important that the apostle John not only describes it but also stops the narration to insist that he saw it himself and testifies that it really happened? John does so because it's so full of symbolism.

First of all, any good Jew who made pilgrimages up to Jerusalem would understand the meaning of the flow of blood and water. During the three great annual Jewish feasts, Jerusalem would swell with hundreds of thousands, or even millions, of pilgrims. During Passover, the Temple priests sacrificed so many lambs for the pilgrims that they built a plumbing system for the Temple that carried the blood out from under the altar, carried it down under the Temple Mount, and expelled it out the side of the Temple Mount, where it flowed down the hill and down into the valley below, which was called the Kidron. This was the valley where Jesus would cross when going out to the Mount of Olives. There the blood flowing down from the side of the Temple Mount would mix with the waters of the Kidron brook, and it would continue to flow down toward one of the main entrance gates of Jerusalem.

So when you approached Jerusalem during festival time, depending on which direction you were coming from, you had to cross a stream of bloody water coming from the Temple. Recall what Jesus said in John 2: "'*Destroy this temple, and in three days I will raise it up*' . . . *he spoke of the temple of his body*" (vv. 19, 21; emphasis added).

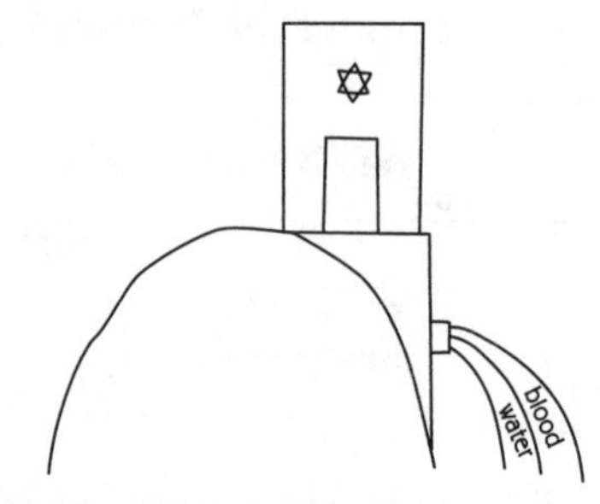

Blood and Water from the Temple

The flow of blood and water pouring out of his side marks his body as the new temple.

The blood and water are also the symbolism of birth. Blood and water come forth from the womb when a child is born. But there is also a parallel to the "birth" of the first woman. Our first father, Adam, had to go into a deep sleep, have his side cut open, and his flesh taken out; from the open wound of his side the first woman, his bride, Eve, was made. In the same way, Jesus is the second Adam. His side is opened when he falls into the sleep of death, and from his side is born his bride, the Church.

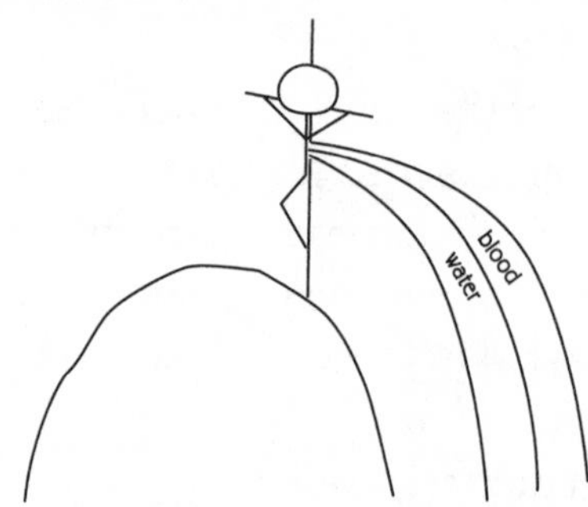

Furthermore, the blood and water symbolize the sacraments. To this point in the Gospel of John, whenever "water" has been mentioned, it has been connected to Baptism, and "blood," when it's been mentioned, has pointed forward to the Eucharist. The blood and water from the side of Christ is the stream of the sacraments: baptismal water and eucharistic blood. But in order to have Baptism and Eucharist, you have to have Holy Orders and the other sacraments as well.

Five hundred years before, Ezekiel had famously prophesied that in the last day there would be a new temple and from that temple would flow a life-giving river (Ez 47). Now we're seeing at the Cross the fulfillment of what Ezekiel foresaw: a life-giving river coming forth from the temple-body of Jesus.

The life-giving river that flows from the body of Christ is ultimately the Holy Spirit. But how does the Holy Spirit come to us? The Spirit comes to us first and foremost through the sacraments: Baptism, Eucharist, and the others. The sacraments give birth to the Church, the bride of Christ. Each sacrament is rooted in Christ's sacrificial death and flows out from the Cross.

Jesus, the Temple to Come

And since we have had no sign so far that has pointed directly to Holy Orders, that's the one we want to pursue at this point. To see the connection, we need to fast-forward to the evening of the first Easter:

> On the evening of that day, the first day of the week, the doors being shut where the disciples were, for fear of the Jews, Jesus came and stood among them and said to them, "Peace be with you." When he had said this, he showed them his hands and his side. Then the disciples were glad when they saw the Lord. Jesus said to them again, "Peace be with you. As the Father has sent me, even so I send you." And when he had said this, he breathed on them, and said to them, "Receive the Holy Spirit. If you forgive the sins of any, they are forgiven; if you retain the sins of any, they are retained." (Jn 20:19–23)

There is a strong connection between the Resurrection and the Sacrament of Holy Orders. Almost the first thing the risen Lord says to the apostles is, "As the Father has sent me, even so I send you." And that's the fundamental nature of Holy Orders. Men who receive Holy Orders undertake this *mission* of Jesus because the word *mission* means "sending."

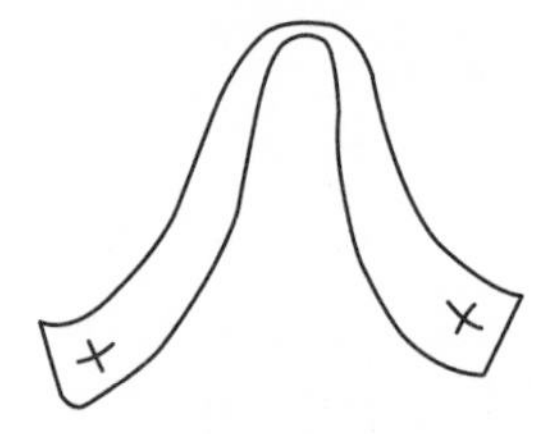

Jesus sent the apostles, the apostles sent the first bishops, the first bishops sent the second generation of bishops, the second generation of bishops sent the next generation, and so on. And each bishop sends his priests on his behalf, and together they send the deacons, who cooperate with them. So it's all one sending, one mission from God the Father.

As part of this mission, Jesus grants the apostles the power to forgive sin: "If you forgive the sins of any, they are forgiven; if you retain the sins of any, they are retained" (Jn 20:23). So they're going to have the power to make decisions about whether to forgive people's sins. This is what the priest does in the confessional. And it's important to note that in the Old Testament, decisions about sins and the rituals involved in the forgiveness of sins were the duty of the priests. For example, "When a man is guilty in any of these, he shall confess the sin he has committed . . . and the priest shall make atonement for him for the sin which he has committed, and he shall be forgiven" (Lv 5:5, 10). Where did you go if you wanted your sins forgiven in the Old Testament? Not to the prophet. Not to the king. You went to the priest; he would lead you through the process to receive forgiveness from God.

So after his death and resurrection, this is the point: Jesus communicates his own priestly authority to the apostles. Up to this point, it's been Jesus who's been forgiving sins (Mt 9:2; Lk 7:48; Jn 5:14). Now he gives that same power to the apostles themselves.

If somebody wants to say this power to retain or to forgive sin stopped with the apostles, my first response would be to say that's not what the Church believed, and we can go back to the very earliest documents, back to things written ten years after the death of the apostle John, and already see the idea that the ministry of the apostles was continued by the bishops, priests, and deacons.[8]

My second response is that if this power to forgive sins didn't continue to other generations, then there is no point in recording the story (Jn 20:30). John is writing the gospel at the end of his life, and he is the last surviving apostle. Why bother recording the story if the power to forgive and retain was about to die with him? Is it there just to rub it in the nose of the next generation of Christians that they were stuck in their sins and no longer had anyone with authority to forgive or retain?

What would be the point? John didn't write these things without reason. He wrote them so that Christians of his own generation and of future generations would see that the powers of the apostles continued in the ministry of bishops, priests, deacons, that is, those who had received Holy Orders.

Summing Up the Gospel of John

Let's summarize. We've gone over the seven signs, and we've connected them with seven sacraments.

We saw that the wedding at Cana reminds us of Matrimony. The healing of the official's son reminds us of Anointing of the Sick. The healing of the paralytic makes us think of Confession. The feeding of the five thousand reminds us of the Eucharist; the healing of the blind man brings Baptism to mind. The raising of Lazarus connects with Confirmation, and we drew a line between the Resurrection and Holy Orders. Keep in mind this is no perfect one-to-one correspondence. Certain signs point to more than one sacrament: the wedding at Cana, for example, is also strongly eucharistic, and all the sacraments could be connected with the Passion and Resurrection. But just for the sake of simplicity and learning, we are linking the seven signs and sacraments in this order.

And it's good to end with Holy Orders because it's through Holy Orders that the sacraments come to us. Each of us have a parish priest. Maybe your parish priest is young, dynamic, and exciting, or maybe he's old, slow, and quiet. It doesn't matter what Father Jim or Monsignor Joe is like; the important thing about them is that they had hands laid on them by guys who in turn had hands laid on themselves and so on, all the way back to the apostles—all the way back to Jesus breathing, "Receive the Holy Spirit. If you forgive the sins of any, they are forgiven; if you retain the sins of any, they are retained" (Jn 20:22–23). This is historical reality. There is a chain of touch from your parish priest back to Jesus over two thousand years. Those outside the Catholic Church do not have this chain of touch.

And so Father Jim might be pretty heavy and Monsignor Joe might be skinny, but they've had the hands laid on them. And it's through their hands, their voice, and their ministry that we're connected all the way back to the signs that Jesus performed in the presence of his apostles. Through their ministry, we come in contact not just with a *memory* of Jesus but also with the *presence* of Jesus.

This helps explain a puzzling passage in the Gospel of John. For five chapters in the middle of the gospel (Jn 13–17), Jesus teaches the disciples in the Upper Room during the Last Supper. We call it the "Last Supper Discourse." Jesus teaches about love, joy, peace, the Holy Spirit, the unity of the Father and the Son, the unity of believers with God, and other topics. Partway into the discourse, Jesus says, "Truly, truly, I say to you, he who believes in me will also do the works that I do; and greater works than these will he do, because I go to the Father" (Jn 14:12). For most of my life I read that line and thought, *What miracles could they possibly perform that would be greater than the miracles that Jesus did?*

But perhaps Jesus isn't talking about *physical* miracles. After all, when we read John closely, we see that Jesus rebukes those who will get fixated on the physical: "You seek me, not because you saw signs, but because you ate your fill of the loaves" (Jn 6:26). "Unless you see signs and wonders you will not believe" (Jn 4:48). From a human perspective, we're impressed with a physical resurrection from the dead; from God's perspective, forgiveness of mortal sin is more impressive. As Father Lagrange said, "Even the raising of the dead to life . . . is almost nothing in comparison with the resurrection of a soul" in the confessional.[9] The sacraments, then, are at least one kind of "greater work" that the apostles and their successors will perform.

What About the Kingdom?

We've been tracing the theme of the kingdom through the New Testament, but in John we've mostly talked about the sacraments. Doesn't John's gospel say anything about the kingdom? It certainly does. When Jesus is teaching Nicodemus, he asserts, "Unless one is born anew, he cannot see the kingdom of God," and "unless one is born of water and the Spirit, he cannot enter the kingdom of God" (Jn 3:3, 5). So Baptism is our necessary entrance into the kingdom, and we can broaden the concept out to include all the sacraments: the sacraments are the necessary way and the primary way that we enter and participate in the kingdom.

Jesus' kingdom is not "of this world" or "from the world," as Jesus explains to Pilate (Jn 18:36–37). But it is in this world because you and I—members of his body and his kingdom—are still in this world. The Gospel of John shows us the perfection of the kingdom, which is when we all become one in God. At the end of the Last Supper he prays,

> I do not pray for these [apostles] only, but also for those who believe in me through their word, that they may all be one; even as thou, Father, art in me, and I in thee, that they also may be in us, so that the world may believe that thou hast sent me. The glory which thou hast given me I have given to them, that they may be one even as we are one, I in

> them and thou in me, that they may become perfectly one, so that the world may know that thou hast sent me and hast loved them even as thou hast loved me. (Jn 17:20–23)

This is the goal of the kingdom of God and also the goal of all the covenants: that we become united to God in perfect oneness. When we get to heaven, we will not sit around talking about kingdom and covenant very much because they will have served their purpose. Instead, we will simply enjoy unity with God and each other for eternity.

In the meantime, the sacraments move us in that direction by *symbolizing* our unity with Christ and *making real* our unity with Christ. So the Eucharist, for example, *symbolizes* the union of our body with Christ's body through the eating of the eucharistic host and also *makes real* our union with him in body and blood, soul and divinity. Those in Holy Orders are royal officers, appointed to provide food for the King's table (1 Kgs 4:7), where we eat as children of the King (2 Sm 9:11; Lk 22:29–30). This eucharistic food makes real our union with God. The goal of the kingdom is to lead us to the perfection of being "*perfectly one*."

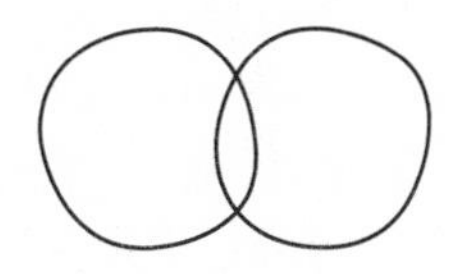

Seven

The Book of Revelation: The Victory of the Kingdom

Congratulations! You are nearing the end of our tour of the New Testament as we take a look at the famous last book of the Bible, Revelation. This book is one of the most sensational in scripture. Believers have become fascinated or even obsessed with the imagery and prophecies of the book and have given it thousands of different interpretations. The full name of the book is The Revelation to John or The Apocalypse of John. The word "revelation" is Latin and "apocalypse" is Greek, but they mean exactly the same thing: "to reveal," "to uncover," or "to remove a veil." The Book of Revelation does "reveal" God's plans for the end of history, but it also "removes the veil" from the bride of Christ at the end of the book, showing her in all her beauty. So Revelation is romantic—it's a wedding book, like the Song of Songs.

Who was the author of Revelation? Early and fairly strong tradition tells us the apostle John wrote Revelation.

John

Yet the Gospel of John and Revelation are written in quite different styles: the Gospel of John has a simple elegance and is grammatically correct. The Book of Revelation is very rough and has some ungrammatical phrases. Many think the same person could not have written them both. However, we all know that a person's writing style changes over his or her lifetime and varies also with circumstances, mood, and audience. We can cite many examples of different styles from the same author in both modern and ancient times. Mark Twain's books can be very different from each other, and the same is true of Plato. St. John Paul II wrote a play ("The Jeweler's Shop") that is almost nothing like his encyclicals (e.g., *Fides et Ratio*).

On the other hand, there are also a number of ideas, motifs, and themes that are only found in John's writings and Revelation. The most obvious are Jesus being called the "Lamb of God" (Jn 1:29; Rv 5:6, etc.) and the "Word of God" (Jn 1:1; Rv 19:13), but there are a great many more examples that are less obvious but still very significant. These connections seem to indicate that, even if the authors weren't the same, they were connected to each other in some way.

My own view is that John wrote Revelation earlier in his life, in the AD 60s, and his gospel near the end of his life, in the AD 90s, with some assistance.[1] Thirty years and many differences in circumstances account for the difference in style. But peace to all who may take a different view.

The Book of Revelation is a record of visions that St. John experienced on the island of Patmos, in the Aegean Sea just off the coast of Ephesus. He was exiled there, perhaps during the persecution of Christians that broke out under Nero in the 60s. This was the persecution in which Peter and Paul died.

John begins by describing how Jesus came to him in a vision. He was in prayer on the Lord's Day (Sunday) when Jesus appeared to him in great glory (Rv 1:10–16). Jesus dictates to John seven letters to seven churches in Asia Minor (modern-day Turkey; Rv 2–3). After this, John is taken up into heaven where he witnesses the heavenly liturgy or "mass as it is in heaven" (Rv 4–5). The heavenly worship leads into three sets of liturgical rituals in heaven that unleash plagues on earth:

- The breaking of seven seals (Rv 6–7),
- The blowing of seven trumpets (Rv 8–11), and
- The pouring out of seven sacred bowls (Rv 15–16).

Between the trumpets and bowls, John sees a series of seven heavenly signs (Rv 12–14). When the seventh bowl is poured out, destruction falls on a "great city" identified as a "harlot" and "Babylon" (Rv 17–19). A vision of the binding of Satan and the final judgment intervenes (Rv 20), and then the "bride of the lamb"—which turns out to be a heavenly city of Jerusalem—descends from heaven to replace the harlot city of Babylon (21–22). Final words of blessing from John the visionary and Jesus himself conclude the book (22).

Our discussion of the Book of Revelation can be outlined as follows:

I. Introduction of John and his vision (Rv 1)

II. Messages to the seven churches (Rv 2–3)

III. The vision of heavenly Worship (Rv 4–5)

A. The seven seals (Rv 6–8:5)

B. The seven trumpets (Rv 8:6–11:19)

1. The seven signs (Rv 12–14)

C. The seven bowls (Rv 15–16)

D. The destruction of old harlot city (Rv 17–19)

IV. A flashback of salvation history (Rv 20)

V. The coming of the New Jerusalem (Rv 21–22)

Let's make a few general comments about the Book of Revelation before we get into interpreting it.

First, the Book of Revelation bounces around like a movie with flashbacks. If you ever watched a movie that involves time travel or some other scrambling of normal time (e.g., *The Lake House*, *Premonition*, *Conception*, or *Interstellar*), you are a little bit prepared for watching the "movie" that is Revelation. Revelation is, after all, very visual, with vivid scenes following upon one another rather abruptly—but the scenes *do not always follow in chronological order*. Big mistakes in the interpretation of the book result when we assume that all the visions refer to historical events that will unfold in the same order we find them in the book. Sometimes there are clear flashbacks (such as Rv 12:1–5). At other times, it's not clear whether a scene is a flashback or in sequence (such as Rv 20). In my view, both the sequence of seven signs (Rv 12–14) and the vision of the binding of Satan, his release, and the final judgment (Rv 20) are flashbacks that don't follow the events that immediately preceded them.

Second, the Book of Revelation is a thoroughly liturgical document. It was meant to be read in church. At the opening of the book, John calls down a blessing on "he who reads aloud the words of the prophecy, and blessed are those who hear" (Rv 1:3), meaning the lector (reader) and the congregation. Then follow letters to seven churches, all meant to be read when the local church gathers for mass. John shows us what the heavenly worship looks like. We see in heaven all kinds of things that Jews and Christians have used in worship in ancient times and today:

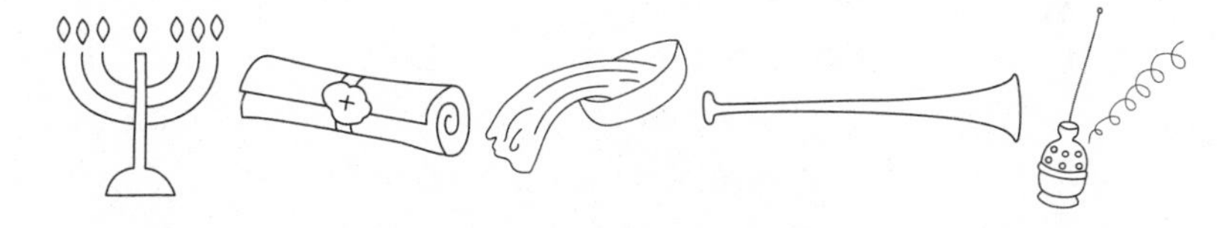

candlesticks, seals, trumpets, bowls for libations, white robes, censers, altars, incense, hymns, and prayers. God communicated to John using images of worship he would understand from his Jewish Christian background. But ever since John wrote this book, his visions have guided what we do in the Mass and the way we do it. So High Mass looks like Revelation.

Further, the number seven plays a significant role. Several times in the Book of Revelation, we read of the "seven spirits" of God. Other English translations say "sevenfold Spirit" of God, which captures the truth better. Seven is the number of oath, covenant, and faithfulness. God's Spirit is "seven" because God keeps his oaths and covenants with perfect faithfulness. A very famous passage, Isaiah 11, lists seven gifts of the Holy Spirit: wisdom, understanding, counsel, fortitude, knowledge, piety, and fear of the Lord. We often teach about these gifts when preparing kids for Confirmation. These seven gifts of the Spirit are behind the expression "seven spirits" or "sevenfold Spirit" used in Revelation.

Third, covenant themes are heavy in the Book of Revelation. This explains the frequent use of the number seven throughout the book. Revelation is famous for its sets of seven: seven seals, seven trumpets, seven bowls, and so on.

Why seven? In the Hebrew language, the word for oath swearing meant literally "to seven one's self," and one of the words for "oath" came from the word "seven." Oath swearing was how you made a covenant with another person (Gn 26:28). So "seven" became connected to covenant. It was the "covenant number." In all the sets of seven in Revelation, we are seeing God fulfilling all his covenants and bringing all his promises to completion. Besides the sevens, there are many references to the earlier covenants of scripture, especially the Davidic Covenant. So at the beginning, Jesus is called "the firstborn . . . and the ruler of kings on earth" (Rv 1:5), a quote about David from Psalm 89:27. And at the end of the book, Jesus says, "I am the root and the *seed* of David" (Rv 22:16). David and his kingdom relate to our final point:

Revelation is all about *the kingdom of God*. A couple times John praises God for having made the followers of Christ into "a kingdom and priests to our God" (Rv 5:10; see 1:6). And at points of victory in the book, various angels proclaim, "The kingdom of the world has become the kingdom of our Lord and of his Christ" (Rv 11:15; see 12:10). At the end of the book, the perfect city of Jerusalem, the capital of David's kingdom, comes down from heaven and rests on earth. The royal city becomes God's home forever. That's why we say Revelation is about the *victory of the kingdom*.

So let's start a quick tour of this fascinating book.

Introduction of John and His Vision *(Revelation 1)*

Revelation is actually a letter to churches, like the other epistles in the New Testament, only the bulk of the letter is taken up describing a vision or visions that John was given by Jesus. After a brief introduction that explains the following account is a revelation to John about what must soon take place (Rv 1:1–3), we get a standard letter opening: "John to the seven churches that are in Asia: Grace to you and peace . . ." (Rv 1:4).

Messages to the Seven Churches *(Revelation 2–3)*

John doesn't write to just one Church but to the seven main churches in Asia Minor or modern-day Turkey, which was an early center of Christianity.

The Seven Churches of Asia (AD 96)

He is going to have a special message for each church and then share with all of them the supernatural vision that he experienced. But first, he explains how Jesus appeared to him on the "Lord's day," Sunday, while he was in prayer on the island of Patmos (Rv 1:9–20). He heard a voice behind him, turned and looked, and saw Jesus in glory. Jesus was dressed as a priest (that's the point of the long robe and the golden girdle), and he is standing in the true holy place of God's temple (that's the point of the lampstands because the lampstands were in the holy place). He commands John to write messages to each of the main churches of Asia.

The churches are listed in order along a road where a messenger would start in Ephesus and travel to Laodicea.

Each of the seven churches has a different major issue they need to overcome:

- Ephesus, the *loveless* church
- Smyrna, the *persecuted* church
- Pergamon, the *self-indulgent* church
- Thyatira, the *immoral* church
- Sardis, the *spiritually dead* church
- Philadelphia, the *powerless* church
- Laodicea, the *lukewarm* church

The messages to the seven churches have enduring significance because these problems remain live issues for parishes, dioceses, and national churches to this day. We need to read these messages with the attitude, "If the shoe fits, wear it!" Is my parish orthodox but loveless like Ephesus, spiritually dead like Sardis, or tolerant of immorality and false teaching like Thyatira? He who has an ear should hear what the Spirit says to the churches.

Jesus tailors each message to the *cultural* and *spiritual* situation in each church. It would take too long to show this in each case, so we'll just examine the best example: the message to the last church, La-odice'a:

> And to the angel of the church in Laodicea write: "The words of the Amen, the faithful and true witness, the beginning of God's creation.
>
> 'I know your works: you are neither cold nor hot. Would that you were cold or hot! So, because you are lukewarm, and neither cold nor hot, I will spew you out of my mouth. For you say, I am rich, I have prospered, and I need nothing; not knowing that you are wretched, pitiable, poor, blind, and naked. Therefore I counsel you to buy from me gold refined by fire, that you may be rich, and white garments to clothe you and to keep the shame of your nakedness from being seen, and salve to anoint your eyes, that you may see. Those whom I love, I reprove and chasten; so be zealous and repent. Behold, I stand at the door and knock; if any one hears my voice and opens the door, I will come in to him and eat with him, and he with me. He who conquers, I will grant him to sit with me on my throne, as I myself conquered and sat down with my Father on his throne. He who has an ear, let him hear what the Spirit says to the churches.'" (Rv 3:14–22)

Jesus criticizes the church of Laodicea for being *lukewarm*, *poor*, *blind*, and *naked*:

Lukewarm

From the city of Laodicea, the townspeople could look north and see the hot springs of their rival city (Hierapolis), which had become a popular resort. Turning around, they could see snow-capped peaks that brought cool mountain water to cities south of them. But the Laodiceans themselves had no good source of water. They had to pipe water in from a spring miles away, and the water was so full of minerals it clogged pipes and didn't wash things clean. Jesus tells the Laodiceans that their spiritual condition is just like their water supply: not hot enough for a healing bath and not cold enough for a refreshing drinking; they were just spiritually "blah."

Poor

The city of Laodicea was extremely wealthy because of their clothing and drug industries. When a major earthquake damaged much of the city in AD 60 or 61, just a few years before Revelation was written (in my view), the Roman Empire offered "federal emergency funds" to help Laodicea rebuild. But the Laodiceans said, *Thanks, but no thanks! We'll pay for it ourselves*. They were so wealthy it was beneath them to accept government assistance. But Jesus says, *You Laodicean Christians* think *you're rich because you look on the outside. Inside, however, you are spiritually poor and needy.*

Naked

One reason Laodicea was so rich was their clothing industry, based on a fine-quality black wool from local sheep. Laodicean black wool garments were in high demand everywhere. The Laodiceans had plenty of physical clothing, but Jesus says they are spiritually naked when God looks at them.

Blind

The other reason Laodicea was so rich was the medicines they produced, especially an eye salve widely believed to have healing powers. They sold ointment to heal people's eyes throughout the empire, but spiritually, they were blind themselves.

* * *

The Christians of Laodicea need to look away from all their material prosperity and turn to Jesus for true wealth and healing. "Behold, I stand at the door and knock; if any one hears my voice and opens the door, I will come in and eat with him, and he with me," Jesus says (Rv 3:20). This is an allusion to the Eucharist, our meal with Jesus. The Lord is calling the Laodiceans to repent and return to the sacraments, where they will find their true wealth, clothing, medicine, and food for eternal life. He says the same to wealthy Christians today.

The Vision of the Heavenly Worship *(Revelation 4–5)*

After Jesus dictates the letters to the seven churches, John is taken in spirit up to heaven to see God's royal courtroom. John sees the Holy Trinity: the Father seated upon the throne; the sevenfold Holy Spirit burning in "seven torches of fire"; and God the Son appearing as a "Lamb that had been slain," clothed with seven eyes that are the sevenfold Holy Spirit since Jesus is always anointed with the Holy Spirit. Before God's throne are twenty-four thrones for the twenty-four *presbuteroi* (*prez-BOO-tur-oy*), translated "elders" but a word that we know becomes the English "priest." Why are there twenty-four? This probably represents the Twelve Apostles plus the Twelve Patriarchs, that is, the combined leadership of the Old Covenant people of God and the New Covenant people of God. Then there are four "living creatures" that resemble a lion, an ox, a man, and an eagle. We know from comparison with Ezekiel 1 and 10 that these "living creatures" are cherubim, warrior angels that guard the holiness of God.

The "Lamb that was slain" comes forward—he is also the "Lion of Judah" and "root of David"—and is prepared to open the scroll with seven seals, which is the Word of God. In early Christian worship, while the apostles were still alive, it is likely that the breaking of seals and opening of scrolls was a common practice when the church gathered for the Eucharist. The apostles wrote many letters to various churches, and when such a letter arrived, the local bishop may have held the sealed scroll up before the congregation—so all the people could see it was authentic—and then broken the seal and read what the apostle had written to the church.

Who is worthy to break the seals on the scroll that holds the secret will and word of God? Only Jesus, the Lamb, is worthy. So we see in Revelation 5 that all the angels and saints sing out in praise as the Lamb steps forward to open the scroll.

When we gather for Mass, we participate in the worship John saw. This is easier to recognize when we gather around our bishop. St. Ignatius of Antioch, who knew the apostle John, wrote to another church in Asia Minor shortly after St. John's death: "Be eager to do everything in godly harmony, the bishop presiding in the place of God and the presbyters in the place of the council of the apostles, and the deacons . . . entrusted with the service of Jesus Christ." So when we go to a solemn Mass at the Cathedral, we see the bishop sitting on this throne like God the Father in John's vision. We see the priests of the diocese, the *presbyters*, gathered around him like the twenty-four elders who represent the apostles and patriarchs. Cherubim and other angels are present though unseen; often our churches are decorated with images of angels to remind us that they are present. Then the deacon, acting in the person of Jesus, comes forward to proclaim God's Word, the Gospel. Through it all, we sing hymns and offer prayers just as the heavenly congregation "sang a new song" and held golden bowls of incense "which are the prayers of the saints" (Rv 5:8–9). Mass represents the heavenly worship, and in fact, since the same Holy Spirit is present at Mass and in the heavenly court, our Mass is joined to the heavenly worship and even *is* the heavenly worship, especially when we behold the Lamb of God who was slain to take away the sins of the world. In the Eucharist, we eat the slain Lamb John saw in heaven.

Seven Seals, Trumpets, Signs, and Bowls: The Judgment on the Earth and the "Great City" *(Revelation 6–16)*

The main body of the Book of Revelation stretches from chapters 6 to 19, and three times we see the same pattern: a set of seven actions are performed in heaven (breaking a seal, blowing a trumpet, and pouring out a bowl). Each action unleashes a plague upon the earth. At the end of each sequence of seven, heaven bursts out in praise, declaring that God's reign or kingdom has finally come.

Seven seals are broken, each unleashing a plague, and after the sixth and just before the seventh, we see a "great multitude" of people gathered around the royal throne of God and the Lamb, who protects them forever and wipes away all their tears—an image very close to the final vision of the New Jerusalem (Rv 21–22).

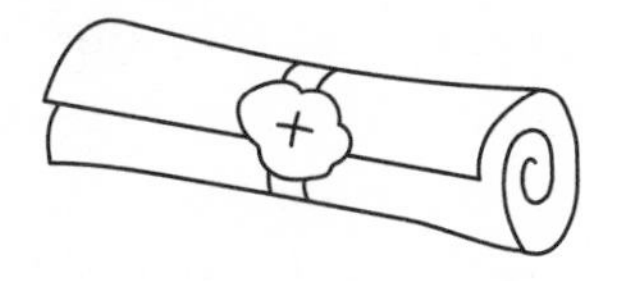

Seven trumpets are blown, each unleashing a plague, and at the blast of the seventh, heaven erupts with praise: "The kingdom of the world has become the kingdom of our Lord and of his Christ, and he shall reign for ever and ever" (Rv 11:15).

Between the trumpets and bowls, John sees seven signs, which symbolically retell major events of salvation leading up to the final judgment.

Then seven bowls are poured out, each unleashing a plague.

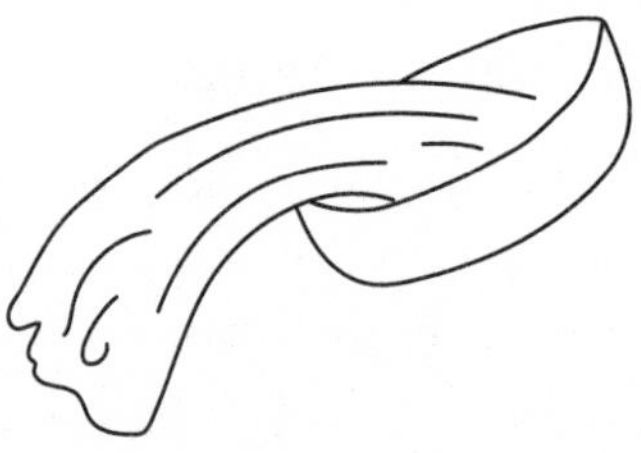

When the seventh is poured out, God says, "It is done!" (Rv 16:17). The great city Babylon is overthrown (Rv 17–18), and heaven erupts in praise: "Hallelujah! For the Lord our God the Almighty reigns. . . . The marriage of the Lamb has come" (Rv 19:6–7).

I would suggest that what we have here is three visions of the same basic series of events: a number of plagues of judgment on the earth that lead up to the destruction of the "great city" opposed to God and the beginning of God's kingdom on earth. Three times John sees the same basic sequence but in different forms. This reminds us of a set of visions in the Book of Genesis: God's visions to Pharaoh of the upcoming judgment on Egypt, which is given to Pharaoh twice in two different forms (ears of grain and cattle), which Joseph the visionary explains to Pharaoh as indicating that the events are soon to come. So John sees the same basic vision three times, meaning it is to come *very soon!* (see Rv 1:1).

But what is the sequence of events that John sees three times in three different ways (seals, trumpets, and bowls)? The third sequence—the seven bowls—is the longest and most detailed, and it ends with the destruction of a harlot city identified as "Babylon" in Revelation. The key to understanding the sequence of events, and the whole book, is to correctly identify this city.

The Destruction of Old Harlot City *(Revelation 17–19)*

Most people identify this city as Rome, and many Protestants identify it as the Roman Catholic Church. However, I think a stronger case can be made that the harlot city is the earthly Jerusalem, which was destroyed in AD 70.[2]

This may sound like a surprising and unlikely identification, and I thought it was farfetched myself until I began to investigate the arguments. There are at least eight major reasons to identify the harlot city of Revelation 17 as the earthly Jerusalem, but let's start with the strongest. The text of Revelation almost tells us outright what the "great city" is in Revelation 11:8. There, describing two witnesses who will testify to Jesus during the great time of trial, it says that their dead bodies "will lie in the street of the great city which is allegorically called Sodom and Egypt, where their Lord was crucified." Now there can be no doubt where "their Lord was crucified." That was definitely Jerusalem, as no one has ever claimed that Jesus was crucified in Rome. This verse, then, identifies the "great city" as Jerusalem for us, and the "great city" is equated with the "harlot city" and "Babylon" in several other texts (Rv 16:19; 17:18; 18:10, 16, 18, 19, 21).

People might be surprised that John would call the earthly city of Jerusalem "Sodom" and "Egypt," but remember that Jerusalem was the early center of anti-Christian persecution (Acts 8:1). Christians were not welcome in Jerusalem: Jesus was crucified there; Stephen, stoned; and James son of Zebedee, beheaded. Saul of Tarsus savagely abused the Christians there (Acts 26:10), and Paul the apostle was nearly torn to pieces there before the Romans intervened (Acts 23:10). Furthermore, people forget that the Old Testament prophets called Jerusalem "Sodom" (Is 1:10) or compared her to Sodom (Ez 16:26; Jr 23:14; Am 4:11) on several occasions. The prophet Amos, in fact, compares God's judgment on Jerusalem with his judgment on both Egypt and Sodom (Am 4:10–11). So calling Jerusalem "Sodom and Egypt" is not very unique. St. John is following the footsteps of the Old Testament prophets, who also prophesied a great destruction to fall on the earthly Jerusalem. In fact, all the great prophets—Isaiah, Jeremiah, and Ezekiel—predicted the destruction of Jerusalem. John is a New Testament prophet doing the same thing.

The great prophets also condemned Jerusalem as a "harlot" in no uncertain terms (Is 1:21; Jer 13:27; Ez 16, 23). Ezekiel devotes two chapters of his book to describing Jerusalem as a harlot (Ez 16, 23). John's description of the harlot city overdressed in a trashy way (Rv 17:4) probably comes from Isaiah's longer description of the trashy "daughters of Zion," who symbolized Jerusalem as a whole (Is 3:16–26). So John's "harlot city" in Revelation fits the image of Jerusalem in the prophets.

Many people note that in Revelation 17 there is a beast with seven heads, and the heads are called "mountains" or "hills" on which the harlot woman sits. Since there was an old tradition that Rome was built on seven hills, they conclude that the woman is Rome. I agree that the idea of "seven hills" probably does indicate Rome, but let's take note: it's not the woman who has the seven hills; it's the beast. So if something is Rome, I would agree that it is the beast. Why then is the woman shown seated on the beast? The woman is sitting on the beast because the Jerusalem establishment rested on Roman power. The Sadducees and chief priests were "in bed" with the Romans, so to speak: they cooperated and collaborated with the Roman authorities in order to keep their power and persecute Christians. The Roman government had given important benefits to the priests of the Jerusalem Temple. For example, the government allowed the priests to collect a Temple tax from every Jew in the empire, which greatly enriched the Jerusalem Temple and those who were in charge of it. The Romans had appointed Herod and his successors as kings. The Romans also appointed the high priest on a yearly basis, contrary to Old Testament law. The Sadducees cooperated with this arrangement and in return held on to their authority by the force of the Roman legions.

At the end of Revelation 17, the "beast" turns on the harlot and consumes her. And that is exactly what happened in AD 66–70. Up until that time, the Jerusalem establishment—the Herodian kings and the Sadducean high priests—had kept power by collaborating with the Romans, but the relationship broke down in the late AD 60s, and the emperor Nero sent the general Titus to destroy Jerusalem. So actual events fit well if we understand the seven-headed beast as Rome and Jerusalem as the harlot city.

Revelation 17:18, however, calls the harlot city "the great city which has dominion over the *kings of the earth*" (emphasis added). That does sound like Rome, doesn't it? However, St. John draws on the Old Testament here. According to the Old Testament, *Jerusalem* is the city that has dominion over the kings of the earth. We see this idea in many psalms (Pss

2, 48, 89) and in the prophet Jeremiah. In fact, in one place Jeremiah speaks of Jerusalem as a city feared by "the kings of the earth" and filled with the "blood of the righteous" (Lam 4:12–13). This is closely parallel to Revelation's picture of the harlot city (Rv 18:24).

Revelation 18 talks about all the merchants of the earth mourning because the great city is destroyed. Now no one will buy their goods. The great city was extremely wealthy and bought all sorts of luxuries. Isn't that Rome rather than Jerusalem? Was Jerusalem really so wealthy?

Actually, Jerusalem *was* that wealthy. The huge number of pilgrims who came to Jerusalem for the three great feasts each year (Passover, Tabernacles, and Pentecost), plus the Temple tax, greatly enriched Jerusalem and whoever was in control of the city. Herod the Great grew fabulously wealthy from the Temple commerce and built himself a dozen outrageous pleasure palaces throughout the country, some complete with large theaters, pools, baths, and race tracks. Before he began the siege of Jerusalem in AD 66, the Roman general Titus asked the Jerusalemites what complaint they had against Rome, since they were wealthier than the Romans themselves.[3] Titus's claim about Jerusalem's wealth is confirmed by archeology: pottery from Jerusalem in this time period contains an unusually high silver content, apparently from all the silver coins in the city that fell to the ground and leeched silver into the ground water.[4] Jerusalem was so wealthy the Roman scholars described it as "the greatest city of the east *by far*."[5] It had no close rival. So, yes, the picture in Revelation 18 of all the merchants mourning because of the fall of the "great city" *does* fit Jerusalem.

One final fact makes the identification of the "harlot city" as Jerusalem almost airtight. John says of this city, "In her was the blood of prophets and of saints" (Rv 18:24). Certainly, Rome could be considered the place of the "blood of the saints." Nero and other caesars martyred thousands there. However, Rome was certainly not the place of the "blood of prophets." There is absolutely no doubt in scripture about where the "blood of prophets" comes to rest: "It cannot be that a prophet should perish away from Jerusalem" (Lk 13:33). Compare what John says and what Jesus says:

> *John about the "harlot city"*: "And in her was found the blood of *prophets* and of saints, and *of all who have been slain on earth*" (Rv 18:24; emphasis added).
>
> *Jesus about Jerusalem*: "Therefore I send you *prophets* and wise men and scribes, some of whom you will kill . . . that upon you may come *all the righteous blood shed on earth*. . . . O Jerusalem, Jerusalem, killing the *prophets* and stoning those who are sent to you!" (Mt 23:34–37; emphasis added).

Understanding the harlot city as Rome just doesn't work. Revelation is about things that will happen "soon," and Rome was not destroyed at any time "soon" to when John gave his vision. Moreover, Rome was never destroyed and burned. It was sacked in AD 410. However, by this time Rome had converted to Christianity. Christians did not rejoice when the city was sacked—instead, they mourned. The Roman Empire had become the protector of the Church, and Christians thought this new alliance was the final goal of human history. St. Augustine was so grieved when Rome was sacked that he wrote his famous *City of God* to try to explain how God could have allowed such a disaster to happen.

Jerusalem, however, was destroyed soon after John wrote (assuming a date in the AD 60s for Revelation) and completely burned to the ground (Rv 17:16). According to the historian Josephus, the destruction of Jerusalem was preceded by frightful plagues and signs in the sky and ended with one of the largest massacres the world had known to that point—similar to the prophecies in Revelation. Jerusalem was where Jesus was crucified (11:8), was where the prophets spilled their blood (18:24), and was the place of early Christian martyrdom (17:6), wealthier even than Rome (18:11–13). Everything fits!

A Flashback of Salvation History *(Revelation 20)*

We can summarize Revelation like this: the Spirit takes John to heaven where he sees the heavenly worship. Then, John witnesses three cycles of seven—seals, trumpets, and bowls—each of which portray the plagues that would fall on earthly Jerusalem leading up to its destruction. Then, after the earthly Jerusalem is destroyed in Revelation 17–19, it is replaced with the heavenly Jerusalem in Revelation 21–22. This heavenly Jerusalem is the Church. After Jerusalem fell in AD 70, a major obstacle to the spread of the Church was removed, and the Gospel began to advance even more quickly.

The Coming of the New Jerusalem *(Revelation 21–22)*

But why should we say the "heavenly Jerusalem," the "bride of the Lamb," at the end of Revelation (chapters 19–22) is the Church? Several verses make this clear.

Most obviously, the "holy city Jerusalem" is called the "bride, the wife of the Lamb," and the Lamb, of course, is Jesus. St. Paul teaches us that the bride of Christ is *the Church* (Eph 5:25–33). In the same letter to the Ephesians, St. Paul says the Church is built on the foundation of the apostles (Eph 2:20). That's the same image John gives us of the "holy city, new Jerusalem," which has twelve foundations with the names of the Twelve Apostles (Rv 21:2, 14).

In Revelation 21, an angel measures the New Jerusalem for St. John and finds that it is a perfect cube (v. 16). The only perfectly cubical structure in the Old Testament was the Holy of Holies (1 Kgs 6:20), the innermost part of the Temple.

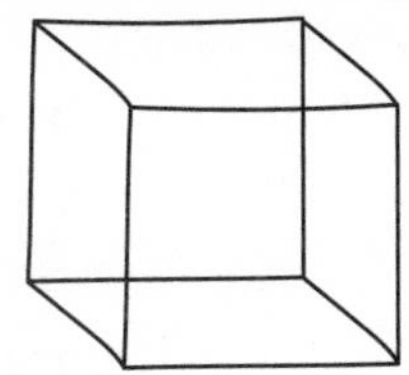

This means the New Jerusalem was a new Holy of Holies, on a massive scale. What was special about the Holy of Holies? It was where God's presence dwelled. Now, St. Paul says this about Christians: "Do you not know that your body is a temple of the Holy Spirit within you, which you have from God?" (1 Cor 6:19). So the Church is one big "Holy of Holies" because every Christian is what the Holy of Holies once was: the special dwelling place of God.

The New Jerusalem is a Temple city, a city that is one massive Holy of Holies. St. Paul calls the Church the new Temple as well, when he says that every Christian is "joined together and grows into a holy temple in the Lord . . . a dwelling place of God in the Spirit" (Eph 2:21–22). The New Jerusalem has the "water of life" flowing from the throne of God, and the "tree of life" growing along the river, producing fruit for food and healing (Rv 22:1–2). These are the sacraments: Baptism is the "water of life," and the Eucharist, as the fruit of the Cross, is the real "tree of life."

The Book of Revelation is very much like those "apocalyptic" chapters of the gospels (Mt 24; Mk 13; Lk 21) that predict the upcoming destruction of Jerusalem. Only Revelation is much longer and more detailed. Three times we see that plagues will fall on the earth, especially the harlot city, earthly Jerusalem, until she is destroyed and replaced by the Jerusalem from above (see Hebrews 12:22–24), the Church. This was fulfilled in the events leading up to and following the destruction of Jerusalem in AD 70.

But wait, I can hear people object, *I thought Revelation was about the end of the world. And there are passages that sure sound like that. So how can it be about the destruction of Jerusalem?*

I agree. Revelation *is* about the end of the world. But it's about the end of Jerusalem at the same time. Both events are being described at once, just as we saw when dealing with Matthew 23. How can this be? This is only because the Temple was a symbol of the entire universe. The Jews believed the Temple was the universe-in-miniature, a *microcosm*. The Jewish historian Josephus, who lived at that time and witnessed the Temple be destroyed, wrote that the furnishings and decorations of the Israelite Temple "were in every one made in way of imitation and representation of the universe."[6] So when you destroy Jerusalem and its Temple—which the Romans did—you symbolically destroy the whole earth. Therefore, the events of the siege, capture, and destruction of Jerusalem in AD 70 are a foretaste of the end of the world.

The Importance of God's Temple

It is hard to exaggerate how important the Temple was to the people of Israel and the Jews of John's day. Ever since Moses, there had been some sort of sanctuary where God had been worshiped except for a span of seventy years between the destruction of the Temple by the Babylonians (587 BC) and its rebuilding (516 BC). How could God not have a Temple? The destruction of Jerusalem and the Temple in AD 70 was traumatic for Jews and Jewish Christians. What did it mean in God's plan? John shows us: the old Jerusalem and its Temple were being replaced by a new one: the Church (Heb 12:22–24).

The Kingdom Is Perfected

The kingdom of God is a major theme in the Book of Revelation. At the beginning of the book, John tells the churches that Jesus has "made us a kingdom, priests to his God and Father" (v. 6). To be a "kingdom of priests" was a promise God made to Israel at Sinai, if they kept the Mosaic Covenant: "If you . . . keep my covenant . . . you shall be to me a kingdom of priests" (Ex 19:5–6). Of course, they didn't keep it. So John sees the Church as the fulfillment of the promised "kingdom of priests" of the Mosaic Covenant.

At the beginning, John also calls himself "your brother" who shares "the tribulation *and the kingdom* and the patient endurance" (Rv 1:9, emphasis added). So somehow the kingdom of God has already come, and we experience it as Christians. We saw this in the gospels. John joins "tribulation" with "kingdom" just as did St. Paul, who used to preach, "Through many tribulations we must enter the kingdom of God" (Acts 14:22). Jesus was and is truly the King, but his only throne in this life was his Cross. That's how it's going to be for each of us. We reign with Jesus in the kingdom even now; but in this life, our royal reign is going to involve the cross!

At the end of the sequence of trumpets, heaven declares, "The kingdom of the world has become the kingdom of our Lord and of his Christ, and he shall reign for ever and ever" (Rv 11:15). We can take this sentence as the theme of the Book of Revelation. The final vision of the book, where we see the New Jerusalem as the bride of the Lamb, is also a picture of the perfect kingdom. Jerusalem was, after all, the royal city. Jerusalem and its Temple were the heart of the kingdom of

David. The New Jerusalem is the perfected kingdom, where the whole kingdom is the royal city and the whole kingdom is the Holy of Holies, the heart of the temple. Kingdom, city, and temple all become one.

What has brought us to this point of perfection? The sacred liturgy has brought us. All through the Book of Revelation, liturgical acts in heaven drive human history forward. The liturgical acts of angels in heaven unleash plagues and other events that bring judgment on the enemies of God, leading to the overthrow of the kingdom of this world and its replacement with the kingdom of God.

You see, the breaking open of seals was a liturgical act, something that was done with letters from apostles in early Christian worship. Blowing trumpets was a feature of the Jewish Temple liturgy, where priests or Levites would blast trumpets to announce feasts or initiate sacrifices. Bowls were used for both Christian and Jewish worship—in Jewish worship, wine or blood was poured from bowls as part of the sacrifices, and in Christian worship bowls held water and wine for the Eucharist.

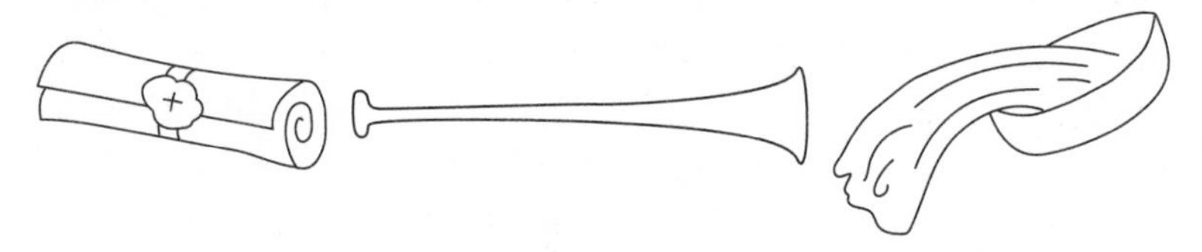

In John's vision, it is the heavenly liturgy going on above that conquers the "kingdom of the world" until it becomes "the kingdom of our Lord, and of his Christ" (Rv 11:15).

That's a powerful concept for Catholics because we believe each Mass is a participation in the liturgy of heaven. To outsiders, the Mass appears as a quiet ritual we do inside our own buildings, at best a harmless set of strange medieval rituals and superstitions. *Those silly Catholics! Why don't they get with the times?*

But in reality, however nonspectacular it may appear, the Mass joins us with "the angels and saints" to worship around the throne of the Lamb, celebrating the wedding feast of the Lamb *right now*. This is the engine of history. The heavenly Mass is pushing us toward the perfect kingdom, and there is nothing more important each Sunday—or any day—than to take the opportunity to pray at Mass.

Bringing All the Covenants to Completion

Seven is the covenant number, and Revelation is full of patterns of seven. This is God bringing all the covenants to their consummation. In the end, the New Jerusalem fulfills every covenant of the Old Testament from the first (the Adamic) to the last (the Davidic).

The New Jerusalem is clearly the New Eden; it has the river of life flowing out of it. It has the tree of life once more. The gold and jewels of Eden are present in even greater abundance. God dwells there in close relationship to mankind (Rv 21:2–5).

The New Jerusalem is everything Eden was but more; Eden was just a garden with a couple, whereas the New Jerusalem is a city with abundant people.

At the same time, the New Jerusalem is the fulfillment of all the promises to David.

David's royal city has taken over the world, transformed the world into one big temple, one Holy of Holies. That is why, even to the end of the book, Jesus still identifies himself with David and his covenant: "I am the root and the *seed* of David, the bright morning star" (Rv 22:16), referring to the prophecy of the royal "star" that will arise for Israel (Nm 24:17).

Revelation Past, Present, and Future

What do we do with the Book of Revelation? It's a book about the past, present, and future.

It's a book about the past because many of the things described in the book actually took place when the old Jerusalem was destroyed by the Roman "beast" in AD 70. This catastrophic event was itself a prophecy of the end of the world. It left the Church as the sole legitimate temple of God on earth.

It's a book about the present because other cities and empires have set themselves up against the Church throughout history, becoming filled with the blood of the saints and martyrs, and ultimately sharing the same fateful judgment that fell on Jerusalem. Surely in the last century, the almost unimaginable carnage that the demonically inspired Nazi empire brought on the earth, followed by the almost unimaginable carnage that was required to end it, had many striking parallels with images in the Book of Revelation. We can say that Hitler surely was an anti-Christ, who purported to be a savior figure of mankind, creating a utopia for the "superior race(s)" and eliminating the "inferior races" that held back progress. Surely many in the midst of World War II wondered, with good reason, if the prophecies of Revelation were coming to pass. And in a sense, they were. Basic patterns in the Book of Revelation repeat themselves through history, with variation, as different cities and nations step forward to take on the role of the "beast" and the "harlot" in persecuting the people of God.

Revelation is also a book of the future. Some Baptists and other non-Catholic Christians try to find in Revelation a program to predict the events leading up to the end of the world. I agree that it does speak of events leading up to the final judgment. But I'm not convinced that we are going to be able to make the correct identifications prior to the fact. If Jesus' first coming is any indication, the way that prophecies are fulfilled is surprising and often only recognized in hindsight. I suspect it will be the same with the second coming. After it is over, we will look back and say, "Aha! I see how it was predicted in Revelation!" Nonetheless, in broad outline, we can be confident that the period leading up to Jesus' second coming will be a time of great trial and persecution, when the forces attacking the Church will have great, even supernatural, power. Nonetheless, victory belongs to God, and he will finally overcome them. It's worth quoting the *Catechism* at this point:

> Before Christ's second coming the Church must pass through a final trial that will shake the faith of many believers. The persecution . . . will unveil the "mystery of iniquity" in the form of a religious deception offering men an apparent solution to their problems at the price of apostasy from the truth. The supreme religious deception is that of the Antichrist, a pseudo-messianism by which man glorifies himself in place of God and of his Messiah come in the flesh. . . .
>
> The Church will enter the glory of the kingdom only through this final Passover, when she will follow her Lord in his death and Resurrection. The kingdom will be fulfilled . . . only by God's victory over the final unleashing of evil, which will cause his Bride to come down from heaven. God's triumph over the revolt of evil will take the form of the Last Judgment after the final cosmic upheaval of this passing world. (*CCC* 675, 677)

This is the final goal of salvation history: the consummation of the kingdom, which is also the Wedding Feast of the Lamb. It seems appropriate that history should begin with a wedding in a garden and also end with a wedding in a garden city. We can draw the bride of the Lamb coming down out of heaven from God. She's a perfect cube—maybe not too attractive when ordering her wedding dress, but we have to look with the eyes of faith:

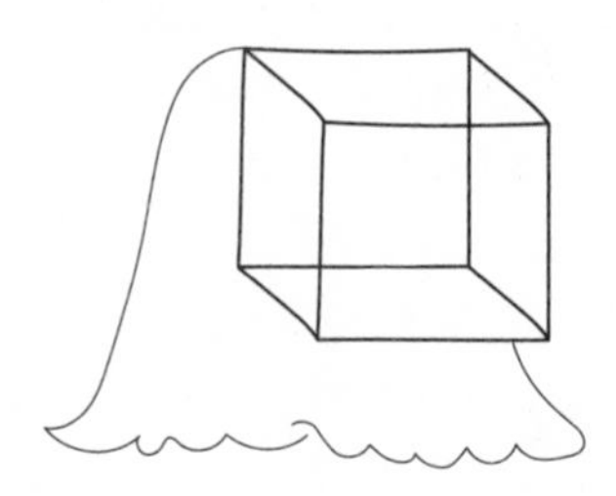

If the bride is a bit unusual, so is the groom, who is a Lamb:

Together, this pair, on top of the heavenly Zion, is the icon for the final covenant consummation of salvation history:

We now have a sequence of eight mountains that sum up the story of the Bible:

Holy
Spirit

Notes

Introduction

1. John Paul II, Wednesday Audience of Jan. 28, 1987.

2. On questions of authorship of the New Testament books, I recommend the introductory essays of the *Ignatius Catholic Study Bible: New Testament* (San Francisco: Ignatius, 2010) as a start and then further D. A. Carson, D. Moo, and L. Morris, *An Introduction to the New Testament* (Grand Rapids: Zondervan, 1992). Vatican II states: "The Church has always and everywhere held and continues to hold that the four Gospels are of apostolic origin. For what they Apostles preached . . . afterwards they themselves and apostolic men . . . handed on to us in writing: the foundation of faith, the fourfold Gospel according to Matthew, Mark, Luke, and John."

1. The Old Testament as "Prequel: Episodes 1–6"

1. "Eucharistic Prayer IV," *The Roman Missal* (Collegeville, MN: Liturgical Press, 2011), 736–744.

2. The Gospel of Matthew

1. See the discussion of Nazareth in Bargil Pixner, O.S.B., *Paths of the Messiah* (San Francisco: Ignatius Press, 2010).

2. See Josephus, *Antiquities of the Jews*, Book 3:180: "For if anyone do but consider the fabric of the tabernacle, and take a view of the garments of the high priest, and of those vessels which we make use of in our sacred ministration, he will find . . . they were every one made in way of imitation and representation of the universe." Likewise the ancient Jewish philosopher Philo, *Life of Moses* 2:143: "Then [Moses] gave [the priests] their sacred vestments, giving to his brother [Aaron, the High Priest] the robe which reached down to his feet, and the mantle which covered his shoulders, as a sort of breast-plate, being an embroidered robe, adorned with all kinds of figures, and a representation of the universe." Compare also *Life of Moses* 2:135; Wisdom of Solomon 18:24; G. K. Beale, "Cosmic Symbolism of Temples in the Old Testament," pp. 29–80 of idem, *The Temple and the Church's Mission: A Biblical Theology of the Dwelling Place of God* (Downers Grove, ILL: InterVarsity Press, 2004); and Jon D. Levenson, *Sinai and Zion: An Entry into the Jewish Bible* (Minneapolis: Winston Press, 1985), 138–39: "The Temple . . . is a microcosm of which the world itself is the macrocosm."

3. See the Mishnah, tractate Pesahim 10:1-7, esp. 10:7 (pp. 150-151 in Herbert Danby, *The Mishnah* [Oxford: Oxford University Press, 1933]). The fourth cup was poured, but before it was drunk, the rest of the Hallel psalms (115-118) were chanted. The disciples appear to sing the "hymn" of the Hallel in Mt 26:30 and depart without drinking the final cup since Jesus said, "I will not drink again of this fruit of the vine until I drink it with you in the kingdom of God" (v. 29).

4. See the Mishnah, tractate Sanhedrin 4:1 (pp. 386-387 in Herbert Danby, The Mishnah [Oxford: Oxford University Press, 1933]). In a capital case, the trial had to be held by day and the verdict reached during the day. A verdict of guilty could not be issued the same day as the trial but had to wait

at least to the following day. Trials could not be held on the eve of the Sabbath or on a feast day.

3. The Gospel of Luke

1. Josephus, *Antiquities of the Jews*, 18:123 and 19:297.

2. For background on the biblical Queen Mother, see Edward Sri, *Queen Mother: A Biblical Theology of Mary's Queenship* (Steubenville, OH: Emmaus Road, 2015)

3. Josephus, *The Jewish War*, 2:119.

4. See my entry on "Genealogy" in *The Westminster Dictionary of New Testament and Early Christian Literature and Rhetoric* (ed. David Aune; Louisville: Westminster/John Knox, 2003).

5. See the Dead Sea Scroll document called "11QMelchizedek" or "11Q13", in any standard edition of the Dead Sea Scrolls, such as *The Dead Sea Scrolls Study Edition*, vol. 2 (ed. F. Garcia Martinez and E.J.C. Tigchelaar; New York/Leiden: Brill, 1999).

6. Moses dies and is buried by God in Dt 34:6. But possibly because his burial place was never found (Dt 34:6b), Jewish tradition around the time of Jesus held that the archangel Michael later took his body to heaven (see Jude 9). A Jewish religious writing called the Assumption of Moses circulated in the time of Our Lord, and probably ended with an account of the ascent of Moses's body to heaven.

7. For a full explanation of the Essene calendar and the Last Supper, see Annie Jaubert, *The Date of the Last Supper* (New York: Alba House, 1965).

4. The Book of Acts

1. Thomas Aquinas, *Summa Theologiae* I–II, q. 106, a. 1.

5. St. Paul and the Letter to the Romans

1. See the introductory essay on Hebrews in the *Ignatius Catholic Study Bible: New Testament*.

2. For the dates of Paul's letters, I follow Bo Reicke, *Re-examining Paul's Letters: The History of the Pauline Correspondence* (New York: T & T Clark, 2001).

3. St. Paul doesn't use the term 'antichrist,' which only occurs in 1-2 John. He does discuss a "man of lawlessness" (2 Thes 2:3) who seems to be an Antichrist figure.

4. Stephen Hawking, *A Brief History of Time* (London: Bantam Press, 1988), 121.

5. Fred Hoyle, "The Universe: Past and Present Reflections", *Annual Review of Astronomy and Astrophysics*, 20 (September 1982): 16.

6. Hawking, *A Brief History of Time*, 125.

7. For a responsible presentation of the argument from cosmic fine-tuning, see Robert J. Spitzer, *New Proofs for the Existence of God: Contributions of Contemporary Physics and Philosophy* (Grand Rapids, MI: Eerdmans, 2010), 1–103.

8. I speak here of the well-known conundrum of the Cambrian Explosion. See most recently Stephen Meyer, *Darwin's Doubt: The Explosive Origin of Animal Life and the Case for Intelligent Design* (San Francisco: HarperOne, 2014).

9. This is clear in the document from the Dead Sea Scrolls known as "4QMMT." This appears to be a letter from the Essene community of Qumran to the leadership of Jerusalem concerning certain "works of the law" or ritual issues. See the translation of 4QMMT in any standard edition of the Dead Sea Scrolls, such as *The Dead Sea Scrolls Study Edition*, vol. 2 (ed. F. Garcia Martinez and E.J.C. Tigchelaar; New York/ Leiden: Brill, 1999).

6. The Gospel of John

1. One of the best treatments of the authorship of the Gospel of John, in my opinion, is to be found in Craig Blomberg, *The Historical Reliability of the Fourth Gospel* (Downers Grove, IL: InterVarsity Press, 2001), 17–67. I believe the apostle composed the gospel. For a careful endorsement of apostolic authorship, see also Juan Chapa, *Why John is Different* (New Rochelle, NY: Scepter, 2013), 25–35; and Raymond Brown, *The Gospel According to John I-XII* (Anchor Bible 29; Garden City, NY: Doubleday, 1966), lxxxvii–cii.

2. Herod the Great began rebuilding the Temple in the eighteenth year of his reign, around 20 BC.

3. St. Ignatius of Antioch, *Letter to the Smyrneans*, § 6–7; emphasis added.

4. This is my translation of the Greek of John 7:37–38. I believe the sentences of this verse should be divided so that it is Jesus' heart from which the rivers of living water shall flow.

5. See Daniel Frayer-Griggs, "Spittle, Clay, and Creation in John 9:6 and Some Dead Sea Scrolls," *Journal of Biblical Literature* 132 (2013):659-670.

6. Reginald Garrigou-Lagrange, *The Three Conversions in the Spiritual Life* (Rockford, IL: TAN, 2002), 15.

7. Josephus, *Antiquities* 3:159–61; emphasis added.

8. I think here of the letters of St. Ignatius of Antioch, available online or in print. A handy edition is *Early Christian Writings* (ed. A. Louth; trans. M. Staniforth [New York/London: Penguin Classics, 1987]).

9. Garrigou-Lagrange, *The Three Conversions in the Spiritual Life*, 15.

7. The Book of Revelation: The Victory of the Kingdom

1. For a discussion of the authorship of Revelation, see *The Ignatius Catholic Study Bible: New Testament* (San Francisco:

Ignatius Press, 2010), 489–91; Eugenio Corsini, *The Apocalypse: The Perennial Revelation of Jesus Christ* (trans. F.J. Moloney; Wilmington, DE: Michael Glazier, 1983); Juan Chapa, *Why John is Different* (New Rochelle, NY: Scepter, 2013), 214–216; and Michael Barber, *Coming Soon: Unlocking the Book of Revelation* (Steubenville, OH: Emmaus Road, 2005), 1–7 but especially 289–292. No less an authority than Raymond Brown concedes, "Even the Greek of Revelation may be from John . . ." in *The Gospel According to John I-XII* (Anchor Bible 29; Garden City, NY: Doubleday, 1966), xcviii.

2. I follow Eugenio Corsini in identifying the harlot of Revelation 17 with the earthly Jerusalem. See Corsini, *The Apocalypse* (Wilmington, DE: Michael Glazier, 1983), 319–346.

3. Josephus, *Jewish War*, book VI, 6:2.

4. See "Silver Anomalies Found in Jerusalem Pottery Hint at Wealth During Second Temple Period," Berkely Lab Research News press release, Sept. 27, 2006 (http://www2.lbl.gov/Science-Articles/Archive/EETD-Jerusalem-pottery.html

5. Pliny the Elder, *Natural History*, 5:70; emphasis added.

6. Josephus, *Antiquities of the Jews*, book 3:180.

Suggestions for Further Reading

If you've enjoyed *New Testament Basics for Catholics* and want to go further in your study of the Bible, here are some recommendations for other good books.

If you haven't already read it, I recommend my brief treatment of the whole Bible, *Bible Basics for Catholics* (Notre Dame, IN: Ave Maria Press, 2015).

If you're interested in historical questions about the New Testament—like how we know who wrote what and whether it really all happened—a great place to start would be Brant Pitre's book, *The Case for Jesus: How We Got the Gospels, Who Jesus Said He Was, and Why It Matters* (New York: Image, 2016). Older books on the same topic include Paul Barnett, *Is the New Testament Reliable*? (Downers Grove, IL: InterVarsity Academic, 2005), and F.F. Bruce, *The New Testament Documents: Are They Reliable?* (Grand Rapids, MI: Eerdmans, 2003).

I can't recommend Pitre's work highly enough. At some point you should really read his other works on the New Testament, such as *Jesus and the Jewish Roots of the Eucharist: Unlocking the Secrets of the Last Supper* (New York: Image, 2011) and *Jesus the Bridegroom: The Greatest Love Story Ever*

Told (New York: Image, 2014). Take them on a retreat for spiritual reading.

If you are looking for a general commentary on the New Testament, the place to start is the *Ignatius Catholic Study Bible: New Testament* (ed. Scott Hahn and Curtis Mitch, San Francisco: Ignatius Press, 2010). The notes in this study bible are so good I ban it from my New Testament courses: if students read it, it would steal all the thunder from my lectures. Both Dr. Hahn and Curtis Mitch have many other books on Scripture that are all good.

For more extensive commentary on individual books, I can recommend two commentary series: The Catholic Commentary on Sacred Scripture Series from Baker Academic Press, edited by Dr. Peter Williamson of Sacred Heart Major Seminary in Detroit, and the *Navarre Bible New Testament* (12 volumes; Princeton, NJ: Sceptre Press, 2002).

When you are comfortable with the New Testament and are looking for something deeper yet, there is the wonderful Jesus of Nazareth series by Pope Emeritus Benedict XVI. The first and third volumes are especially helpful: *Jesus of Nazareth: From the Baptism in the Jordan to the Transfiguration* (San Francisco: Ignatius Press, 2007) and *Jesus of Nazareth: The Infancy Narratives* (New York: Image, 2012).